layers

Unfolding the Stories of Chester County Quilts

Published by Chester County Historical Society

2009

This book is dedicated to those who enjoy creating quilts, to those who preserve them because they are part of the family, and to those who save them but aren't sure why. All of it counts.

Editor: Catherine E. Hutchins

Book Designer: Suzanne D. Gaadt, www.gaadt.com

Photographer: Laszlo Bodo

Printer: Pearl Pressman Liberty, Philadelphia, PA

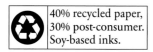

40% recycled paper, 30% post-consumer. Soy-based inks.

(Front cover) Friendship Quilt detail, 1847
Finished quilt top made for Mary Worrall; overall on page 39. Cotton; 78" x 78"
Courtesy of Sally Berriman

(Top left) Star of Bethlehem, 1840s
Made by Martha Thomas Lewis (1825 – 1912), a Quaker from Chester County.
Cotton top; cotton back; 98" x 97"
Courtesy of Joann H. Lewis

(Back cover) Star, 1840 – 1850
Made by Guenne S. Hall (1806 – 1875) of East Goshen. Cotton top; cotton back; 106" x 103". Courtesy of Ron and Nancy Harper/Doug and Amy Harper

This book and companion exhibition were generously funded by a grant from the Institute of Museum and Library Services. Additional support for marketing and publicity was provided by the Chester County Conference and Visitors Bureau.

Funding for the quilt documentation project planning in 2002 was provided by the Greater Philadelphia Cultural Alliance. The documentation in 2002/03 was funded by a grant from the Pennsylvania Historical and Museum Commission.

All dimensions for quilts are in inches and height is preceded by width.

Unless noted otherwise, photographs of quilts were taken by Laszlo Bodo. The Chester County Historical Society wishes to thank all photographers and institutions who provided images.

14, 61 lower right, 87 upper right, Edward Huberty; 19, 21, 22, 23, 26, 27, 35 upper left, 38 lower left and right, 82, 89 top, 132 top right, quilt documentation archives; 31, 43 lower right, Ellen Endslow; 52, 81, Cliff Parker, Chester County Archives; 54 (2.1), Kory Berrett; 59, Jim Schneck; 60, 67, 93 upper left George Fistrovitch; 61 lower left, Heritage Center of Lancaster County; 61 lower right, Patricia Keller; 63, The State Museum of Pennsylvania; 80, 93 lower right, 95 lower left, 96 lower left, 98, Hagley Museum and Library; 87 lower left, Royal Ontario Museum, Toronto, Ontario; 97, Winterthur Museum and Library; 99 bottom, Dallas Knight; 113 top, Gloria Schelling

contents

acknowledgements

Considering the many people who deserve unstinting thanks, it is easy to envision the metaphor of the project being a quilt and all of those who participated as the quiltmakers, whether or not they ever literally sewed a stitch. First and foremost are the community members who, since 2002, brought their quilts to the documentation days and freely shared their quilting heritage and family stories. It has been gratifying. They are the fabric of many colors and patterns and we thank them for enriching all of us.

Equally important are the community volunteers who were undeterred through rain, snow and freezing cold. The documentation, this book and exhibition simply would not have happened without them. They helped to collect the community fabric by taking photographs, writing physical characteristics, and collecting stories. Thank you, Julie Henderson for keeping the train on the tracks in 2002/03 and a memorial thank you to Bill Billet who helped to set up each documentation day.

We are grateful to the Pennsylvania Historical and Museum Commission for funding for the documentation phase. For this phase, we are greatly indebted to the Institute of Museum and Library Services. Their support has made our ability to reach the community far greater than we could possibly have achieved on our own. Institutional partnerships, created by Bernie Herman and Karin Gedge with their respective universities, were also instrumental in our success.

In a largely solitary activity since 2002, Maggie Alleva and Jane Brosius completed data entry of the collected information. We are forever beholden to Bill Hoag, the primary designer of the database who, regrettably, is no longer with us to see the finished product. And thank you to Bill Parker for completing the version for the exhibition.

The project went to school in 2008. Teachers and principals from all over Chester County welcomed Carol Samuelson, Sue Knight, Nicole Krom, Shannon Almquist, Karin Gedge, Jane Fenicle, and Barbara Perrone to their classrooms. The results have added a vibrant dimension. We hope that the more the 1,000 students and their teachers enjoyed the outreach as much as we did.

Engaging conversations with Bernie Herman, Pat Keller, Adrienne Hood, Karin Gedge and Dawn Heefner opened avenues of thought that helped to stitch the pieces together in thought-provoking ways. Margaret Jerrido's ability to keep us focused was especially helpful. We hope this publication offers new insight into the realm of quilt research.

Thank you to the volunteers who helped to create the framework for the exhibit, selected quilts for the three rotations, many of which are in this book, and conducted oral history interviews. They are: Barbara Garrett, Jane Davidson, Betty Voorhees, Sandy Day, Kathleen Wagoner, Jane Hamilton, Suzy Brody, Pat Keller, Barbara Perrone, Joanne Brown, Ellen Richardson, Karin Gedge, Marian Mackey, Stella Parry, Barbara Schneider, Nancy Papay, Nicole Krom, Teri D'Ignazio, Dawn Heefner and Anita Regester. Thanks go to Ed Huberty and Dallas Knight for taking photographs as needed and to Linda Eaton whose suggestion of the multi-voiced labels was brilliant.

Institutions have generously provided quilts or images of manuscripts from their collections. They are: The American Geographical Review; Ginger Tucker, Chadds Ford Historical Society; Jon Williams, Hagley Museum and Library; Wendell Zercher, Heritage Center of Lancaster County; Deborah Estep, John Ross and Karen Marshall, Hibernia House Museum, Chester County Parks and Recreation; Mary Dugan, Kennett Underground Railroad Center; Sandy Reber, Longwood Gardens; Nicola Woods, Royal Ontario Museum; Beatrice Hulsberg, The State Museum of Pennsylvania; and Helena Richardson, Winterthur Museum and Library.

Three people to whom we are all indebted are photographer Laszlo Bodo, editor Catherine Hutchins and graphic designer Suzanne Gaadt. Their excellence helped to make an extremely complex task seem possible. They sewed this quilt together with unwavering skill. Any errors, or missed stitches, are mine.

Thank you to the Chester County Historical Society staff and administrative leadership who, over the years through which this project spanned, completed a variety of unsung tasks behind the scenes. Your contributions were appreciated more than you know.

And thank you, Ina, for lighting the fire.

EEE
December 18, 2008

We are indebted to the many community participants for their inspiration, time and talent. We sincerely apologize for the omission of anyone who helped with this project in any way.

LENDERS TO THE EXHIBITION
2009 – 2010

Margaret P. Anderson
Patricia Patterson Baily
Marlene Baker
Lois Bassett
Ann McAfee Bedrick
Drema Benson
Sally Berriman
Carol Biggs
Susan Bravo
Barbara Breen
Jane Pengelly Brigman
E. Worth Brown
Jane Brown
Joanne C. Brown
Martha M. Cameron
Jane Cannard
Barbara Hickman Carozzo
Helen Carr
Susanne A. Carson
Naomi R. Catenese
Chadds Ford Historical Society
Dessa Crawford
Gladys Coates
Anne Gates Copley
Rene Cottrel
Barbara Crocker
Crosslands Community

Elaine B. Cumens
Jane L. S. Davidson
Sandra Fulton Day
Eliza Jane Scott Dering
Mark E. Dixon
Iris Gray Dowling
Geri Dulis
Esther Dusinberre
Bonnie Fennant
Helene Rooke Ferrantello
Sarah Taylor Finnaren
Marjorie Falese
Sharon S. Fogg
Gordon and Florence French
Friends of Hibernia Park
Diane Fields Funk
Carol Gerhard
Carolyn Ginther
Pamela Gray
Ronald and Nancy Harper
Douglas and Amy Harper
Ruth Harrison
Linda D. Hawley
Hibernia County Park
Helen Hickman
Mary C. Hickman
Linda Hicks
Barbara P. L. Hill
Vanessa Horstead
Barbara Huston
Margaret R. Ireson
Ina Jacobs
Nell Jameson
Lena Jenkins
Gay G. Johnson
Mary Ann D. Keefe
Kennett Underground
    Railroad Center
Ruth Keim

Pat Keller and Kory Berrett
Sara Hamilton Kent
Margaret Koch
Dorothy Lammer
Mary E. Larsen
Ann Pusey Heess Lee
Joann H. Lewis
Wendy Lofting
Longwood Gardens
Ella Nieweg Luff
Jean Mansur
Sidney Matthews
Sara Meadows
Charles Buster McAfee
Ann Y. McCarney
Edith McElroy
Richard McIlvaine
Gail K. Miller
Joanne Moll
Anne H. T. Moore
Sally Moore
Gladys Mosteller
Virginia Musser
Carolyn L. Neff
Judy Nelson
Rachel Neville
Leslie O'Brien
Jean A. Patrick
Patricia L. Patterson
Carolyn Payne
Viola M. Patton
Barbara Loftus Perrone
Nancy H. Plumley
Roberta L. Pettit
Susan Podolin
Barbara Wood Pusey
Denise Rash
Marguerite N. Rector
Wilson B. Reynolds

Judith Rigney
Jacqueline Robinson
Margaret Schmoyer
Barbara Schneider
Virginia Graul Shainline
Susan Cloud Schofield Sleichter
Marian Stoner
Edith Sumner
Nancy Swisher
Grace D. Tait
Beatrice Thomas
George Thomas
Terry L. Thomas
Ruth Smedley Thompson
Elsa E. Walters
Jenny Watson
Katherine Burton Way
Connie L. Webster
Margaret Welcomer
Jean Weller
Susann E. Welsh
Marjorie Williams
Velma Wilson
Esther Grealy Wise
Carolyn W. Wonderly
Elizabeth S. Voorhees
Katherine Yerkes
Mary Ann Zeiders
Barbara Morris Zorn

VOLUNTEERS 2002 – 2009

Joanna Aaron
Maggie Alleva
Jo Ann Badasarian
Susan Beach
Kory Berrett
Bill Billet
Jean Billet
John Blubaugh
Denise Bowie
Lindsay Brinton
Susannah Brody
Joan Broge
Mary Brooks
Jane Brosius
Joanne Brown
Vickie Brown
Andrea Cakars
Janet Caldwell
Lucinda R. Cawley
Joan Cobb
Anne Congdon
Helen Daiuta
Peggy Danie
Jane L.S. Davidson
Doris W. Davis
Sandy Day
Marnie de Carville
Teri D'Ignazio

Justin Donaldson
Gertrude Dougherty
Esther Dusinberre
Linda Eaton
George Ehrgott
Lauren Fagan
Betty Fiske
Sharon Fogg
Carole Forsythe
Nancy Fowler
Lois Fulton Halpern
Joy Gardiner
Sheri Gardner Von Urff
Barbara Garrett
Karin Gedge
Mary E. Giny
Karen Glasthal
Sue Greenwood
Gretchen Guidess
Judith Hagerty
Dagmar Hall
Joan Halpern
Jane Hamilton
Joy Hartshorn
Carol Jo Heald
Dawn Heefner
Karen Helm
Julie Henderson
Barbara Hennigan
Mary Kay Hitchner
Bill Hoag
Doris Hoag
Lynne Hoyt
Barbara Huberty
Edward Huberty
Sandy Jackson
Ina Jacobs
Carmen James
Barbara Jobe
Mary Ellen Josephson
Bill Kashatus
Patricia Keller
Kathleen Kiefer
Dallas Knight
Sue Knight
Sandra Kwisz
Nicole Krom
Yadin Larochette
Terri Leamer
Rob Lukens
Rosemary Lynch
Marion Mackey
Ida McIntyre
Kelly Meanix
Lori Memmen
Vivian Miller
Denise Nordberg
Adelia Ocklerbloom
Peggy Olley
Mary Painter
Nancy Papay

Stella Parry
Anne Peranteau
Barbara Perrone
Shirley Phillips
Liz Plane
Julie Powell
Pamela Powell
Sandy Reber
Anita Regester
Lillian Reiss
Frances K. Reyburn
Ellen Richardson
Lisa Rodgers
Diane Rofini
Sara Rubino
Carol Samuelson
Josephine Sanders
Barbara Schneider
Martha Schreiner
Terry Seeley
Suzanne Simmons
Marian Stoner
Stacey Swigart
Kathy Talley
Kathy Tauber
Karen Terry
Amy Tetlow
Nan Tischler
Barbara Tuft
Greta VanDenBerg-Nestle
Yolanda Van der Kroll
Kate Verbeke
Elizabeth Voorhees
Kathleen Wagoner
Sandy Weaver
Deborah Weinberg
Ruth Whittaker
Carolyn Wonderly
Mary Ann Zeiders

PRINCIPALS, TEACHERS AND STUDENTS 2008

Avon Grove High School
Thomas Alexander - *Principal*
Shirley Shenker

D.J. Ross

Bayard Rustin High School
Dr. Phyllis Simmons - *Principal*
Fran Butler
Kevin Diehl

Manli Avallino, Kelly Baxter, John Bender, Trever Bergwall, P.J. Bernacki, Carlie Bold, Alex Bolte, Annalise Curtin, Chris Denison, Sherif Ehaggar, Rachel Ewing, Austin Flanagan, Dave Handy,

arah Hayes, Steven Hughes, Mike
elly, Nicholas Lauasseur, Adrienne
McKean, Raedora Rawl, Curtis
iddle, J.J. Rudisill, Matt Soojian,
an Swalm, Julie Tatios, Brian
reichel, Aubree Williams

Downingtown Middle School
Thomas Mulvey - *Principal*
Laura Fredd
haron Jackson
na Kean

elli Follett, Camryn Hess, Kelly
hatcher, Michael Townsend

East Goshen Elementary School
Dennis Brown - *Principal*
Clare Chevalier
Ellen Hulnick
usan Jones
Linda Romeika

Michael Ceribelli, Will Delaney,
ammy Fenimore, Eric Gassenmeyer,
Caprice Harvey, Andrew Henry,
Victoria Lawrence, Morgan
Mancuso, Katie Quinn, Sarah
Richard, Saige Schramm, Meg Ward

Elk Ridge Elementary School
Nicole Addis - *Principal*
Gina Gagliardi
Leslie Gambrell

Thomas Baires, Alvaro Bedollaklz,
Katie Bird, Sabreena Byrd, Brian
Cordova, Maddy Lehr, Hannah
Lindsey, Tori Kinsella, Bryan Nieves,
Dayana Torres, Emily Webster

Exton Elementary School
Roberta Gettis - *Principal*
Penny Arndt
Cyndy Roth

Michaela Cephas, Ben Donovan,
Madison Machado, Anne Pena,
Laura Richardson, Michael
Ridgeway, Leah Ritchey, Natalie
Shulkawski, Emily Xu

Glen Acres Elementary School
Dr. Susan Huber - *Principal*
Paula Miller
Marilyn Steines
Deborah Whitmire

Madie Ahearn, Stephanie Batog,
Gillian Bonner, Lauren Bruce, Jamie
Cohen, Andrew Dunscomb,

Matthew Gallagher, Benjanim
Klucznik, Brian Mulcahy, Lucas
Naylor, Joel Paskings, Logan Prann,
Ann-Laurie Razat, Olivia Sarkisian,
Anne Subach, Linda Ziminsky

Henderson High School
Robert Sokolowski - *Principal*
Grace Threadgill

Mel Ent, Ashley Frame, Carly Hahn,
Emily Mccammon, Nicole Salvaggio,
Stephanie Zinman

Kennett High School
Dr. Michael Barber - *Principal*
Shawn Duffy
Dan Falcone

Dannielle Callen, Ashley Evans,
Devon Goddard, Eliza Spear

New Eagle Elementary School
Dr. Beth Ann Kob - *Principal*
Bill Adlin
Katie Moyer
Amy Newns
Walt Thompson

Julianne Connors, Divya Srinivas,
Tommy Ausonder, Erin Willgruber,
Olivia Lanchaney, Eric Muchorski,
Sophie Schwartz

Nottingham Elementary School
Paula Voshell - *Principal*
Pam Anderson
Carin DeWitt
Laura Miller
Marilyn Steines

Joseph Casey, Josh Freese, Grace
Hennessey, Andrew Leonard,
Rebecca Shine, Samantha Shirk,
Deborah Vandrick, Kelsey Winters

Octorara High School
Scott Rohrer - *Principal*
Aimee Blochberger
Sarah Callaway
Amy Rios
Stephanie Rusen
Elena Wilson

Cassidy Clark, Matt Muchow,
Danielle Murray

Owen J. Roberts High School
Dr. Richard Marchini - *Principal*
Brad Creswell

Michaela Shaw

Peirce Middle School
Diane Smith - *Principal*
Danielle Teeple

Julie Anderson, Allison Barnes,
Abby Cosgrove, Austin Dando,
Colleen Driscoll, Mary Lawrence,
Jenica Narducci, Kylie Naughton,
Frank Nocella, Matthew Pistritto,
Noah Sneddon

**Tredyffrin-Easttown
Middle School**
Mark Cataldi - *Principal*
Jean Cook
Gloria Schelling

Robbie Campbell, Niall Carlson,
Michael Chappelear, Jenn Fisher,
Richard Fritzgerald, Steven
Hildebrand, Maya Jankowska,
Marley Jennings, Tara Malloy,
Elizabeth Manton, Bree Pecci,
Megan Reckmeyer, Elise Romberger,
Danielle Schepanik, David Siah,
Amanda Simon, Ally Weigand

Westtown Middle School
Nancy van Arkel - *Principal*
Judy Asselin

Nic Arnold, Emily Blackman, Brian,
Molly Coates, Sage Garrettson,
Olivia Geddes, Sarah Gilroy, Evan
Gross, Chris Infantino, Natalie
Kaplan, Katherine Keyes, Alex
Kimmel, Sarah Latta, Ali Lodner,
Taryn McFadden, Paige Norris,
Claudia Nunes, Tessa Schwarz, Will
Slotznick, Steven, Ryann W.,
Charlotte Wagner, Rachel Workman

There is on earth a friend I prize
More dear than aught beneath the skies.
That bless'd word, brother from my heart.
While life remains shall never part.
Thou lovest thy parents neighbors too,
Art an Abolitionist true blue.

My brother Caleb.

Memorabilia and daguerreotype of Sarah Jones Pusey (1823 – 1858)
of Parkesburg. See her quilt on page 112. Courtesy of Nancy Plumley

foreword

Quilters are a group of dedicated and highly skilled individuals, and with humor and not a little self-deprecation, I share my one personal thread to their world: "I have one child because I only had enough patience to make one quilt!" That humbling experience gave me great respect for those who produced the marvels this book reveals.

When we examine a quilt, we can readily see that its essence goes beyond the function of providing physical warmth. Each one represents a connection to people who have a shared commitment to create an object of beauty intended to be cherished for years. In my case, my act of creation was a solitary one; however, some quilts involve large amounts of collaboration that reveals a tremendous sense of community and resourcefulness. Often quilts were made with fabric that remains silent witness to many tales. Why was it made? Was it a church or civic group seeking to raise money? A gift to a bride's dowry? By friends or family looking for an excuse to gather? Or simply out of the love of the process?

As our world moves faster and faster, the time people used to take to connect with each other becomes further removed from daily life. This changed reality illuminates the reasons to cherish these works of art even more and to work toward keeping this tradition alive. Whether each of us has been involved in the creation of a quilt or not, we all can appreciate the otherwise untold stories they tell of the communities from which they originated.

Like the quiltmakers, the people responsible for this book and the accompanying exhibition approached this project with meticulous care. More than six years ago numerous community members began the process of documenting local quilts. They avidly continued their participation in the past year by interpreting and selecting quilts for this exhibition. Consultants helped to develop the publication and write chapters. West Chester University of Pennsylvania added its support in this second phase with project internships. Through educational outreach efforts by volunteers at more than thirty of the county's primary and secondary classrooms, we involved multiple generations in our efforts to refine the interpretation of and label writing about the wide variety of quilts that had come to light.

With heartfelt gratitude, on behalf of Chester County Historical Society I thank the Greater Philadelphia Cultural Alliance for providing the seed money with which we could put this vision into motion; the Pennsylvania Historical and Museum Commission for the funding necessary to implement the documentation stage in partnership with the University of Delaware's Center for American Material Culture Studies; and the Institute of Museum and Library Services for supporting the exhibition and this publication through its Museums for America program.

The CCHS staff and volunteers have overseen the coordination of the project from start to finish. I proudly extend especial thanks to them for their shared, and enduring, commitment to creating a book and exhibition that, like a quilt, will be cherished for years to come.

Kimberly A. Hall
President

Bars, 1850 – 1910
Descended in the Scattergood family.
Silk top; cotton back; approx. 90" x 90"
Courtesy of Margaret Chalfant

introduction

There is something intriguing about quilts. Millions of people in the United States are intensely interested in them, yet millions of others have little knowledge of what quilts are. This contrast provided the focus for many discussions that have shaped this publication and concurrent exhibition. Community participants and consultants vidly considered the ideas revealed in quilts and focused on the stories of the people who made them, what quilts are, and how they came to be. We also pondered the value of another quilt book among the many fabulous works that have come before. We found the answer when the questioning devolved to a very basic issue: why do quilts matter?

They matter a great deal to the quilting community that instigated the Chester County Quilt Documentation Project (CCQDP) in 2002, on which both this book and the exhibition are based. With more than twenty years of quilt documentations nationwide and at least twenty-eight quilt projects in Pennsylvania alone, the absence of quilt fieldwork in Chester County, a region known for this artisanship, stood out as a glaring omission. Community members, led by Ina Jacobs, clamored for such research. As a deft leader of the Chester County Historical Society's volunteer Quaker Quilters who made fundraising quilts for more than eighteen years, she and many others understood the layers of meaning that quilts represent. During the processes of construction, quilts present makers with countless opportunities for creativity, decision-making, and even community interaction. Once finished, quilts

become objects that possess both artistic values and practical uses.

Quilts are a colorful example of local and personal history that is cut apart, rearranged, and sewn up; thus, they provide undeniable evidence of each quilter's existence. That precept informed the entire project. Throughout the original nine documentation days in 2002 and 2003 it was not unusual for relatives to bring family quilts that other members of the extended family, who attended the same documentation day, did not know existed. Similarly, our own discoveries during the publication process allowed us to connect friendship quilts with neighborhoods, whether virtual or actual, that existed 150 years ago. Today some current owners accept the challenge of having family quilts, yet feel the burden of their care. Others know little of the origins of their quilts and keep them out of duty or mild curiosity. Stories of connection and separation abound; they are far too numerous to recount within these covers.

The value of quilts to academic analysis was less clear when we began the study. On one hand, some of the writers have done considerable work in this area. Bernard Herman, a professor who has specialized in the study of everyday architecture and material culture, expanded his research area to include quilts. His institutional partnership with CCHS was instrumental in phase one as we undertook the bulk of the actual fieldwork. Patricia Keller, a curatorial consultant, designed the CCQDP, basing it on similar projects elsewhere and dovetailing it with her dissertation research

into historic quilts and their cultural origins. Professor Adrienne Hood, who has spent years examining the very fabric of quilts, brought an international scope to illuminate the global trade that quilts embody. By contrast, Karin Gedge, a historian of American women and culture, embarked on the project knowing that the new direction of her research would meet with some resistance among her peers. An appreciation of quilts as the focus of serious historical examination is far from universal.

The many stories that came out of this effort were partially captured through the oral history portion led by Margaret Jerrido. Her extensive professional involvement in oral history projects helped project volunteers to understand the value of conversation as part of the historical record. With the opportunity to look inward, oral historians began to find more layers in their own family stories and to examine their own ideas about why quilts matter. For most of these individuals, quilts are important because they are part of their families' past. Quilts represent people they once knew or never met and are objects that were touched by people from a time to which many owners regret no longer having any connection. If they themselves are quilters, these individuals also sense a creative kinship to their quiltmaking foremothers.

The more layers we pulled aside, the more layers we discovered. As Herman analyzed the virtuosity of the community's quilts, a quilt long cared for by the CCHS took on monumental proportions and raised the tantalizing promise of more in-depth research for other quilts in the Historical Society's collection. Embedded within the stories willingly shared is the on-going debate between myth and reality that Gedge revisited. Our differing perceptions of why and how people in both the past and the present make quilts is a question that invites continuing study. Keller scrutinized estate records to discover when and where quiltmaking emerged as a womanly craft, and her results suggest that the longstanding assumptions underpinning previous studies may well be in error. Hood focused on the widespread availability of imported textiles in the eighteenth century, which were augmented by fabrics

(Top) Valley Forge Homestead Quilters' Guild, King of Prussia. Show and tell, June 2008.

(Bottom) Calico Cutters Quilt Guild, West Chester. Show and tell, June 2008.

(Far right) Bear Paw detail, 1892 See quilt on page 126. Courtesy of Edith McElroy

roduced in American mills in the nineteenth entury. The manuscripts in numerous regional ollections, some of which are published here for he first time, have revealed an important part of ocal history yet to be fully uncovered.

Dawn Heefner's essay brings us full circle, back o the community. A self-described "serial quilt ocumenter," her analysis is in part a firsthand view f the extraordinary grassroots movement of quilt ocumentations. She sums up what we endeavored o accomplish: the CCQDP represents one step in n ongoing process of learning and discovery.)ozens of community quilt enthusiasts have articipated in this effort. They donated hundreds f hours to make the project a success, and with the ielp of graduate and undergraduate students they lso provided the legwork necessary to make that nformation accessible to other scholars and uiltmakers.

Perhaps most fascinating of all is that this roject has raised more questions than answers. tudents supervised by Gedge, volunteers and onsultants tirelessly tackled provocative questions. imple ideas, such as what is a scrap, turned into iscussions about perception and reality. A critique f the myth of systemic Underground Railroad

code quilts sparked another energetic debate. Unafraid of controversy, the students looked at this notion of quilts as symbolic guides for freedom seekers and discovered the irony in the idea that an enslaved population produced the very cotton fabric from which many so called Underground Railroad quilts were made.

Not everyone relates to quilts in the same way. We hope that this book appeals to a wide range of interests. In producing it we know that it is only the tip the iceberg. We have become convinced that there is still much opportunity for quilts to help us examine who we are and from where we have come. The diversity of the project to date has been in the varied cultural backgrounds of the primarily European descendants who have so far participated. There is even greater diversity in the people of Chester County, and there are many more stories that we hope to tell. And that alone is why quilts matter.

Ellen E. Endslow
Director of Collections/Curator

Friendship Quilt, 1850
Made for Emza (Baldwin) and William Jackson of Marshallton. Emza's sisters' and their
husbands' names are written in the center column. Names of other family members and friends
are included, most from Chester County. Cotton top; cotton back; 82 ¾" x 81"
Gift of Mrs. Robert J. Merrick, Chester County Historical Society, 1981.15

Bernard L. Herman

"A cloak for all my errors":
Voice, Virtuosity,
and the Art of the Quilt

Imagining an "art of the quilt" exposes an array of celebrations, anxieties, and prejudices related to the ways in which we as viewers, makers, and critics talk about and assign aesthetic value. The larger conversation about the relationship between quilts and art focuses on questions of discernment and cultural power. Discernment means the ability to render judgment on the basis of a privileged body of knowledge. Deeply rooted in concepts of taste, discernment also reflects a community sensibility in which the ability to make distinctions between good / bad, beautiful / ugly, sophisticated / simple defines relationships between individuals, assigning not only values but also creating hierarchies. There is little creative work in our lives that is neither subject to judgment nor part of a culture of conversation which simultaneously brings us together and yet maintains differences between us. Thus, the "art of the quilt" at the outset is both affirming and competitive. How we engage and prize Chester County's historic quilts springs from continuing acts of discernment that valorize some objects and sideline others.

Judgments about quilts are themselves artifacts of critical assessment that speak to, from, and for the modern quiltmaking community. Guidelines for judging quilts in competition implicitly shape any quilt exhibition. So, too, does the creation of categories for recognizing merit. The judges at quilt shows across the United States adhere to a uniform set of standards in their evaluations and these are organized into three broad categories. In her essay "How to Create an Award Winning Quilt: You Can Do It!" "Quiltingal," an online author, identifies the three key aspects that the judges focus upon: design, workmanship, and appearance.[1] The first "includes the design of the quilt top, as well as the design of the quilting." Judges scrutinize the relationship between the quilting and the overall work as well as the complexity, proportion, and thoughtfulness of the total composition. The second aspect, evaluation of workmanship, both front and back, assesses multiple factors such as "the use of quality fabrics, points and corners that meet precisely, smooth appliqué, flat seams, sashings of an equal width, straight borders, evenly spaced quilting stitches, pucker free binding sewn down with neat and nearly invisible stitches, square mitered corners with no 'cupping,' and a quilt that hangs evenly or lays flat, with no bumps or ripples." The third aspect the judges assess is the general appearance of the quilt—what some quiltmakers and collectors term the "wow" factor.[2] Unlike workmanship, which requires close and detailed inspection, general appearance forces the viewer to stand back and see the quilt as a whole. As Marilyn Maddalena Withrow once asked and answered: "So what does a judge look for? Design, technique, workmanship, skill level shown by the quilter, creativity, overall effect."[3]

Significantly, the judging process is one that examines the quilt on the wall and not on the bed, and that very gesture aligns the quilt with art. The framework for judging quilts is a curious fusion of art exhibition and county fair.[4] Quality, lodged in technique, links the quilt to domestic work; yet quality, located in creativity and visual affect, connects the quilt to art. When we look at historic quilts, the tension between these two modes of looking shapes our perception of the art of the quilt.

Quilts, then, are elusive things. The rich associations of quilts and domestic life, family, and the home are also fraught with assumptions about craft and use. When we turn to assessing how quilts fit into the realm of art, those very associations translate into what we might think of as the four damnations that consign quilts to the sidelines: the connections to handicraft, domesticity, femininity, and community.[5] Paradoxically, the world of quilts is subject to the same canonical actions that keep it on the margins in the world of art. (A canon in the context of art is most easily understood as a privileged and essential category of objects or texts. The objects and texts that populate a particular canon are imbued with a critical authority that defines not only standards for judgment but also the possession and application of cultural literacy. Simply put, canons are about particular forms of aesthetic knowledge and power.) In the world of quilts, the canonical emanates from a variety of critical gestures centered generally on the three categories deployed for judging quilts in competition: technique, design, and the "wow" factor.

To move beyond the conventions and canons of modern quilt judging and asserted hierarchies of artistic production, we must first explore the two defining qualities of the quilt that fall outside the connoisseurial concerns of quilt show and art exhibition: voice and virtuosity.

Stand to the side at any quilt exhibition, eavesdrop on viewers' conversations, and you will overhear variations on two laments: "If only this quilt could talk"; "If only the quiltmaker were here to tell us about her work." These commentaries expose the viewers' desire to engage the voices of the quilt through the object and its maker—and the remarks betray a wistfulness and a sense that those voices have been somehow muted and even lost. Objects, however, are not nearly so silent as some people imagine. Quilts communicate to us

through the design, materials, and construction; their makers speak through the quilts they have fashioned. Each quilt reflects individual and community creativity, ability, and judgment; the maker's voice is at once singular and plural. Although we may discern the hand of an individual maker in each quilt, we simultaneously apprehend the quilt as belonging to a community of objects and creative practices. The voice of the quilt endures, and what it communicates is always changing in response to a volatile mix of physical evidence, historic context, and the narrative needs of the present. The problem we confront is how to find and engage those voices and the conversation they superintend.

A mid-nineteenth-century friendship quilt dedicated to William and Emza Jackson of Marshallton, Chester County, eloquently illustrate this point (fig. 1).[6] Nearly seven feet square, it has forty-eight appliqué blocks surrounding a central square in an oak-leaf-and-reel composition. Separated from its neighbors by yellow print sashing, each block bears a name and the date 1850, all apparently inscribed by the same hand. With a single exception, the blocks on the right bear the names of women and those on the left (again with a single exception) the names of men. The center square reads "William W. Jackson / Emza Jackson / Sept. 30th 1850" over the verse:

Fig. 1. Friendship Quilt detail, 1850
Made for Emza (Baldwin) and William Jackson of Marshallton. See overall image opposite page 13. Gift of Mrs. Robert J. Merrick, Chester County Historical Society, 1981.15

When the last loud trump shall sound / To wake the King of terrors, / Then may this work in heaven be found, / A cloak for all my errors." A number of features distinguish this quilt, and these serve, in turn, to raise core questions about the complex relationships between voice and object.

The inscription at the heart of the Jackson quilt draws on I Corinthians 15:50–55 (King James version):

> 50 Now this I say, brethren, that flesh and blood cannot inherit the kingdom of God; neither doth corruption inherit incorruption.
> 51 Behold, I shew you a mystery; We shall not all sleep, but we shall all be changed,
> 52 In a moment, in the twinkling of an eye, at the last trump: for the trumpet shall sound, and the dead shall be raised incorruptible, and we shall be changed.
> 53 For this corruptible must put on incorruption, and this mortal *must* put on immortality.
> 54 So when this corruptible shall have put on incorruption, and this mortal shall have put on immortality, then shall be brought to pass the saying that is written, Death is swallowed up in victory.
> 55 O death, where *is* thy sting? O grave, where *is* thy victory?

In concert the verse on the quilt and the passage from the Bible suggest an extraordinary connection between object, righteousness, redemption, and salvation. The first two lines of the quilt verse neatly rehearse the advent of the Resurrection. The last two lines project the writer into that moment of divine judgment where the quilt with which she wraps or shrouds herself conveys a degree of virtue that warrants salvation. What is it about this quilt, however, that enables redemption? A clue comes from the biblical verse: "So when this corruptible shall have put on incorruption, and this mortal shall have put on immortality, then shall be brought to pass the saying that is written, Death is swallowed up in victory." The Jackson quilt, dedicated by their family, friends, and neighbors, is an object that evokes the incorruptible and the immortal. It is a human work that its makers and owners understood would outlive the human body—and, important, they understood it as virtuous work. As a worldly signifier of virtue and transcendence, the quilt through its very materiality signaled the defeat of mortality.

The verse also suggests a deeper meditation on quilts and quiltmaking that compels us to pause and consider the extraordinary significance objects exert in everyday life.[7] As a "cloak for all my errors" it evokes multiple possibilities. Bearing the names of friends and family, the quilt is a physical emblem of community in which the Jacksons belonged. The word "cloak" connotes the symbolic network of virtuous relationships that surround and bind the signatories together as one and in that unity protects them. In this sense the quilt doubles as an epitome of spiritual warmth and as armor against darkness. The particular associations of a quilt as a cloak also hint at its role as a shroud. As the earthly body passes away, the soul arises humble and triumphant. Whatever the frailties of flesh and the sins occasioned in life, the quilt with its talismanic register of names enfolds the body, becoming an emblem of greater virtue. It is a powerful object that transports the goodly life of this world into the eternal good of the next.

The reference to virtue and redemption encountered in I Corinthians found its way into the Jackson quilt through the popular culture of sentimental verse. Robert Stevenson Coffin, popularly known as "the Boston Bard," published his poetry in newspapers and collections of his work.[8] Significantly, Coffin worked for a period in the early 1800s as a typesetter for the *Village Record, or Chester and Delaware Federalist,* a West Chester newspaper. Reportedly published in a Philadelphia newspaper around 1818 and subsequently reprinted in other papers and anthologies, *The "Boston Bard" to His Old Coat* explored themes of humility and vanity, worldliness and salvation, foppery and wisdom through the poetical conceit of a soliloquy addressed to his frayed and mended coat:

> Long time has past, old ragged friend,
>   Since first we met together,
> And then to me thy aid didst lend,
>   To shield me from the weather.
>
> But envious *time* relentless king!
>   Has rent thy seams asunder,
> And thou hast now become a thing
>   For every blockhead's wonder.
>
> The coxcomb as he passes by
>   Condemns each *holy* feature:
> And *modest* virtue with a sigh,
>   Exclaims, *"Oh wretched creature!"*

The ladies—kind obliging souls!
  As through the streets they dash on,
When'er they view [a] thousand holes,
  Cry, *"Mending's out of fashion."*

But as thou'st been a friend in *need,*
  Thro' half life's rugged journey,
'Twould be a graceless thing indeed,
  Now out of doors to turn *ye.*

No, no, old friend—'twere better now
  To brave the world's dread laughter
Than e'er to thoughtless folly bow,
  And meet with scorn hereafter.

The cringing wretch who turns aside
  To spurn a wretched brother,
Will feel the sting of injured pride
  In this world or an *other.*

And he who leaves an aged friend
  Forgotten and neglected,
May be himself when earth shall end,
  By heaven itself rejected.

Then come, old friend for thou canst yet
  Protect me from the weather,
And when my sun of life shall set,
  We'll both lie down together.

And when the last loud trump shall sound
  To wake the King of Terrors,
Oh, may my rags in heaven be found,
  A cloak for all my errors.

First published thirty-two years before the dates inscribed on the Jackson quilt, Coffin's poem concerns itself with similar themes of reflection and redemption. As historian Patricia Keller notes, however, the concluding stanza on the Jackson quilt substitutes "Then may this work in Heaven be found" for Coffin's "Oh, may my rags in heaven be found." Where Coffin speaks to the rags he literally wears upon his back, the makers of the Jackson quilt address them themselves to the work of the quilt. The quiltmakers' labors, however, are neither about mending nor rags, but celebrate instead the creation of new work out of fabric acquired for this particular quilt. In their choice of the concluding stanza from Coffin's poem, the makers of the Jackson quilt jettison the poet's larger sentimental meditation in favor of the stark evocation of the final judgment and salvation of I Corinthians (the

ultimate source for Coffin's stanza). In this sense, the Jackson quiltmakers approached popular poetry in much the same way they worked with fabric, cutting and piecing whole cloth and word into a new and meaningful design that expressed the bonds between the quilt's makers and celebrants and the larger spiritual, recuperative, and redemptive power of their art.

The Jackson quilt also raises issues about quiltmaking practices in Chester County and beyond. First, as a friendship quilt bearing multiple names (all seemingly penned by a single hand), it broaches the question of authorship, as the inscription in the center is in the singular, but the names surrounding are plural. Second, it is an object that negotiated the space among the popular (a vogue for objects that occurred within the larger mid-nineteenth-century pursuit of sentimentality), the ideological (the union of family and community), and the conventional (the lexicon of then contemporary quilting practices). Third, friendship quilts generally commemorated unions and departures, signified group and family identity, and sustained social networks.[9] Fourth, the Jackson quilt literally embedded the object within the larger community of its signatories.

The physical attributes of objects also speak loudly, making the assorted associations audible. The Jackson quilt is symmetrical and uniform in it use of appliqué. Individual names adorn the blocks. A central block identifies the Jacksons as a couple, links them with biblical reference, and places them at the heart of a community. A close look at both the fabrics and their placement, reveals the subtle care given to the quilt's composition. The appliqué work consists of twenty-three distinct turkey-red prints. With two exceptions, each print appears in only two squares. (The exceptions are a print that is used in four squares, and the prints used for the central square, which swatches are identical to those in the adjacent blocks.) Fabric choice and placement provides a narrative that identifies couples, underscores kinships, and suggests these individuals constitute an inner circle of intimates. We cannot know the precise nature of these relationships, but we can understand the Jackson quilt as a map that delineates—through pattern, fabric, and text—a complex topography of familial and social relationships. This raises an important question: Why deploy a quilt as a map?

If we think of quilts through an architectural metaphor, a provocative answer emerges. Drawing distinction between place and space, we can describe place as location, and describe space as the universe of experience and understanding that renders that location lived in and meaningful.[10] The distinction between house and home parallels this division. A house is a designed object brought to actuality through construction. Home is the realization of the house around experience and, more importantly, deeply held, often unarticulated values about one's self, family, neighborhood, and community. Scale, organization, elaboration, materials, and workmanship place a house in a larger comparative universe of houses. These attributes also provide the space that inform the ways in which we see ourselves and others see us. Thus, *home* space reveals a great deal about the people who inhabit it and their values. Because those values may not be apparent on the surface, they can be challenging to grasp, demanding a good deal of reflection and interpretation on our part. The architecture of a quilt relies on a similar interplay between place and space. In the Jackson quilt, the physical object is the location; whereas the making, viewing, and our understanding of it (on multiple levels) constitute the spaces. The central verse describes the quilt and its making as "this work"—not "my work." While it is easy to

presume that the quilt is the "work," we need to remain mindful that the word instead may refer to the names on the quilt, as both the object and the relationships it describes constitute enduring and aesthetic work.[11] Within its design lay spaces dedicated to praise, family, community, craft, art, tradition, and narrative. This *voice* of the quilt is an essential element in its larger architecture.

Hannah Grubb of South Coventry Township completed her Lone Star quilt sometime during

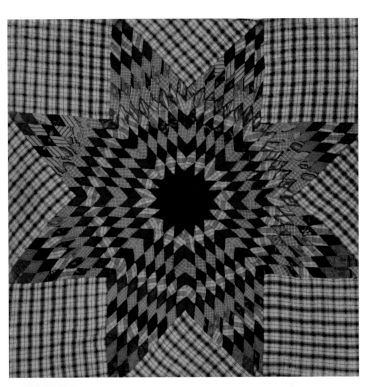

the 1920s using cotton-wool blend fabrics likely purchased in nearby Pottstown (fig. 2.1 & 2.2). Stored in a chest along with partially finished quilts, the seventy-eight-by-seventy-four-inch quilt descended through the family, first to a niece and in turn to her daughter. No one in the family recalls the quilt being used on a bed, suggesting instead that the maker conceived of it as an heirloom from the start. As Grubb's grandniece describes the quilt, "it's just part of my family," a tangible link between women through succeeding generations. She also captured her great aunt's confidence in design and execution, remarking simply that "they just did it." The descent of the quilt through the family followed a familiar course of actions that

Fig. 2.1 & 2.2. Lone Star front and back, 1920 – 1930
Made by Hannah Grubb, South Coventry Township.
Cotton, synthetic blend top; wool, rayon, synthetic blend back; 78" x 74"
Courtesy of Judy Nelson

amplified its voice:

> My mother wanted me to have these quilts. She told me they were from "down home," the farm where she grew up in South Coventry Township, Chester County. They were probably made by her aunts, possibly her Aunt Hannah. She came to help the family after my mother's mother passed away. The women in the family did a lot of needlework and my mother knew I would appreciate the quilts and the piece of family history that they are.[12]

The voice in the quilt created a conversational space that reaches across generations, creating continuity and connection. Hannah Grubb's quilt is the place that anchors and sustains narrative spaces defined by memory and genealogy.

Often, though, the only voice we encounter is through the object. Its family history lost, a circa 1880–1910 quilt, roughly six feet square and pieced with cotton and wool fabrics, possesses a front laid out in a neatly ordered fan pattern and a back composed of an explosive array of nine-patch squares and fabric scraps (fig. 3.1 & 3.2). Although the quilt looks like those created in Dauphin County, it possesses a Chester County history of ownership. United in a single object, two compositions offer a dramatic counterpoint between the regularity of the formal top laid out in sixty-four geometrically uniform squares and the pragmatic asymmetry of the back. The fans on the formal side suggest a maker of modest abilities, as the design elements are irregularly cut and the piecing comparatively tentative compared to other quilts made in Chester County. The *informal* side, however, tells a very different story. In its ad hoc collection of nine-patch squares and scraps, this face exudes confidence and ability. The distinction seems to reside in a suggestion of intent: formal composition in a popular pattern that offers a public display of a kind of polite competency; informal composition in a make-do composition that privately displays qualities of practiced ability and playfulness. In a larger contemporary art context, the top might be considered emblematic of the quilt alienated from the everyday into an object animated by aesthetic display; the back speaks directly to the inseparability of art and life.

Virtuosity amplifies the voice with which a quilt speaks. Virtuoso quilts display heightened skill levels in their design and construction, transforming the object through the affective power of art. Affect, the emotional response to an object, reaches into shared and individual frameworks that shape the reception of the quilt in the viewer's aesthetic imagination. Virtuosity in the art of the quilt is about transformative magic—the capacity of a quilt to evoke a rush of feeling: wonder, awe, peace, anger, warmth, anxiety. Virtuosity invokes passionate responses to individual quilts, enabling narratives of creativity, history, and family to emerge. Thus, the notion of

Fig. 3.1 & 3.2. Fans front and back, 1880 – 1910
Possibly Schuylkill County, PA.
Cotton, wool top; cotton, wool back; 74" x 72 ½"
Courtesy of Susan Bravo

rtuosity is key to nderstanding the art of the uilt.

Virtuosity manifests self in quilts as two ntwined elements: nactment and discernment. nactment springs from uiltmaking, thus, for xample, surpassing ability s revealed in the ccomplished design and onstruction of quilts. Discernment encompasses ur ability to appreciate and ppraise those qualities. Although enactment and iscernment can be eparated for purposes of iscussion, in reality they re inextricably entangled in very quilt we encounter rom the most basic to the most rarified nterpretations. A virtuoso quilt, then, is the roduct of at least two types of performance: one lisplays technical and aesthetic abilities of the ighest order, the other recognizes those qualities nd places them in context. Assessments of irtuosity rely on viewers' abilities to compare, liscern, and articulate the relative quality of objects vithin hierarchical systems. Those systems, in turn, ranslate physical characteristics in fabric choice nd placement, regularity and fineness of needlework, and composition into values and udgments. Quiltmakers acknowledge that the basis of judgments of virtuosity on technique and lesign are never absolute, but subject to other ariables like originality, inventiveness, and visual mpact. None of these judgments, however, refers back to a quilt's function as bedding—and in that lisjuncture locates the virtuosity of the quilt in the ealms of the visual (design and technique) and way from utility (bodily comfort).

Virtuosity is not about complexity, but onfidence and ability—and it resides in the naturality of the quilt as an object. A mid-nineteenth-century quilt, made by a member of Schuylkill Friends Meeting, exhibits two key aspects of virtuosity: deliberate formality and practiced improvisation (fig. 4). The thirty-by-thirty-five-inch quilt is composed of three-inch-square pieced blocks with a cotton print border. Drawing on the idiom of a nine-patch quilt, the maker's composition plays with color in the clustering of blue, green, and dark brown in asymmetrical arrangement. The resulting effect is one of visual subtlety and movement within a larger field of tan and light brown cotton prints. The simple geometry of the quilt coupled with its gently nuanced palette is the work of an artist thoroughly versed and immersed in this medium. Pattern and color overlap and inform each other in sophisticated play but without undue showiness.

A late nineteenth-century strip quilt pieced by Isabella Deery Gill of Chester Springs similarly exemplifies a practiced quiltmaker's virtuosity (fig. 5). Twenty-one strips of pieced and continuous fabric compose the roughly six-foot-square quilt in a straightforward symmetrical arrangement. The quilt top incorporates cotton fabrics including solid colors, woven patterns, and floral and paisley prints. Gill, a lifelong quiltmaker, and her daughter Erma worked in a sewing circle at St. Peter's Lutheran Church. Her strip quilt demonstrates the confidence and ease of a lifetime of quiltmaking. Gill put symmetry at risk in her quilt. Within an overall composition of alternating strips of tan and buff floral prints contrasting vividly with red

Fig. 4. Crib Quilt, 1880s
Unidentified maker from the Roberts family, of either Valley Friends Meeting or Schuylkill Friends Meeting.
Cotton top; cotton back; 30" x 35"
Courtesy of Susann E. Welsh

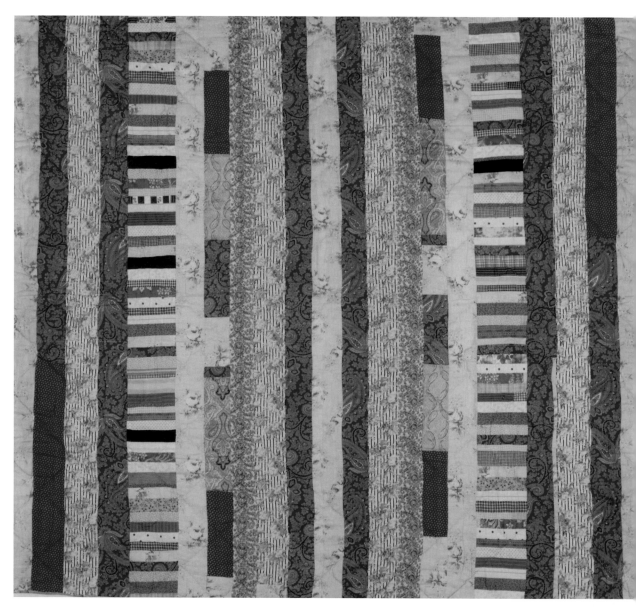

prints, Gill carefully created something of a mirror image. The reversal of patchwork elements, however, is on somewhat of a diagonal and is masked by the two horizontally pieced strips that create a visual distraction and draw the eye away from other compositional irregularities.

Three categories of quilts—those that map the lexicon of quilting, those that privilege the mastery of quilting conventions, and those that highlight creative play and invention—illuminate aspects of virtuosity associated with deliberate formality. Lexicon quilts incorporate multiple patchwork and appliqué decorations in a heightened and self-conscious display of mastery. The individual components offer a recitation of established and generally well-known patterns. Their distinction derives from their ability to display the quiltmaker's vocabulary; their originality stems

from the ways in which they bring that vocabulary together in a uniform composition. Elizabeth Shaver Voorhees and Joanne Campbell Brown produced pieced quilts in this idiom. Voorhees, who moved to Pennsylvania from Illinois, learned quilting as an adult when she joined a sewing circle in West Chester (fig. 6). Drawing on a block-of-the-month design obtained through a local quilt shop, she undertook this quilt using reproduction antique fabrics and arranged the more than sixty individual blocks into seven columns. Completed when Voorhees was seventy-one years of age, this final work, undertaken for personal pleasure, earned her a first-place ribbon at an American Quilter's Society juried show. Brown, who also learned to quilt as an adult, was similarly inspired (fig. 7). Although she conceived of the quilt as a learning project, she entered it in a local context

Fig. 5. Striped Quilt, 1880 – 1918
Made by Isabella D. Gill (1843 – 1918) of Chester Springs.
Cotton top; cotton back; 72 ½" x 75 ½"
Courtesy of Marjorie Williams

here it received a ribbon.

The quilts made by Voorhees and Brown demonstrate the extent to which voice and virtuosity remain lodged in contemporary popular culture and community life. Conceived as bed quilts constructed for personal satisfaction and the home, the two quilts map two additional contexts: popular convention and group competition. Both makers drew on published and commercially available sources for their designs, but chose their own fabrics—opting in each case for reproduction material. That choice reveals a shared aesthetic foundation informed not only by color and pattern but also by perceptions of time and history in ways that connect the makers not just to the present but also to their perceptions of tradition. A competitiveness tempered that connection. Both women entered the quilts in a contest and won recognition in them. But their competitive nature runs much deeper and is revealed in the makers' self-conscious decisions to employ a design lexicon. The result for each was a quilt that comments on the variety of design in ways that only an accomplished maker could achieve—even when a maker like Brown claims that this is the first quilt she made. Significantly, the demonstration of individual ability is located exclusively in the quilt top and does not extend to the actual quilting, as in both cases that task was contracted to other needleworkers.

Quilts that deploy a conventional pattern in a manner that display the artists' abilities, particularly in terms of their composition, constitute a second aspect of virtuosity (fig. 8). A circa 1900 center-square quilt made by Harriet Miller of the Royersford–Spring City area demonstrates virtuosity through the simplest of patterns. Although the maker's descendants claim that Harriet Miller made her quilt out of necessity, they preserve it as a family heirloom. The roughly seven-foot-square quilt consists of a centrally placed block within a much larger rectangle of dark brown paralleled by two narrower tan rectangles and framed with a gray border. The solid fabrics of the front and back are knotted with green, teal, yellow, red, royal blue, and variegated perle cotton or yarn. As a virtuoso

object, the quilt relies on the simplest of geometries, quoting the square-in-square and diamond-in-square patterns common in early twentieth-century Pennsylvania-German Amish communities. In lieu of quilting, colorful yarns bind the layers of the quilt and create a spangled spray of color.

(Top right) Fig. 6. Sampler Block Quilt, 2001
Pieced by Elizabeth Shaver Voorhees (b. 1929) of West Chester and quilted by Melinda Miller.
Cotton top; cotton back; 101″ x 93″
Courtesy of Elizabeth S. Voorhees

Fig. 7. Sampler, 1978 – 1980
Pieced by Joanne Campbell Brown (b. 1925) of Phoenixville and quilted by a woman in Harrisburg, PA who charged $35.
Cotton top; cotton back; 94 ½″ x 85″
Courtesy of Joanne Brown

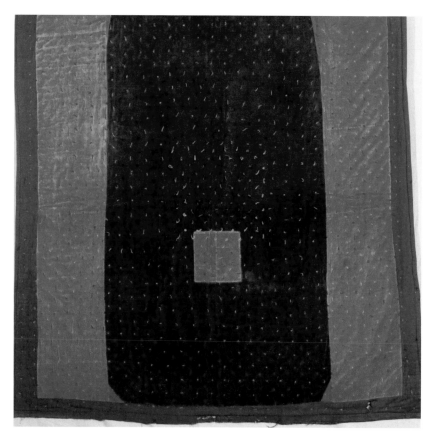

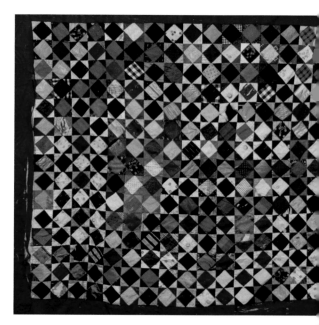

bands of red-and-white sashing to emphasize each patchwork square as an independent element. Finally, Alic Mae Springer's circa 1900 approximately five-by-six-foot geometric medley incorporates square-in-square elements as a framing device for a patchwork cente medallion. Her square-in-square fram nests inside a series of borders radiating out from pieced strips to nine-patch blocks, to a yellow surround with dark edging. The maker of each quilt in this group delved into the same design lexicon and from it made a confident work that was distinctly her own.

Key to the art of the quilt illustrated by the four square-in-square compositions is the relationship between the object as an aesthetic work and the work of the object as bedding. Few quilts make this point more sharply than Mary Eliza Rakestraw's twenty-five patch with its blue-and-white sashing and borders (fig. 13). Born into a Quaker farming family, Rakestraw lived the span of her eighty-seven years in Chester County. At the age of sixteen (ca. 1858), she traveled alone to Philadelphia to buy a sewing machine. She made her twenty-five patch quilt nearly twenty-five years later, and a great-great-great-grandniece "found this quilt inside a ticking mattress that was sewed

A group of square-in-square quilts with varied histories further illustrate the degree of variation within a simple convention (figs. 9, 10, 11, 12). We might think of each of these quilts as an individual voice speaking in a shared conversation. Ruthanna Brown Sharpless of West Grove designed and completed her roughly five-by-six-foot square-in-square quilt in the late 1800s. Made of pieced silks and brocades, framed with a wide purple border and both tied and quilted, this quilt descended mother-to-daughter through her family. Her daughter Elizabeth Sharpless Smedley Painter produced a similar quilt in 1901 at the age of sixteen. Similarly composed, the nearly six-foot-square quilt incorporated solid as well as printed and woven pattern silks contained in green, blue, and white checked border. Although the two quilts are virtually identical in pattern and geometry, the color choices and border proportions render them distinctly different. The mother's quilt possesses a visual stillness enhanced by the framing fabrics while the daughter's work radiates an almost explosive kinetic energy accentuated by its border. These quilts differ dramatically from a parallel example documented in Pocopson Township. Just over six feet square and pieced from calico and other print cotton fabrics, that quilt deploys broad

Fig. 8. Center-Square, circa 1900
Made by Harriet Miller (d. early 1930s) of Royersford.
Cotton top; wool back; 86 ¼" x 84 ¼"
Courtesy of Gail E. Clauser

Fig. 9. Square-in-Square, 1880 – 1900
Made by Ruthanna Brown Sharpless (1846 – 1927) of West Grove.
Silk top; cotton back; 68" x 76"
Courtesy of Ruth Smedley Thompson

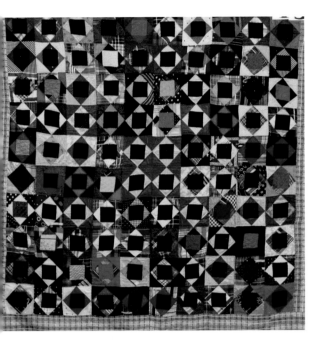

to mattress stuffing. The Rakestraw quilt and its history highlight the degree to which the art of the quilt is often lodged in the process of design and making. The quilt in this context survives as an artifact of aesthetic process—an index to artistic practice, rather than a work of art.

The third arena (the first two being the mastery of lexicon and convention and the creative play of innovation and invention) for the display and reception of virtuosity constitutes quilts that embody *collective* or *group* effort. Friendship quilts, like the Emza and William Jackson quilt, are the most widely documented examples in which individually crafted blocks are joined in single composition. Collectively made quilts emerged both from sewing circles where a group of family and friends gathered together for art and conversation, and from individuals working alone and sometimes at great distance. In either instance, all collaborative quilts are literally conversational, bringing people together (either physically or via imagination) through the creation of an object intended as a touchstone for memory and affection. The collaborative process of quilting is, of course, not limited to friendship quilts. Although piecing and appliqué work appears to have been a typically solitary or small group (for example, immediate family) pursuit, quilting offered an occasion for greater sociability.[13] In any context, the finished effect of collaborative art making is one that combines aspects of gallery and album.

ogether about 1922 and used at a cabin in Maryland for eighty years." The quilt embodies the qualities ascribed to a bed quilt: commonplace cotton print fabrics and straightforward design define an object made for use—but not without aesthetic consideration. Simple details set it apart: black-and-pink and orange-and-brown cotton, wool, and silk blocks stand out as exclamation points in the regular geometry of her composition; a sequence of nine alternating blocks on the center left creates a quilt within the quilt. The history of the quilt, however, suggests the degree to which those aesthetic qualities were relegated to a secondary consideration—after the quilt had served its utilitarian purpose it had been demoted

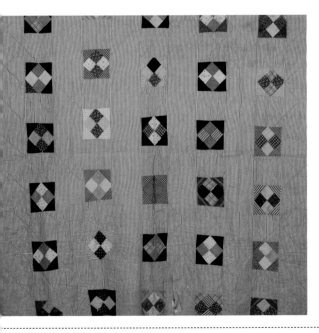

(Top) Fig. 10. Square-in-Square, 1901 Made for or by Elizabeth Sharpless Smedley (1884 – 1977) of Elk Mills. Silk top; cotton back; 68 ½" x 68 ¼" Courtesy of Ruth Smedley Thompson

(Above left) Fig. 11. Square-in-Square, 1930s. Possibly made by a McAllister family member of the Marshallton area. Cotton top; cotton back; 76" x 76" Courtesy of Alice E. Fling

Fig. 12. Patchwork Center Medallion, 1860 – 1910. Made by Sally Ann Arters (d. 1941) who lived at Green Tree Farm in Downingtown. Cotton top; cotton back; 61 ½" x 72" Courtesy of Joyce Arters

The completed work of many hands represents an inherent competitiveness and affirmation located in the relationship between the individual blocks and the literal unity in their coming together.[14] A signed and inscribed friendship quilt from 1846–1847 documents a dynamic mix of virtuoso work assembled into a single composition (fig. 14). Associated with the Reynolds family in the Oxford area of southern Chester County, the large, over seven-and-a-half-foot square quilt contains thirty-one individually signed blocks, several of them aggregated in clusters of four. The geometrically irregular pieced and appliquéd top consists of solid and print cotton fabrics sewn into a sampler of popular patterns reflecting varied degrees of ability and sophistication. Two blocks in particular stand out. An appliquéd American eagle bearing a shield and encircled with a wreath occupies the broad border around the nine centrally placed squares. A second block within the central grouping showcases a floral print of blooming roses springing from a flowerpot. The range in quality of the blocks communicated distinctions and connections between friends and family members. This visual tension between the individual contributions suggests something of a paradox that lies at the heart of shared artistic work.

The association of intimates that occasioned their coming together through their contributions to the Reynolds family quilt remains elusive. The signatories on the quilt identified themselves by place (Baltimore and Harford County in Maryland, Wilmington, the state of Delaware, and Nottingham Township in Chester County), mapping a community that extended well beyond the local. Signed and dated, each maker's block contributed to the finished quilt that combined individual effort into an asymmetrical collective composition. The uniform fabrics employed in the sashing and plain printed intermediary blocks indicate that a single person collected and arranged the individual contributions to the overall composition.

One block, inscribed by Eliza Ann Cheney bears an inked verse:

> Come while the blossoms of thy years are
>   brightest
> Er the dim phantoms thou art chasing die
> Er the gay spell which is round thee
>   throwing
> Fades like the crimson from a sunset sky.
> Life is but shadows, save a promise given,
> Which lights up the future with a fadeless ray;
> O, touch the sceptre!—win a hope in Heaven:
> Come turn thy spirit from the world away!

The lines come from *An Invitation* by Philadelphia poet Willis Gaylord Clark.[15]

"They that seek me early shall find me."

Fig. 13. Twenty-Five Patch, 1860 – 1890
Made by Mary Eliza Rakestraw (1842 – 1929) of Willowdale.
Cotton, wool, silk top; wool, linen back; 98" x 72"
Courtesy of Nancy Plumley

Come, while the blossoms of thy years are
    brightest,
        Thou youthful wandered in a flowery
        maze,
Come, while the restless heart is bounding
    lightest,
        And joy's pure sunbeams tremble in thy
        ways;
Come, while sweet thoughts, summer-buds
    unfolding,
        Waken rich feelings in the careless breast,
While yet thy hand the ephemeral wreath is
    holding,
        Come—and secure interminable rest!

Soon will the freshness of thy days be over,
        And thy free buoyancy of soul be flown;
Pleasure will fold her wing, and friend and
    lover
        Will to the embraces of the worm have
        gone;
Those who now love thee will have pass'd
    forever,
        Their looks of kindness will be lost to thee;
Thou wilt need balm to heal thy spirit's fever,
        As thy sick heart broods over years to be!

Come, while the morning of thy life is glowing,
        Ere the dim phantoms thou art chasing die:
Ere the gay spell which earth is round thee
    throwing
        Fades, like the crimson from a sunset sky;
Life hath but shadows, save a promise given,
        Which lights the future with a fadeless ray;
O, touch the scepter!—win a hope in Heaven:
        Come turn thy spirit from the world away!

Then will the crosses of this brief existence
        Seem airy nothings to thine ardent soul;—
And, shining brightly in the forward distance,
        Will of thy patient race appear the goal:
Home of the weary!—where in peace reposing,
        The spirit lingers in unclouded bliss,
Though o'er its dust the curtain's grave is
    closing,
        Who would not, early, choose a lot like this?

The poem taps into a popular culture of religious sentimentality that weighed the ephemeral blush and pleasure of youthful earthly existence against the eternal spiritual beauty of Heaven. An early biographer neatly summarized this verse and the poet's larger *ouvre*: "The sadness which pervades them is not the gloom of misanthropy, but a gentle religious melancholy; and while they portray the changes of life and nature, they point to another and purer world."[16] Like the stark fusion of biblical allusion and sentimental verse on the slightly later William and Emza Jackson quilt, the lines on the Reynolds family quilt point to redemption and the promise of a better world—but in markedly different terms: refined sentiment rather than divine judgment.

Anthologized multiple times in the nineteenth century (slightly altered in some iterations; abbreviated in others), Clark's verse entered the popular creative imagination in much the same manner as the patterns for the blocks in the Reynolds family quilt.[17] As part of the quiltmaker's creative process, the choice of verse was not so different from the selection of sewn motifs in the sense that the maker dipped into a reservoir of options and picked the one that answered the moment. Block and verse contributed together to the production of a larger meaningful composition that displayed virtuosity not only in making but also in signifying shared values.

The collective virtuosity in the Reynolds family quilt brings us full circle to the question of voice and the art of the quilt introduced through Emza and William Jackson, Isabella Deery Gill, Mary Eliza Rakestraw, Elizabeth Shaver Voorhees, and Joanne Campbell Brown. Each block possesses voice in the sense of a presence encountered through its design and construction. The simplest are plain pieced squares; the most complex are immaculately executed geometric, floral, and figural appliqués. The diversity of blocks in the Reynolds family quilt also documents elements of the lexicon that informed every quiltmaker's creative endeavor. The knowledge of that lexicon, however, was not enough to demonstrate virtuosity. Quoting biblical scripture or sentimental verse paralleled the ability to draw on a popular design repertoire. The voice, virtuosity, and art of the quilt emerged from a quiltmaker's ability to reinvent the familiar and the comfortable through a creation that was fresh and original.

Endnotes

Bernard L. Herman is the George B. Tindall Professor of American Studies at the University of North Carolina at Chapel Hill where he also serves on the faculty of the Department of Art. Formerly the Edward and Elizabeth Rosenberg Professor of Art History at the University of Delaware, he co-founded the Center for Material Culture Studies and the Center for Historic Architecture and Design. He has published and lectured on vernacular architecture, history of the quilt, self-taught and outsider arts, contemporary foodways, and material and visual culture.

1. Quiltingal, "How to Create an Award Winning Quilt: You Can Do It!" (April 25, 2007), http://www.associatedcontent.com/article/213148/how_to_create_an_award_winning_quilt.html.

2. Robert Plant Armstrong, *The Affecting Presence: An Essay in Humanistic Anthropology* (Urbana: University of Illinois Press, 1971).

3. Marilyn Maddalena, http://www.marilynquilts.com/id22.html (2000).

4. Leslie Mina Prosterman, *Ordinary Life, Festival Days: Aesthetics in the Midwestern County Fair* (Washington: Smithsonian Institution Press, 1995).

5. Susan E. Bernick, "A Quilt Is an Art Object when It Stands Up like a Man," in *Quilt Culture: Tracing the Pattern*, ed. Cheryl B. Torsney & Judy Elsley (Columbia: University of Missouri Press, 1994), 134–50; N. C. M. Brown, "Theorising the Crafts: New Tricks of the Trades," *Craft and Contemporary Theory*, ed. Sue Rowley (St. Leonards, Australia: Allen & Unwin, 1997), 3–17.

Fig. 14. Friendship Quilt, 1846 – 1847
Unknown maker from the Nottingham area.
Cotton top; cotton back; 90" x 94"
Courtesy of Margaret Schmoyer

I thank Barbara Huberty and Ellen Endslow for sharing their research on the origins and associations of this remarkable quilt

Jessica F. Nicoll, *Quilted for Friends: Delaware Valley Signature Quilts, 1840–1855* (Henry Francis du Pont Winterthur Museum, 1986), 10, 14–15, 36–37.

I am indebted to Patricia Keller who identified *The Boston Bard" to His Old Coat* as the ultimate source for the verse inked onto the Jackson quilt. Keller also provided the background information and insight on Robert Stevenson Coffin (1797–1827), the publication history of the poem that reportedly first appeared in the *Philadelphia Union* and reprinted in the *Vermont Gazette* (August 4, 1818) and *Oriental Harp: Poems of the Boston Bard* (1826), and the poetical conceit surrounding the culture of mending and sewing. The *Philadelphia Union* likely referred to one of two newspapers: *Union, United States Gazette and True American* or *Union, United States Gazette and True American for the Country.* See, John Thomas Scharf and Thompson Westcott, *History of Philadelphia, 1609–1884* (Philadelphia: L. H. Everts & Co., 1884), 3:1969.

Barbara Huberty and Ellen Endslow compiled the following details about the individuals whose names appear on the quilt: At the time of the 1850 Federal Census and the year the quilt was dated, 40-year-old Amza Jackson and William Jackson, a 51-year-old stonemason, lived in Marshallton, but no children lived with them; Jonathan Livezey and his wife Euphemia (née Powers) and their three children John, Elizabeth and William, lived in Warwick Township (townships with this name exist in Chester, Bucks, and Lancaster counties). Rachel Lesley may be the Rachel Lasley (age 45) who lived Marshallton, her second child, Sarah Ann (age 8), was another signatory, but Rachel's husband (a farmer, age 33) and four other children were not. Lydia Speakman (age 66) was the head of household in Marshallton, but the names the others who lived in her home that year are not on the quilt; however, the name of her fourth child Ebenezer (age 28 and a farmer), who lived elsewhere in Marshallton, is on the quilt.

10. Michel de Certeau, *The Practice of Everyday Life,* trans. Steven Rendall (Berkeley: University of California Press, 1984). Dell Upton, "Architecture in Everyday Life," *New Literary History* 33, no. 4 (Autumn 2002): 707–23.

11. Jacques Ranciére, *The Politics of Aesthetics,* trans. Gabriel Rockhill (New York: Continuum, 2004), 20–30.

12. Helen Grubb's grandniece as quoted by Ellen Endslow to the author, June 23, 2008.

13. See for example, Bernard L. Herman, "Architectural Definitions," in *Gee's Bend: The Architecture of the Quilt,* ed. Paul Arnett, Joanne Cubbs, and Eugene W. Metcalf, Jr. (Atlanta: Tinwood Books, 2006), 207–19.

14. Francesco Panese, "The Accursed Part of Scientific Iconography," in *Visual Cultures of Science: Rethinking Representational Practices in Knowledge Building and Science Communication,* ed. Luc Pauwels (Hanover, N.H.: University Press of New England, 2006), 63–89.

15. Rufus W. Griswold, *Poets and Poetry of America* (2d ed.; Philadelphia: Casey and Hart, 1842), 366–71. According to Griswold, Clark published *The Invitation* in the *Columbian Star,* a Baptist "religious and literary periodical, of high character," sometime prior to 1831.

16. Griswold, *Poets and Poetry,* 366.

17. Examples of anthologies that published this poem prior to the 1846–1847 date on the quilt, include S. J. Hale, *Flora's Interpreter: Or, the American Book of Flowers and Sentiments* (Boston: Marsh, Capen, & Lyon, 1832), 115–16, and George B. Cheever, ed., *The American Common-Place Book of Poetry, with Occasional Notes* (Philadelphia: Hooker & Agnew, 1841), 89. The poem continued to appear in anthologies of sentimental and religious poetry throughout the century, one of which was, Henrietta Dumont, comp., *The Language of Flowers: The Floral Offering; A Token of Affection and Esteem; Comprising the Language and Poetry of Flowers* (Philadelphia: H.C. Peck & Theo. Bliss, 1852).

Fig. 15. Square-in-Square detail, 1880 – 1900.
See quilt on page 22, fig. 9.

Friendship Quilt, 1847
This quilt, made by a Quaker living on a rural farm, offers a fireworks display of turkey-red prints and, at the center, intricate appliqué work. Made by Sarah Webb Cloud (1817 – 1899) of Kennett Township as a wedding gift. Cotton top; cotton back; 93" x 90"
Courtesy of Sara Meadows

Karin E. Gedge

Tension and Transition:
Quilts as Carriers of
Competing American Values

Chester County, Pennsylvania, epitomizes the slow change from agriculture to suburbia that has taken place in the nation as a whole over the past two centuries. Almost one in five of Chester County's nearly half-million residents today still lives in a rural area. Remnants of an agricultural past remain in its farms, nurseries, and mushroom houses, in its fields of horses, cows, and sheep, and in the Amish horse-drawn carriages and farm equipment of its westernmost reaches. Towns like Coatesville, Phoenixville, and West Chester supported heavy industries, while the relentless push of suburban development followed the Main Line from Philadelphia out to the northern and western edges of this sprawling county of 760 square miles.[1] Chester County quilts, their makers, and their owners reveal how the county's residents have negotiated an evolving shift from a rural, agricultural way of life to a suburban and urban way of life, from a world where women worked mostly at home to a world where they often work in and outside the home. The stories people tell about their quilts all have a *moral*, one that often upholds the very values that historical changes, and the quilts themselves, made obsolete.

When asked what is so fascinating about their quilts, owners and makers often reply that it is the *stories* that accompany them, stories that historians have so often dismissed as *myths*.[2] In contrast to most historians, I believe the stories that accompany quilts impart meaningful moral values to makers, owners, and viewers of quilts. The quilt sto-

ries of the Chester County Quilt Documentation Project bridge the gaps between the nineteenth, twentieth, and twenty-first centuries. Yet the quilts and quilt stories often seem out of step with their historical contexts; they reflect the issues and values of a receding past rather than their present circumstances.

Textile production, and especially cotton thread and cloth, was the engine that led the industrial revolution. Eli Whitney's cotton gin plus the inventions and industrial espionage by Samuel Slater, Francis Cabot Lowell, and others, inspired Americans to build the water-powered spinning machines and looms that propelled Americans into the industrial age. The changes they produced were profound, especially for American women of the nineteenth century.[3] Gradually freed from the endless hours at spinning wheels, young unmarried women could earn wages in textile mills. A new middle-class of married women could purchase fabrics with husbands' income. Since quilts are a product of the initial phase of the industrial revolution, they should logically demonstrate what women gained as a result: freed from spinning, women acquired increased leisure time and new buying power in a national market. Instead, the stories that accompany quilts in the twenty-first century reach back to women's roles and worth in the decades prior to the industrial revolution. They describe a maker's hard work, her frugality, and her ingenuity under the trying conditions of a premodern existence, precisely what was lost as a result of the industrial revolution. To be sure, even many of Chester County's twentieth-century women still lived on farms and worked to produce much of their family's food and clothing, but few of them performed the chores of textile production.[4]

American women making quilts at home were directly linked to the massive changes of the industrial production of textiles and the larger market revolution that connected farms, cities, towns, and frontiers. The desire to fashion quilts from mass-produced cotton fabric fed the ambition for wealth from cotton production that, in turn, fueled the impressive growth of technological innovations. Cotton plantations spread westward, pushing Native Americans from their land and pulling African American slaves into the Deep South. Sophisticated institutions of credit developed to finance the farming, manufacture, and distribution of goods. An increasing division of labor offered (mostly men) wages in construction, transportation, mercantile businesses, manufacturing, warehouses, and banks. Working for wages or profits and purchasing the necessities of daily life rather than producing them at home required men and women to change their thinking about their values and their gender roles.[5]

Optimists in this period touted the new political and economic virtues of free trade, competition, and self-interest. They urged Americans to maintain the personal virtues of independence, hard work, thrift, and sobriety, explaining that these virtues would pave the God-given natural path to individual and national prosperity. Pessimists, on the other hand, worried that the new market system fostered competition, pride, a "passion for accumulation," and growing economic inequality, in short, an immoral market economy incompatible with Christian values.[6]

One way to resolve the conflict between old and new values was to encourage men to compete in the sometimes-immoral sphere of politics and business and to encourage women to maintain morality in the domestic sphere. Men should demonstrate the new virtues of the capitalist economy, although with moderation, as too much profit taking was greedy, too much competition was heartless, and too much exploitation of wage earners or slaves was unchristian. Women should be the nation's moral guardians and maintain traditional values by staying at home, raising moral children, and creating for their husbands a "haven in a heartless world."[7]

Recognizing the important historical changes that gave rise to the popular activity of quiltmaking among women should encourage all of us as viewers to see both sides of quilts: as celebrating both women's hard work and their liberation from the endless responsibility of spinning and sewing, as recognizing women's frugality as well as their increased power in the market, and as appreciating women's continuing commitment to family and community in addition to their expanded responsibilities and opportunities in a world beyond the home.[8]

The Tension between Industry and Leisure

The English Quakers and Presbyterians and the German Reform Protestants who immigrated to Pennsylvania between 1682 and 1800 shared an enduring Protestant work ethic. To be idle was to be purposeless or even sinful. To be busy and productive gave spiritual meaning to one's life and brought one closer to God. Even though machines and markets gradually relieved American women of much tedious and time-consuming labor during the ensuing centuries, many women remained reluctant to give up the notion of the virtue of hard work.[9]

Today's quiltowners and quiltmakers still value the relentless labor of the preindustrial past. They express a reverence and awe for hand stitching, for instance, even though sewing machines became one of the first popular home appliances more than a hundred and fifty years ago. The quilts that garner the most attention and respect from quilters and owners alike are those that display the careful hand-stitching skills required to piece tiny squares, triangles, or hexagons or to create elaborate feathered or flowered designs when quilting through three or more layers of fabric and batting. Even if the handwork is not of the finest quality, as is the case in an 1840s heirloom quilt belonging to Sara Meadows of Kennett Square, it has more value than does machine stitching. For Meadows and many other owners, such quilts recall a time, now long past, when needlework was a principal measure of women's worth.[10]

Quilters reinforce the value of hard work by explaining their quiltmaking as the result of a carefully cultivated work ethic. The five Nieweg sisters, all quilters born between 1918 and 1930, grew up on a farm near Nottingham, members of family that is always busy." "We don't want to waste the time," they say. "Nobody's a slacker." Their recollections of making quilts are framed in the context of the many chores—weeding gardens, feeding chickens, cleaning house, making fires, canning foods, caring for younger siblings—required of women in a farm family that still produced much of its own food.[11] Quiltmaker Ina Jacobs grew up near Elizabethtown, Lancaster County, but spent most of her life in Cochranville. She recalls that her father discouraged idleness: "You'd find something to do," or he'd give you something to do "like sweeping the grass with a broom."[12] Coatesville quiltmaker Margaret Anderson remembers, "I was always doing something." When not in active worship, she found time to sew scraps at Quaker meeting. "I felt like that was a good enough thing to be doing, to keep your fingers busy while you're listening. Also it keeps you awake!"[13]

Providing a counterpoint to these stories, though, is evidence that making quilts was essentially a leisure activity. The Niewegs quilted after dark when other chores were done and did so as they conversed with family, listened to the radio, or later, watched TV. When asked whether quiltmaking was a chore, they replied, "Quilting was good.... We all loved to do it." It was "our relaxation," "fascinating," a "satisfaction," "something you wanted to do." "Once you start you hate to quit cause you want to do another square and another square and pretty soon you say, that's it, I have to quit for now." "That was our leisure pastime."[14] The four retired women interviewed at the Tel Hai retirement community echoed these sentiments: "You're happy," one said, when you have one quilt in design, one in the piecing stage, and one in the

quilting stage. Quiltmaking's special pleasure stems from its combination of "work" and "fun," purposeful rather than purposeless activity, "not vegging out," as Tel Hai quilter Joanne Belsen put it.[15] Quiltmakers derive pleasure from their active leisure hours because their "work" produces a material object, one that is neither strictly utilitarian nor merely decorative (figs. 1, 2).

The *moral* of the stories that celebrate and appreciate women's labor and work ethic tells us that women work hard even when they have access to laborsaving appliances and leisure time, but that same moral tends to gloss over the rich enjoyment that women have long taken from this activity. As Joanne Belsen reflected, "we think of women [in the past] as downtrodden and overworked, but they had a sense of humor and beauty ... they wanted to brighten up their lives."[16] Quilts communicate that women don't waste time even when they have more of it.[17]

Tension between Thrift and Consumption

Quilts also provided the opportunity for women to continue to demonstrate frugality and thrift even in their uses of mass-produced fabrics. The tension springs from the very act of purchasing fabrics just for quilts. Author Lydia Maria Child recognized this tension in her household manual of 1835. She applauded women who made good use of otherwise unusable scraps but scolded those who wastefully cut up perfectly good fabric to create

Fig. 1. Joanne Belsen (left) and Esther Burtner (right) pause in their quilting at Tel Hai retirement community, Honey Brook, 2008.

Fig. 2 Alta Hershey (left) and Gladys Mosteller (right) quilting at Tel Hai retirement community, Honey Brook, 2008.

grocery items. Adaptive uses of quilts also reinforced the value of thrift. Lancaster County resident Helen Smoker remembered using them to cover windows and doors and t serve as walls in a childhood home under construction.[20] He daughter Jane Smoker Davidson, a resident of Glenmoore, documented humble quilts that recycled old bedspreads, showed signs of repair, or were so worn that, with ties sewn to their edges, they became even humbler mattress protectors (fig. 3).[21]

elaborate designs.[18] The stories told by quiltmakers and quiltowners still emphasize thrifty use of fabric. Quilts made in both the nineteenth and twentieth centuries are accompanied by stories and construction histories that celebrate the reuse of old or "found" fabrics, whether from special event clothing, cast-off clothing, scavenged fabric, or bags of bargain fabric scraps from factories.[19] The moral running through all of these stories is that women created warmth for their families and beauty in their lives by "making something from nothing," by avoiding a waste of money on luxuries. Makers and their stories reinforce the concept of frugality with the repeated use of the word "scrap." In their lexicon, though, scraps have dual meanings: leftovers that connote "thrift," and tiny pieces of fabric that allow the creation of intricate, elaborate, and even extravagant, designs.

The oral history interviews overflow with references to frugality. The Tel Hai quilters admired a "scrap" quilt made of used clothing cut in triangles and then declared unequivocally that "it tells you they [the makers] were thrifty." Practical and utilitarian quilts also imply thrift. Ina Jacobs recalled that many of her family quilts were fashioned from feedbags. Her family also recycled "old blankets called sheet blankets, and when they were worn out, that was your middle material for your sandwich for [the] quilt." They tied, not quilted, the layers together with the string used to secure the brown paper wrapped around bread and

Life during the Great Depression produced many instances of thrift. The Niewegs' childhood memories include wearing remodeled worn adult clothing, making a variety of rugs (braided, crocheted, or sewn from petal shapes) from "rags" and paper bread wrappers, and fashioning old ties and scraps from a shirt factory into the tops of quilts. Their family's habit of frugality has endured into the twenty-first century. During the interview, one sister remembered a request to make a pair of pajamas for a grandson and said she still needed to "hunt up some pieces of material that have enough for him" to make the clothing. Listening attentively her niece then offered some brown plaid flannel she had in her possession. Fabric can be acquired from family and friends, who can then feel thrifty when they give their scraps to a quilter. Another Nieweg sister now makes crib quilts to donate to charity, using squares given to her by another church member: "They know that I make quilts and I've got all these patches. And I figure, I've got to do something with those patches. The lady cut them all out, now I've got to make something out of them."[22]

In their construction, too, quilts demonstrate the makers' value of frugality or, at least, a propensity to save fabric that implies frugality. Some quilts present old fabrics mingled with newer fabrics in the pieced blocks.[23] Others combine old tops or old blocks that had never been turned into finished quilts with new sashing or borders, backing, quilting, or embroidery.[24]

Fig. 3. Dresden Plate, 1920 – 1940
This mattress pad with ties sewn to its front began its existence as a Dresden Plate design quilt. Made by Helen Kathryn Buch Smoker (b. 1916) of Lancaster County, PA.
Cotton top; cotton back; 61 ½" x 69"
Courtesy of Jane L.S. Davidson

Quilters sometimes inherit old collections of fabric pieces or even entire pieced tops if family and friends have identified them as people "who can use this stuff." Some quilters purchase old pieced tops and finish them, others turn the best parts of old worn quilts into wall hangings or pillows.[25] Timberton resident Anna Wilson, who does not quilt, has inherited a stack of old quilt tops that she wants to finish by hiring other women to back and quilt them (fig. 4).[26] Sometimes being thrifty requires spending more money.

While all this reuse of fabric speaks loudly of frugality, the sheer abundance of fabric pieces, quilt blocks, and quilt tops is the product of a huge commercial industry that has long relied on the purchase of extra fabric, on clothing designs that "waste" fabric, or on the ability to make and purchase new clothing before the old completely wears out. Ina Jacobs gives voice to a central paradox of quiltmaking when she says, "we don't do it [make quilts] because we have to keep our families warm, but because we're frugal."[27] In other words, the abundance of fabric, not its scarcity, induces women to make quilts. Because they have so much, they feel compelled to recycle rather than throw it out. Such paradoxes abound in quilts. It seems industrious to make, rather than buy, quilts only if the labor invested is viewed as work rather than leisure. It seems virtuous to use up remnants only if the wealth of fabric that initially created those scraps is ignored.

Quiltmakers justify a hobby by invoking the language of industry and thrift, and owners reinforce this rationale by associating quiltmaking with using up materials. Owner Sara Meadows sees thrift displayed in her mid-nineteenth-century

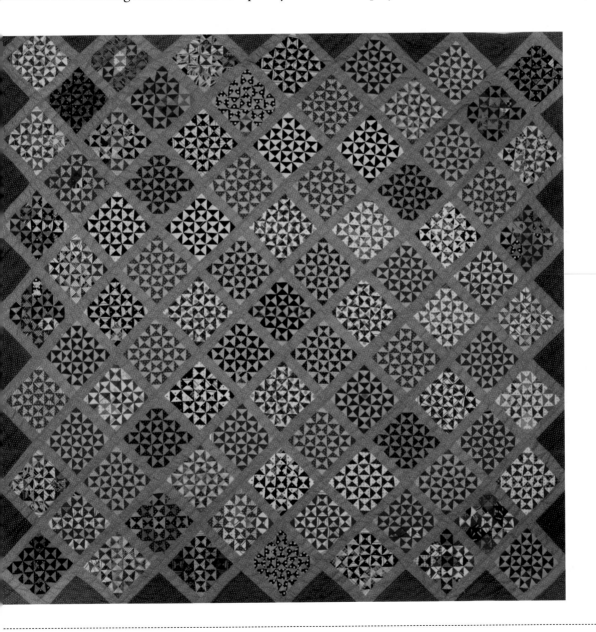

Fig. 4. Square-in-Square Quilt Top, 1940
This is one of several striking unfinished quilt tops that Anna Wilson inherited.
Descended from the Heistand and Yeager families of East Pikeland Township.
Cotton; 85" x 85"
Courtesy of Anna Wilson

quilt because it has only very plain quilting stitches and because she presumes it is made from remnants. She terms it "a frugal Quaker thing," and because Quakers valued plainness, Meadows "can't imagine that they would have gone out and purchased fabric for a quilt" as doing that "defeats the purpose" of piecing the fabric. Nonetheless, the variety of turkey-red fabrics in the quilt puzzles her. After wondering about their initial use, she has settled on the notion that perhaps her plain

Quaker foremothers wore bright-colored petticoats under their drab-colored dresses. Meadows reinforced her image of ancestral frugality by defining this as an "honest" quilt of cotton, a type she considers preferable to those made of "satiny, fancy fabrics" (fig. 5).[28]

Strasburg resident Ron Harper inherited a quilt he believes was made by his Quaker ancestor Guenne Hall Wetheral during the antebellum era. He, however, sees neither "plainness" nor frugality in it. The maker had a comfortable life, as her husband William was a prominent stage driver and businessman in both West Chester and Philadelphia. Guenne had what Harper terms both "time and ability" to lavish on quiltmaking. Yet Harper also considers that buying cloth to accomplish its impressive design would have defeated the purpose of quiltmaking. In two crazy quilts made later in the nineteenth century by Guenne's daughters Sarah Jane Swain and Susan Entricken, Harper has identified fabrics and trade labels that resemble clothing preserved in the

family.[29] Yet, as with Sara Meadows's quilt, no evidence confirms that Guenne Wetherall relied on scraps or remnants when she constructed her quilt. The multiple turkey-red fabrics in it could have come from separate purchases of new fabrics or from trading fabrics with other women in her circle of family and friends (fig. 6).

Some makers intentionally incorporated mementos into their efforts. Quilts made from wedding dresses (or other special clothing) display a sentimental worth that cannot be considered mere frugal use of textiles. West Chester resident Barbara Loftus Perrone, for example, still fashions crazy quilts from scavenged materials like her husband's old ties (fig. 7). Much more than testaments to her thrift, her quilts memorialize her long and happy marriage to her dear husband, Charlie. One of them includes photographs printed on fabric as well as pieces of his old clothing. It is embroidered with his nicknames and his favorite old songs; layers of meaningful and memorable images, labels, and sounds, are represented by the various fabrics.[30]

Today's quilters may acquire fabric in even more ways than their nineteenth-century ancestors did. Margaret Anderson recalled that "we all traded fabrics around because we had this little group here in the neighborhood. And we'd go to shops where they sold fabric and barrels, you just dug into the barrel and pulled out what you wanted ... and you bought it by the pound." At one point, Anderson attended a quilting conference in New Mexico where she was the lucky winner of a large

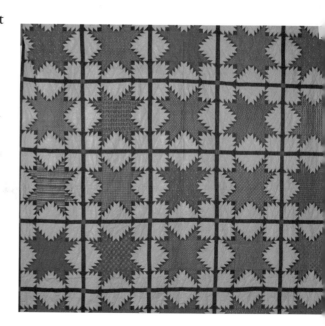

Fig. 5. Friendship Quilt detail, 1847
Made by Sarah Webb Cloud (1817 – 1899) of Kennett Township as a wedding gift. See overall image opposite page 29.
Courtesy of Sara Meadows

Fig. 6. Feathered Star, 1850 – 1880
Made by Sarah (Sallie) Jane Wetheral (1836 – 1902) of East Goshen Township.
Cotton top; cotton back; 99" x 97"
Courtesy of Ronald and Nancy Harper/Douglas and Amy Harper

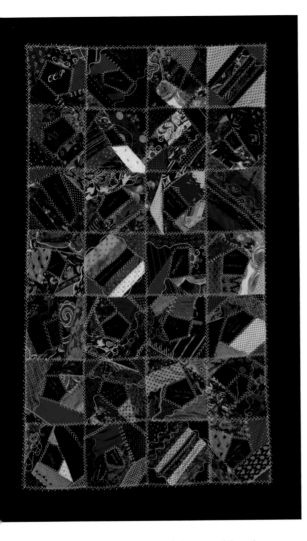

she carefully salvaged from clothing from six generations on her mother's side and five generations on her father's side (fig. 9). Her mother "had a habit of collecting clothing from relatives that had passed on," leaving them carefully starched, pressed, and neatly packed in boxes in the attic. Loath to "burn them," Jacobs searched for sections that remained bright, such as "underneath the hem of the nightgown, and underneath the pocket of aprons," collecting swatches that date back to the 1800s.[33] Though made from material that others might consider trash, her quilt rises far above utility and frugality. It is an artist's masterpiece, crafted of saved and found objects that transform and transcend their materials, just as creators of folk and high art have done for years. Yet sometimes the constraint of using scraps provides both challenge and relief. The incredible variety in today's fabrics, Jacobs believes, actually creates too many choices. Phoenixville resident Joanne Campbell Brown echoes this sentiment and prefers limiting her choices to piecing scraps because "you don't have to worry about a color board" or carefully search quilt shop inventories for the perfect color match.[34]

Memories of a frugal use of fabric reverberate through the accounts recorded by many of the Chester County women in the oral history project.

ag of quilt squares made and donated by the ttendees (fig. 8). One of the Tel Hai quilters, ormer Mennonite missionary Alta Hershey, still ashions crib quilts from the colorful fabric used by African women to carry their babies. Perhaps a etter way to see quiltmakers, then and now, is as vid collectors of fabric, in which case the quilts are heir artful ways of displaying those collections. his perspective elevates women's shopping to a ind of connoisseurship—the ability to bring a nowledgeable, critical eye to their acquisition and rrangement of colorful fabric.[31] Seen in this light, quilts become far more than expressions of mere rugality.

A maker's *use* of a variety of fabrics also nhances our understanding of a quilt as a work of reativity and ingenuity. Quiltmakers like poets nd composers exercise "creativity within onstraints," piecing words or notes together within ometimes rigid patterns of rhythm and rhyme.[32] na Jacobs's Grandmother's Flower Patch quilt ncludes more than 2,700 small hexagons of fabric

Fig. 7. Charlie's Memory Quilt, 2000
Made by Barbara Loftus Perrone (b. 1930) of West Chester as a memorial to her husband Charles C. Perrone. Silk, rayon top; silk back; 62" x 39" Courtesy of Barbara Perrone

Fig. 8. Cactus Bud, 1989
Margaret Anderson (b. 1915), having won these quilt squares at a quilting conference in New Mexico, skillfully composed the background to recall the Western desert, mountains, and sky. Cotton top; cotton back; 72" x 59 ¼" Courtesy of Margaret P. Anderson

They grew up during the Great Depression, imbibing the values of recycling that economic hard times inculcate. Yet Helen Smoker recalls that even during the 1930s, she battled crowds of women shopping for bags of scraps and remnant material from shirt factories—the seemingly paradoxical act of purchasing scraps. Sara Meadows observes, too, that so few women today still sew their own clothes, that accordingly most of them must buy their fabric.[35] Thrift as a motivation for making quilts, then, should only occasionally be applied to Chester County quiltmakers today, as most are now frank about their consumerism. They may have been children of the Great Depression, but they delight in shopping for quilt fabric, acquiring large "stashes," and displaying their neatly folded fabric arranged by color. They convert basements, spare guest rooms, garages, or home offices into studios and storage spaces for their craft materials.[36]

Joanne Brown believes that it is actually wasteful to use some scraps. She prefers new cotton fabric because "you don't know whether it [old fabric] will hold up." She uses wool scraps because it is more durable, recycling her family's old clothing and items she picks up at yard sales. She describes her vibrant pieced cotton Pineapple Log Cabin as a "scrap quilt" but defines it as made of lots of "different colors and patterns." Quilters make scrap quilts when they "have more fabric than they know what to do with," she explains. "Even though you don't need it," you buy lots of fabric because "variety is the spice of life." Joanne Belsen, one of the Tel Hai quilters, terms quilting "not the cheapest hobby" because it requires time, room, and money.[37]

Perhaps the quilts of the Amish, the Gee's Bend women, and the folk artists of rural Appalachia are so popular today because they seem to speak more honestly of plainness and frugality, because they were made by more "authentic" quiltmakers, and more to the "point," because they more nearly live up to the stories and ideals that Americans have attached to quilts when viewing them primarily as products of frugality. Their makers seem to reflect the lack of technology, the closeness to the land and the past, the poverty, and the thrift of a past era.[38] Such a perspective ignores historical reality. Only the very wealthiest of women in preindustrial American had access to an abundance of fabrics. Similarly when we as viewers assess quilts as folk art—primitive and original, constructed of scavenged or found objects, serendipitous accident of beauty—we prevent ourselves from considering quilts as careful craft or even high art. Craftspeople and artists invest in good tools and materials, devote years to develop their skills and their vision, and many cultivate patrons to support or purchase their work. Seeing all quilts as examples of "making do" ignores the investments in time, skills, tools, and materials, and it prevents us from elevating quiltmakers from clever and thrifty housewives to careful craftswomen and innovative artists.[39]

The Tension between Selflessness and Self-expression

Quilts also convey special values that are specific to women in American culture. Quilts speak lovingly and admiringly about women's essential care for their families, even as twentieth-century women increasingly joined men in work outside the home and shared family responsibilities with men and other caregivers.

Many Americans tend to assume that until the last few decades of the twentieth century women's roles have remained static. According to that view, the "traditional" woman was timeless in her duties and in the characteristics that define the ideal

Fig. 9. Grandmother's Flower Garden, 1958 – 1959
The 2,700+ creatively combined hexagons in this quilt are made from swatches of clothing that had belonged to numerous ancestors of the maker. Pieced by Ina Ruth Hippensteel Jacobs (b. 1928) of Cochranville and quilted by her and her mother-in-law Jennie Jacobs. Cotton; 98" x 81"
Courtesy of Ina Jacobs

woman. Contemporary quiltmakers generally share those views. Margaret Anderson believes that by making quilts, she is "following along" in the footsteps of her female ancestors. As Helen Smoker puts it, sewing was "the thing that women did. All along." Quiltowner Ron Harper quips, men do the "killing, hunting, digging," while women's work is sewing, and "always has been." Even schoolchildren have trouble imagining many men making quilts.[40]

Yet the roles and the ideals about women that many Americans generally think of as traditional are not age-old but instead, like quilts themselves, are products of the nineteenth-century industrial revolution. Quiltmaking blossomed in the nineteenth century, emerging roughly when the prescription that women "stayed home and took care of the children" became the ideal for middle-class families. Prior to then married women

generally worked alongside husbands on farms and in small shops, and in families the father was the childrearing authority. As the nineteenth century progressed, new work opportunities took men away from the home during the day and women increasingly shouldered the duties of childrearing. Perhaps quiltmaking helped to compensate for women's tangible loss of responsibility in running a shop or a farm and ennobled their newer caretaking responsibilities. Quilts decorated and elevated the bed in which so much of nineteenth-century women's functions increasingly centered—fulfilling their sexual responsibilities, giving birth, and caring for the sick and the dying. As West Chester quiltowner Pamela Gray has phrased it, women "are closer to life's transitions."[41]

In this context, quilts speak clearly and eloquently about the family relationships that

Fig. 10. Family Tree, 1959
The Nieweg sisters made this Family Tree quilt at their river house, the location of the family's many reunions, for their mother Ella Weir Crowl Nieweg's 69th birthday. Makers were from the Elkdale, New London, Kelton area. Cotton top; cotton back; 85" x 82"
Courtesy of George Thomas

reinforce women's maternal roles. The Nieweg sisters' elaborate Family Tree quilt makes those bonds explicit, celebrating an extended family and their frequent reunions at a cherished river house (fig. 10). Every contemporary quilter recites many stories of making quilts for children, grandchildren and great-grandchildren, of celebrating weddings, housewarmings, and reunions. Makers take pride in the fact that their progeny, both boys and girls, request their quilts. In turn, the makers work hard to create objects that reflect the children's interests and desires. Joanne Brown, for example, is working diligently to grant a grandson's plea for a quilt made in his middle school's colors of black and gold, colors she would never have chosen herself.[42]

The adult recipients of quilts also view them a tangible expressions of strong bonds between family members. Patricia Baily of Kennett Square and Betty Andersen of Oxford received similar quilts from their mother, long-time Avondale resident Alice Chase Patterson. One quilt helped her grown daughter cope with widowhood, servin as a comforting "hug" from her mother. The other quilt reminds a daughter of her mother's uncomplaining, positive attitude even as she reached one hundred years old. Similarly, Susan Sleichter of Wagontown still prizes the childhood quilt her grandmother made, "just for me" (figs. 11, 12).[43]

The most spectacular, historic, and distinctively Chester County quilts brought in for documentation (as well as those in the Historical Society's permanent collection) are the red-and-green signature quilts from the mid-nineteenth century. They celebrate the closeness of families as well as church, community, and friendship ties with an impressive variety of turkey-red prints, pieced and appliquéd quilt patterns, and drawn, stamped, or embroidered names. They also demonstrate how those interwoven webs could stretch across the country. One signature quilt migrated westward to Colorado, discovered in a thrift shop by a former Chester County resident who recognized the place names under the signatures (fig. 13).[44]

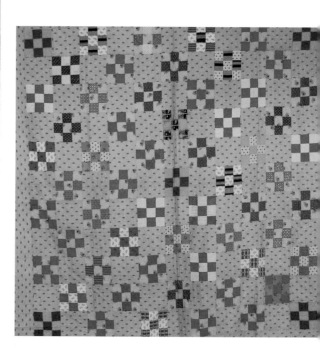

(Top) Fig. 11. Dresden Plate, 1985
Patterson made similar quilts for her two daughters. This one has a rose quilted border as a reminder of the family's rose business. Made by Alice Elisabeth Chase Patterson (b. 1902) of Christiana, Lancaster and Chester Counties, PA.
Cotton top; synthetic blend back; 86 ¼" x 87 ½"
Courtesy of Patricia Patterson Baily

(Above left) Fig. 12. Eighteen-Patch Sawtooth, 1949
Made by Eva Viola Cloud Delaney (1883 – 1965) of West Chester.
Cotton top; cotton back; 89" x 69 ½"
Courtesy of Susan Cloud Schofield Sleic

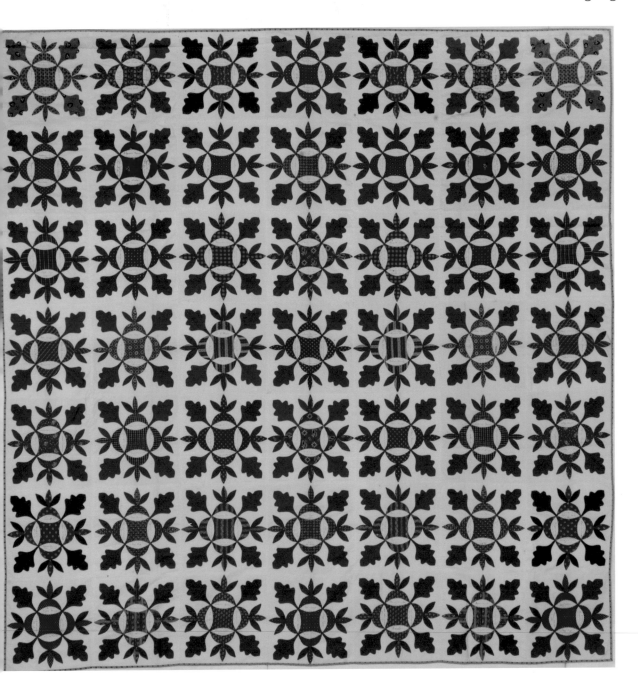

Quilts also come with stories that highlight the fragility of family life, exposing the tensions—the broken or frayed threads—that exist in any family. Honey Brook quiltowner Marian Stoner inherited an 1840s quilt that acquired the nickname "Spite Quilt" because upon the death of its maker, Sarah Logan, one of her sisters hurried to retrieve the quilt just "so the other sister wouldn't get it" (fig. 14). Other quilts bear witness to the sorrow that death inflicts on a woman and her family. Coatesville's Ruth Thompson inherited a childhood dress that she believes may have belonged to Florence Graham, whose untimely death as a young woman may have inspired her grieving mother, Libby Graham, to include swatches of its fabric in a quilt (fig. 15). Finally, quilts created in love cannot prevent a marriage from unraveling. The maker of one beautiful wedding quilt enlisted family members and friends to create "special little patches," then over a "matter of years" bound and stitched the squares together. With regret she acknowledged that "Yes, it is . . . too bad. In those days we never foresaw there would be a divorce." As these examples illustrate, quilts are neither trivial artifacts of domestic life nor impersonal abstract works of art. They offer personal and powerful testimony to the pain as well as pleasure of family life and illustrate the

(Opposite page right)
Fig. 14 Nine-Patch, 1850 – 1870
Made by Sara Logan of Romansville.
Cotton top; cotton back; 87 ⅝" x 87 ⅝"
Courtesy of Marian Stoner

(Above) Fig. 13. Friendship Quilt Top, 1847
Made for Mary Worrall by Chester County friends and family with sentiments such as "Think of me when far away." Found in a thrift shop in Colorado.
A detail is on the front cover. Cotton; 78" x 78"
Courtesy of Sally Berriman

powerlessness to produce happy endings that even the strongest women suffer in their roles as mothers and family members.[45]

Confinement often characterizes women's lives, and quilt stories emphasize the constraints of women's lives while showing how quilts helped to ease the confinement. Ina Jacobs stitched pieces of fabric together as she waited for children in school and doctors' appointments or during long evenings when her husband was on military duty and she was isolated on a babysitter-less military base. Joanne Belsen credited quiltmaking with "saving her sanity" during the seven long years she cared for her husband who was ill with Alzheimer's. She set up her quilt frame in view of her husband because he became agitated when he couldn't see her. Ina Jacobs spent the long months she cared for her dying father enlisting his help during the day in piecing a postage stamp quilt and then spending the long night at his bedside sewing the tiny scraps together.[46]

Quiltmaking also eased the pain of confinement caused by the quiltmaker's illness or

by bad weather. Helen Smoker learned to sew while recovering from polio, and when stricken by rheumatic fever as an adult, quiltmaking remained one of the few activities open to her. Ina Jacobs spent months in a hospital bed during which she couldn't read but could craft "yo-yos," small strips of fabric sewn into doughnut shapes, that she pieced into a quilt after her recovery. One quilt brought in for documentation was accompanied by a story of its maker, Miss Clara Dilks, who was "an invalid and could only move her fingers" (fig. 16). Stories of men making quilts also bolster the notion that the activity is both a result of, and an antidote to, confinement. Dementia, strokes, heart attacks, and the loss of limbs all induced men to engage in this activity usually pursued by women. Some quilters actually looked forward to some periods of confinement. The Nieweg sisters welcomed snowstorms that limited all activities except quiltmaking. Ina Jacobs planned ahead, freezing soups for the children to prepare so that she could devote the frigid month of February to quiltmaking. Drema Benson credited the winter storms in 1993 and 1995 with helping her to finish her quilt.[47]

Though quilts repeatedly reaffirm women's family relationships and responsibilities, they also speak of a wider women's world beyond the home. The quilting bee has been a favorite American icon, a symbol of cooperative labor in the same spirit as the barn raising or the husking bee. It has also become a powerful symbol of what one historian of nineteenth-century women called a "female world of love and ritual." For some of today's quiltmakers, the activity can be a similar social occasion. Ina Jacobs helped to organize Chester County Historical Society's Quaker Quilters group that met regularly for years, much like the women who regularly quilt together at their retirement community at Tel Hai and much like the church members who stitch quilts for charity. While such groups certainly continue a tradition of collaborative female labor, socializing may be a secondary reward. According to Jacobs, her Quaker Quilters raised tens of thousands of dollars in quilt raffles for the Historical Society. Quite a few quiltmakers belong to guilds and sometimes work with those groups. These, too, provide opportunities for fundraising and charity, but they also allow members time to "show and

Fig. 15. Modern Blocks, 1880 – 1900
Made by Ruthanna Brown Sharpless (1846 – 1927) of West Grove.
Silk top; cotton back; 67" x 68"
Courtesy of Ruth Smedley Thompson

ell" or to learn techniques from experts and each other. In this light, socializing is the means to accomplish quiltmaking rather than the purpose of quiltmaking. As one quilt author has recognized, "Whatever [a quilting bee's] function as a social occasion, quiltmaking's main reason for being has always been a private one—the personal satisfaction it gives."[48]

Most of the quilters interviewed for the Chester County Quilt Documentation Project spend the majority of their quilting time working alone, and that is a positive aspect for many of them. They prefer the solitary activity, enjoying a meditative state that some experts have endorsed as conducive to mental and even spiritual health. Many enjoy a peaceful setting in front of a sunny window or the rhythmic and calming repetitive motion of stitching. Some of them "multitask," planning and taking notes for other activities as they work. For others, focusing on the quilt helps to exclude other worries, or in Joanne Brown's words, it "takes your mind off your problems."[49]

Although quilts and their stories communicate the many images and obligations of domesticity, making quilts represents a choice of activity even when choice may not have been available to women in other areas of life. Today's young women are encouraged to consider a wide range of career choices, but women who came of age before or during the middle decades of the twentieth century had far fewer options. Although several women who brought in quilts and consented to be interviewed attended college and went on to teaching, nursing, or other careers, and others had

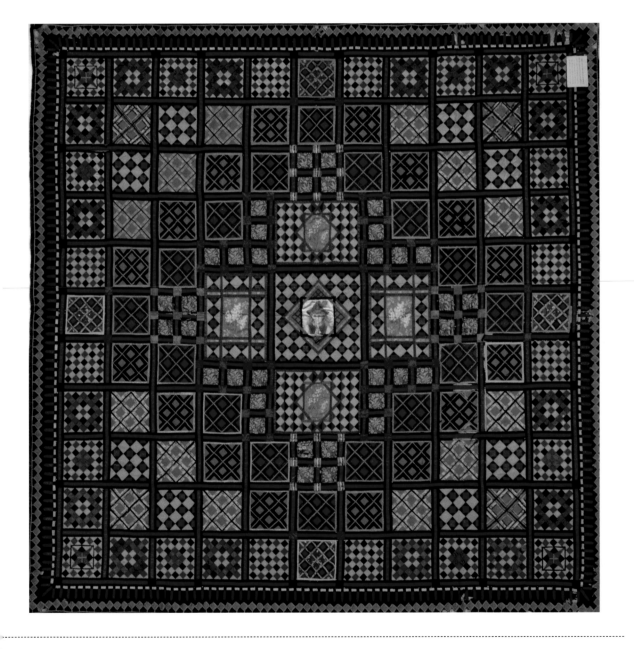

Fig. 16. Dilks Quilt, 1881
Although only able to "move her fingers" invalid Clara Dilks fashioned a quilt of sumptuous fabrics combined in a highly original design. Made by Clara Dilks (d. 1885) and descended in the Pierce family of Kennett Square. Silk top; cotton back; 69" x 69"
Courtesy of Longwood Gardens

worked at least temporarily as domestic servants or factory workers or "took in boarders to make ends meet," most of the women had spent considerable time tending children, homes, and farms. These obligations, though, did not prevent these women from choosing to undertake quiltmaking instead of purchasing widely available, and generally inexpensive, blankets or spreads. They chose to make quilts, too, as part of a range of creative activities that went far beyond the essential care of family and farm. Twentieth-century Chester County quiltmakers engaged in dressmaking, knitting, crocheting, tatting, embroidery, cross-stitch, painting canvases, braiding rugs, making furniture and other decorative objects, doing upholstery and furniture repair, gardening, landscape planning and planting, among other activities. A few supplemented the family income by performing these activities for others, for pay, though none could be said to have supported herself from the activity. Several women had models for quiltmaking—grandmothers, aunts, and other women friends who enjoyed the activity—but others did not. Quiltmaking was a conscious creative choice.[50]

Now, as in the past, choosing to make quilts allows women to remain within the domestic sphere while gently expanding its boundaries. Quiltmakers reinforce nineteenth-century ideals of

Fig. 17. Bicentennial Quilt, 1975 – 1976
Helen Smoker wears the subdued apparel of her Mennonite faith but possesses an artist's love of color and design. This is evident in the quilt she and her daughter Jane Davidson made in 1976 to commemorate both the American Bicentennial and Jane's housewarming. Made by Helen Kathryn Buch Smoker (b. 1916) of Ronks, Lancaster County, PA and Jane Louise Smoker Davidson (b. 1939) of Glenmoore. Cotton top; synthetic blend back; 100" x 99 ½"
Courtesy of Jane L.S. Davidson

femininity when they express a modesty and ambivalence about their efforts. In interviews as well as in quilt guild meetings, these women often express an unwillingness to draw attention to their accomplishments, interests, or talents, voicing comments such as "I'm just a beginner," or "I'm not nearly as good as some of these women"; however, quiltmaking provides a safe space for women to express some individuality and pride in their work. Many take advantage of the "show and tell" part of the meeting to hold up their quilts and explain their significance or techniques, an effort that invariably meets with appreciative comments from the audience.[51] Nevertheless, the women also take risks in their choices. Barbara Perrone makes crazy quilts even though she doubts others share her enthusiasm for the genre. She eagerly brought in many quilts and vests for documentation, shared her quilts in shows, and pointed with pride to the quilt she made for the Paoli Hospital Gift Shop that now hangs in the hospital lobby. Joanne Brown gained satisfaction from exhibiting her quilts and winning ribbons. Even the modest Mennonite Helen Smoker admitted, "You want people to see the pride you took in your work." Her Bethlehem Star quilt is an exuberant testament to her individual creative vision and artistic originality (fig. 17). Though expressions of modesty confirm feminine ideals and recall a time when "pride" was often considered a vice, quiltmakers resist such stereotypes when they share or exhibit their work, enter quilts into competitions, or gain self-esteem from their work and their abilities. The documentation project and the exhibition of community quilts are the result of these women's pride in their work and the quilting tradition.[52]

Quilt historians have argued that since the nineteenth century women have employed quilts to challenge restrictions on their speech and speak out politically. For example, historians have traced the Drunkard's Path pattern to its use by women who supported the temperance movement, a powerful political group that eventually secured the passage of a constitutional amendment that brought Prohibition to the nation.[53] The documented Chester County quilts, however, generally fail to convey such

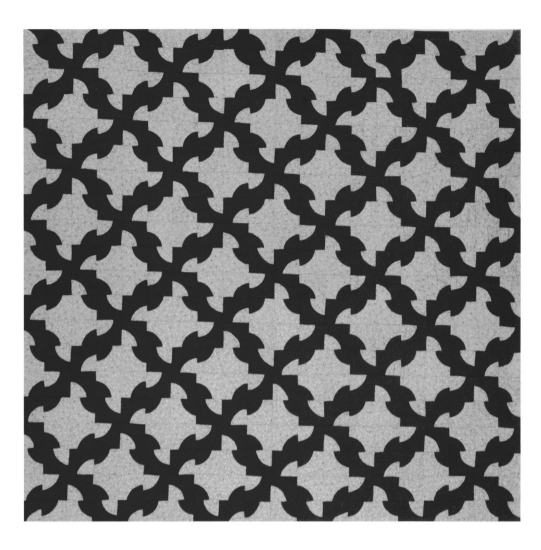

lear political messages, and few current owners
an interpret a political message in their older
uilts. Margaret Anderson, for instance, recognized
he Drunkard's Path pattern on her quilt and knew
hat its maker, her great-great-grandmother, was the
vife of a busy Presbyterian minister. Yet Anderson
xpressed confusion when asked about the
neaning of the design, perhaps worrying that the
nessage indicted the minister as a drunkard rather
han conveying his spouse's support of his position
gainst drinking alcohol. Ruth Keim's grandmother
lso made a Drunkard's Path quilt. Keim, however,
ived for a while with her grandmother,
emembered that Phoenixville woman's active
nvolvement in the Women's Christian Temperance
Jnion, and confidently confirmed the pattern's
olitical message (fig. 18).[54]

When former West Chester resident Gay Gilpin
ohnson joined with her sister Quaker quilters to
reate a Peace quilt, they intended to express their
eligious and political beliefs in nonviolence. More
ecently quilt guild members have created

hundreds of patriotic red-white-and-blue Quilts of
Valor to send to troops wounded in Iraq and
Afghanistan. Beyond their colors, these
contemporary quilts carry no explicit political
messages about the justice of the war but instead
convey expressions of feminine and maternal
concern for the young people who fight for their
country (fig. 19).[55]

(Top) Fig. 18. Drunkard's Path, 1930 – 1950
Made by Mary Ellen Detweiler Rapp (1869 – 1952)
of Phoenixville.
Cotton top; cotton back; 75″ x 73″
Courtesy of Ruth Keim

(Above right) Fig. 19. Friendship Quilters
clothesline display in the Oxford area. These quilts
were sent to troops wounded in war zones of Iraq
and Afghanistan, 2008.

she just admired the bold pattern by a published quilt designer and simply adapted its "far out, arty design" (fig. 22).[57]

Messages in quilts can be difficult to discern, thus makers, owners, viewers, and historians can come to very different interpretations. When Pamela Gray read a message in her late nineteenth-century crazy quilt, she saw the "connections between [three generations] of strong women."[58] This timeless and positive message combines all the best qualities that Americans want to see in quilts and their makers: the strength of women and

When quiltmakers are asked if they send any messages in their own quilts, most respond in the negative, although when the point is pursued, some change their mind. For example Gay Gilpin Johnson explained that the message in her wedding quilt expresses "affection for your kids" because each square made by friends and relatives symbolizes the makers' special relationship with the couple (fig. 20). "So I guess the message is," Johnson says, "'Three cheers for the kids!'" West Chester quiltmaker Elizabeth (Betty) Shaver Voorhees may not try to send a message in her quilts, but her reliance on traditional patterns and reproduction fabrics announces her strong and enduring allegiance to the styles and designs of older quilts (fig. 21). [56]

Chester County's schoolchildren can read messages into many quilts. They combine their imaginations and their own social and political backgrounds and discern multiple messages of maternal love and interesting stories, but also political messages about multiculturalism, nearly all of which were unintended by their makers. For example, Joanne Brown was surprised to learn that so many children were drawn to her "Illusions" quilt and that two middle-school girls had examined it carefully and dubbed it the "Gay Jew Quilt." "You're kidding," she exclaimed. These politically aware girls had perceived an elongated Star of David and read the rainbow colors in between the bold triangles as symbolic manifestations of gay pride. Brown, however, says

their relationships with their families and with each other. When Chester County quilts overwhelmingly send messages of love, friendship, or charity, rather than overt political messages, when they are made for giving rather than for selling, and when they tell stories of confinement or express modesty, they reinforce an ideal of feminine domesticity. That ideal, though, has been threatened in the last four decades by some feminist ideology as well as the increasing opportunities for women to pursue new career opportunities beyond the home.

It is dangerous to allow generalizations about quilts and domesticity to obscure the ways that quilts also challenge notions of femininity and women's domesticity. A careful examination reveals

Fig. 20. Friendship Quilt, 1984
Made by Gay Gilpin Johnson (b. 1924), Germantown, Philadelphia County, PA. Blocks made by friends and family, some from Chester County, for Emily Johnson and Rick Mohler. Cotton, linen, polyester top; polyester back; 94 ½" x 96"
Courtesy of Gay Gilpin Johnson

Fig. 21. Contemplation, 1994
Made by Elizabeth Shaver Voorhees (b. 1929) of West Chester.
Cotton top; cotton back; 41" x 34"
Courtesy of Elizabeth S. Voorhees

how quilts can disguise newer, and less-prized, behaviors and motivation—leisure and consumerism, or women's individualism, pride, competitiveness, and desire for recognition, self-expression and self-fulfillment. Drema Benson's Story Quilt documents the migrations of two generations of an African-American family through several states, visibly linking Benson to her extended family through maps, photographs and memorabilia. The quilt aptly shows, too, Benson's development as an individual—a journey that took her from Cleveland, Ohio, to Chester County, Pennsylvania, where she has become a mother, an artist, and a teacher (fig. 23).[59]

Quilts have been at the center of an ideological tug-of war, working to resist the social and economic changes that pulled women away from their central role as producers in the nineteenth century and struggling to resist those twentieth-century changes that have pulled women away from primary roles as mothers and homemakers. When industrialization changed life in the home, quilts served to reclaim the values of the previous era. When twentieth-century politics and economics drew women themselves from the

Top) Fig. 22. Illusion, 1997
Made by Joanne Campbell Brown (b. 925) of Phoenixville.
Cotton top; cotton back; 70 ½" x 52 ½"
Courtesy of Joanne Brown

Fig. 23. The Road Traveled, 1995 – 1997
This story quilt reads clockwise and highlights the migration of Drema Benson's grandparents and parents to various states, and, most recently, herself to Chester County. Made by Drema Benson (b. 1950) of West Chester, her mother and grandmother. Cotton top; 73" x 105". Courtesy of Drema Benson

home, quilts worked to reclaim the feminine virtues that domesticity represented. Quiltmaking has allowed women, then and now, to maintain an allegiance to powerful, even if confining and restricting, models of womanhood while simultaneously negotiating transitions to changing roles.

Consequences of Tension in Quilts

Whether quilts speak of industry or leisure, of thrift or consumption, of women's selflessness or self-expression, the tensions inherent in quilts and the stories about quilts contribute, in part, to their ambivalent value in families and society. Despite the many people who lavish time and effort on making quilts, or those who carefully save and research their makers and their families, quilts do not retain a universal appeal. Some quilts documented in the last five years have already ended up in thrift shops. Current owners worry about who should inherit quilts, whether the quilts will be appreciated, and whether historical societies or museums are interested in family quilts and the objects and documents that go along with them. Susan Sleichter owns a quilt her

(Above and opposite top right) Fig. 24. Crazy Quilt and detail, 1887
Made by Rachel Shoemaker (1804 – 1883) of West Grove.
Silk top; cotton back; 52" x 52"
Courtesy of Pamela Gray

andmother made for her, and she knows it will
ot have the same intrinsic value to her daughter.
mela Gray's crazy quilt is in such mint condition
aradoxically increasing its value) precisely
cause it was not valued by previous generations
d lay forgotten in a barrel in the attic of a West
rove home for almost a century (fig. 24).
onically, too, the humble, worn, simple utilitarian
ilts that best illustrate the values of industry,
rift, and domesticity are those most likely to have
en left at home on documentation days, or to be
ssed over in the selection of quilts to exhibit. A
ajority of quilts do not garner automatic
preciation even among other quilt-makers.[60]

My initial lack of interest, knowledge, and
preciation of quilts is a deficiency shared by
any other Americans, women and men. Quilts
ow hold new significance for me because I better
nderstand their construction: the thoughtful
eativity required in their design and the skill
quired in their execution. I was aware, for
stance, that combining complementary colors,
atching the corners of pieced squares and
iangles or executing tiny, decorative quilting
itches was aesthetically pleasing, but I did not
alize that failure to choose colors carefully could
e jarring, or that mismatched corners and
nskilled basting and stitching techniques
roduced a quilt that was lumpy and "all wobble-
wed," in Helen Smoker's words. As objects, quilts
re complex constructions.[61]

Quilts now hold new significance for me as an
istorian, too. They embody the tensions inherent
 American history: the tug of old values under
e relentless pressure from new competing values;
e lure of comfortable stories and the lack of
ttention to uncomfortable realities. Quiltmakers
nd owners tell stories sometimes quite different
om those related by quilt historians. Makers and
wners sometimes fail to appreciate the larger
ntext of the development of quiltmaking in the
ineteenth century, and historians sometimes fail
 appreciate the importance of the values those
dividual and collective quilt stories convey. These
nduring tensions make quilts rich and complexly
yered historical artifacts.

Endnotes

Karin E. Gedge, who received her Ph.D. from Yale University, is Associate Professor of History at West Chester University and the author of Without Benefit of Clergy: Women and the Pastoral Relationship in Nineteenth-Century American Culture *(New York: Oxford University Press, 2003).*

1. U.S. Census Bureau Chester County Quick Facts at http://quickfacts.census.gov/qfd/states/ 42/42029.html.

2. Historians of quilts have long been preoccupied with the degree to which stories, and histories, perpetuate myths. See Laurel Horton, ed., *Quilt Making in America: Beyond the Myths* (Nashville: Rutledge Hill Press, 1994); Judy Elsley, "Making Critical Connections in Quilt Scholarship," *Uncoverings* 16 (1995): 229–43, takes a literary historian to task for perpetuating the "myth" of piecing old fabric. For a recent "myth" about slave quilt codes that has generated much controversy, see Jacqueline L. Tobin and Raymond G. Dobard, *Hidden in Plain View: A Secret Story of Quilts and the Underground Railroad* (New York: Anchor Books, 1999); and Laurel Horton, "The Underground Railroad Quilt Code: The Experience of Belief," *Uncoverings* 28 (2007): 207–16.

3. For an excellent discussion of the relationship of women, quilts, and for a more detailed historical context, see Pat Ferrero, Elaine Hedges, and Julie Silber, *Hearts and Hands: The Influence of Women and Quilts on American Society* (San Francisco: Quilt Digest Press, 1987). Janet Floyd, "Back into Memory Land? Quilts and the Problem of History," *Women's Studies* 38, no. 1 (January 2008): 38–56, notes the "heyday" of popular quiltmaking in the decade of the 1840s by examining the ambivalence of women to the historic changes in several short pieces of fiction on quilts from that period.

4. Pat Baily and Betty Andersen, interview by Karin Gedge, April 16, 2008, Chester County Quilt Documentation Project (hereafter cited as CCQDP), recall their mother spinning wool.

5. For a comprehensive overview of these massive changes see Daniel Walker Howe, *What Hath God Wrought: The Transformation of America, 1815–1848* (New York: Oxford University Press, 2007).

6. Stewart Davenport, *Friends of the Unrighteous Mammon: Northern Christians and Market Capitalism, 1815–1860* (Chicago: University of Chicago Press, 2008).

7. For early examples, see Nancy Cott, *The Bonds of Womanhood: "Woman's Sphere" in New England, 1780–1835* (New Haven: Yale University Press, 1977); Christopher Lasch, *Haven in a Heartless World: The Family Besieged* (New York: Basic Books, 1977).

8. Ferrero, Hedges, and Silber, *Hearts and Hands*, 96; Rachel Maines, "Paradigms of Scarcity and Abundance: The Quilt as an Artifact of the Industrial Revolution," in Jeanette Lasansky et al., *In the Heart of Pennsylvania: Symposium Papers* (Lewisburg, Pa.: Oral Traditions Project of the Union County Historical Society, 1986), 84–89.

9. Max Weber, *The Protestant Ethic and the Spirit of Capitalism*, Talcott Parsons, trans. (New York: Scribner, 1958). Robert N. Bellah, Richard Madsen, William M. Sullivan, Ann Swidler, and Steven M. Tipton, eds., *Habits of the Heart: Individualism and Commitment in American Life* (Berkeley: University of California Press, 1985), also inform my thinking on American values.

10. Sara Meadows, interview by Karin Gedge, April 7, 2008, CCQDP. Lasansky, Foreword, *Heart of Pennsylvania:19th & 20th Century Quiltmaking Traditions* (Lewisburg, Pa.: Oral Traditions Project of the Union County Historical Society, 1985), 7, observes that the hours spent making a quilt "elevates" it, "even the most mundane, in the eyes of the owner" raising it above other inherited objects. Roszika Parker traces the development of the association between needlework and feminine worth in *The Subversive Stitch: Embroidery and the Making of the Feminine* (London: Women's Press, 1984).

11. Velma Nieweg Wilson (b. 1920), Marguerite Nieweg Rector (b. 1928), Beatrice Nieweg Thomas (b. 1918), and Ella Nieweg Luff (b. 1930), and Jenny Thomas Watson, daughter of the late Muriel Nieweg Thomas (b. 1921), all interviewed by Patricia Keller, October 25, 2003, CCQDP. Unfortunately, it is difficult to identify each individual by her voice on the recording.

12. Ina Jacobs, interview by Ellen Endslow, November 27, 2007, CCQDP. Jacobs lived for years in Cochranville.

13. Margaret Anderson, interview by Anita Regester, December 6, 2007, CCQDP.

14. Nieweg family interview.

15. Gladys Mosteller, Alta Hershey, Joanne Belsen, and Ester Burtner, December 10, 2007, interview by Ellen Endslow and Karin Gedge, CCQDP. When I can identify the individual voices on the recording, I cite the individual by name in the text.

16. Marybeth C. Stalp, "Negotiating Time and Space for Serious Leisure: Quilting in the Modern U.S. Home," *Journal of Leisure Research* 38, no. 1 (January 2006): 104–32. Quiltmaking for these 20th-century quilters is as much pleasurable pastime as it is productive work, hence the need to "negotiate." It probably was for many of their foremothers, too, but diaries only explicitly record the work done and not the pleasure gained; for example, Mary Blanche Jackson wrote: "Mother and I went up to ——'s and helped quilt till 5:30" (August 12 1924, diary, Chester County Historical Society).

17. Chester County schoolchildren often said that women, not men, made quilts because "women had more time," implying that women did not work as hard or as long men. Perhaps women who made quilts chose a leisure activity that looked more like work than leisure, that it was important to maintain an appearance of work even when they had leisure. One study of Georgia families moving from farm to factory in the early 20th century found that women continued the duties they had on farms, but successfully used new free time for care of families and neighbors. Their men, though, drifted to unproductive leisure activities like drinking and gambling. Teresa Beyer-Sherwood "From Farm to Factory: Transitions in Work, Gender, and Leisure at Banning Mill, 1910–1930s," *Oral History Review* 32, no. 1 (Winter/Spring 2005): 65–94. Journalist Michael Hall had a difficult time finding an analogy for quilts in men's lives today and likened quiltmaking to men's "poker nights"; see Hall "The Fabric of Our Lives," *Texas Monthly* 36, no. 1 (January 2008):116–21, 175–76, 185–89. Thanks to William Haff for advising me of this article.

18. Lydia Maria Child, *The American Frugal Housewife* (30th ed.: New York: Samuel S. & William Wood, 1844) Historians like to remind readers that frugality is a myth, and that quilts were an "artistic endeavor, rarely . . . an economic one" (Joel Slater, *The Patchwork Quilt* [Ephrata, Pa.: Science Press, 1981], as quoted in Holstein "American Block Quilt," in Lasansky, *Heart of Pennsylvania . . . Symposium*, 26).

19. The Tel Hai quilters, for instance, recall that the cheap remnants of pastel velvet and satin from the Boyerstown casket company showed up in local crazy quilts.

20. Roderick Kiracofe, *The American Quilt* (New York: Clarkson Potter, 1993), 131, cites similar uses in frontier families. Helen Smoker (Lancaster County) and daughter, Jane Davidson (Glenmoore), interview by Karin Gedge, November 20, 2007, CCQDP, brought in

---

...any quilts of the type that others chose to leave at ...ome, the homely and worn rather than the spectacular ...d pristine. Both the Nieweg family and Sara ...eadows, among others, assumed that their well-worn ...ilts were not worthy of documentation. "Oh, you ...on't want us to get started on that pile," remarked one ...ieweg sister referring to a stack of plain quilts. ...ikewise, the community members choosing quilts for ...e exhibition largely avoided selecting quilts in a worn ...ondition.

...1. Besides Davidson's quilt (145 FF), see quilts 34A, ...6B, 158C for examples of repairs.

...2. Nieweg family interview.

...3. See 228A as well as 26V, 77A, 94A, 115 E, 118E, 145V, ...00A.

...4. For examples of new sashing or borders, see 64 E, ...25A, 125 B, 125D; 184J, 235A; for new quilting, see ...3D, 130C, 138D, 160C, 220C; and for new embroidery, ...e 146F.

...5. See 272C for example.

...6. Anna Wilson, interview by Ellen Endslow, April 23, ...008, CCQDP.

...7. Jacobs interview.

...8. Meadows interview.

...9. Ron Harper, interview by Karin Gedge, April 17, ...008, CCQDP.

...0. Barbara Perrone, interview by Barbara Schneider, ...ecember 10, 2007, CCQDP.

...1. Burton J. Bledstein, *The Culture of Professionalism: The Middle Class and the Development of Higher Education in America* (New York: W. W. Norton, 1976). Besides fabrics, Barbara Perrone has collected books, eggcups, teapots, ...ddy bears, and figural hands.

...2. Thanks to Jane Kircher for pointing out this ...imilarity. See Patricia D. Stokes, *Creativity from Constraints: The Psychology of Breakthrough* (New York: ...pringer, 2005) for a discussion of this phenomenon.

...3. See also 29B; and quilts including flags or souvenir ...abric 34A; and socks 41J.

...4. Jacobs interview; Joanne Brown, interview by Karin ...edge, May 5, 2008, CCQDP.

...5. Smoker interview; Meadows interview.

...6. Elizabeth Shaver Voorhees, interview by Karin ...edge, January 16, 2008, CCQDP; Brown interview; & ...elsen interview.

37. Brown interview; Belsen interview.

38. Geraldine N. Johnson, "More for Warmth than Looks: Quilts of the Blue Ridge Mountains," in *Pieced by Mother: Symposium Papers*, ed. Jeannette Lasansky (Lewisburg, Pa.: Oral Traditions Project of the Union County Historical Society, 1988), 47–59.

39. Susan E. Bernick, "A Quilt Is an Art Object when It Stands Up like a Man," in *Quilt Culture: Tracing the Pattern*, ed. Cheryl B. Torsney and Judy Elsley (Columbia: University of Missouri Press, 1994), 134, challenges the idea that quilts were not seen as art within their own traditions, yet Chester County's quilters are reluctant to call their work "art." Gay Gilpin Johnson (interview by Margaret Jerrido, December 5, 2007, CCQDP) concedes, "I guess you would say it is an art form." Voorhees (interview) distances her work from high art when she says, with a wry smile, that she does not like "artsy-fartsy" quilts. Quiltmakers can resist the label of artist that scholars apply or the messages that scholars read into quilts. For examples, see Fabvienen Taylor, "Mississippi Quilters Shun 'Artists' Label," *National Catholic Reporter*, March 17, 2006; Amei Wallach, "Fabric of Their Lives," *Smithsonian* 37, no. 7 (October, 2006): 66–75.

40. Smoker interview; Harper interview; and writing assignments for Chester County schoolchildren conducted in Spring 2008 by CCHS staff and volunteers.

41. Historians trace shifts in notions of the ideal woman at the nation's founding (the Republican Mother) and during the 19th century's market and industrial revolutions (the Cult of True Womanhood) and the development of "separate spheres" for men and women. Barbara Welter, "The Cult of True Womanhood, 1830–1860," *American Quarterly* 18, no. 2, pt. 1 (Summer 1966): 15–74; and especially Patricia J. Keller, "The Quilts of Lancaster County, Pennsylvania: Production, Context, and Meaning, 1750–1884" (Ph. D. diss., University of Delaware, 2007), which helped me to refine my thinking here. Pamela Gray, interview by Ellen Endslow, April 23, 2008, CCQDP.

42. Nieweg family interview; Brown interview.

43. Baily and Andersen interview; Susan Sleichter, interview by Susannah Brody, November 29, 2007, CCQDP. Examples of such bonds are also evident in other interviews, specifically: Gray interview; Nieweg family interview; Smoker interview; and Joanne Brown interview. See also the scenes in Drema Benson's Story Quilt.

44. Only after current owner Sally Berriman, formerly of Chester County, purchased it in a Colorado thrift shop did she recognize its connections to the county and realize its great value.

45. Ruth Smedley Thompson, interview by Sandy Reber, December 2, 2007, CCQDP; Marian Stoner, interview by Ellen Endslow and Karin Gedge, December 20, 2007, CCQDP; Johnson interview. See also Perrone interview; and Carolyn H. Krone and Thomas M. Horner, "Quilting and Bereavement: Her Grief in the Quilt," *Uncoverings* 13 (1992): 109–26.

46. Jacobs interview; Belsen interview. The sadness that informs these stories about care giving to the dying seems permanently attached to the quilts and quiltmaking these women undertook during these periods.

47. Smoker interview; Jacobs interview; and Nieweg family interview; Drema Benson, *Drema's Quilt* (np: np, 1993), a pamphlet.

48. Carroll Smith-Rosenberg, "Female World of Love and Ritual," in *Disorderly Conduct: Visions of Gender in Victorian America* (New York: Alfred A. Knopf, 1985); Jacobs interview; Tel Hai interview; Kiracofe, *American Quilt*, 131–32.

49. Perrone interview; Anderson interview; & Brown interview. Sociologist/psychologist Mihaly Czikzentmihaly termed this phenomenon "flow" in his "Ten Paradoxical Traits of the Creative Personality," *Psychology Today* 29, no. 4 (July/August 1996): 36–41. He recognized that creative people enjoy the process for its own sake. See also Nancy Monson, "Quilts, creativity, and healing," *Quilter's Home*, 2 no. 6 (January/February 2008): 65–66. Thanks to Rhonda R. Newton for this reference. Heather Lenz, "Learning to Quilt with Grandma Mary Sibley: Gift Labor, Traditional Quiltmaking, and Contemporary Art," *Uncoverings* 19 (1998): 109, quotes quiltmaker Mary Sibley, who had a similar response: "You can be worried about this, or that, or the other thing, but when you start to make a quilt, the only thing you worry about is finishing that quilt."

50. See Jane L.S. Davidson, "Quilting: A Family Tradition," *Mennonite Family History* 10, no. 1 (January 1991): 4–8, for one such family.

51. Quilt guild meetings: Friendship Quilters of Southern Chester County, March 31, 2008, Elk Ridge School, Oxford; Calico Cutters, April 9, 2008, Fame Fire Co., West Chester. I am indebted to Sandy Day for correspondence and invitations to attend these and other meetings.

52. Perrone interview; Brown interview; & Smoker interview. Sara Reimer Farley and Nancy Hornback, "The Quilting Records of Rachel Adella Jewett and Lucyle Jewett." *Uncoverings* 18 (1997): 26, describes one 19th-century diarist's possible guilt at the pride she took in recording her quilts and the prizes they were awarded: "These records demonstrate some pride in her work, which may not have been considered a positive character trait by these Quakers turned Methodists. Lucyle's Scrapbook is inscribed with some irony: 'Ecclesiastes 12:8' ['Vanity, vanity, all is vanity']."

53. Ferrero, Hedges, and Silber, *Hearts and Hands*, provides the best background on political quilts.

54. "But, the funny thing, kind of, is that her husband, my great-grandfather [confusion over relationship], was a minister. So maybe, I don't know what, whether there's a connection, but I thought that was funny that she chose that path [i.e., Drunkard's Path pattern]." (Anderson interview). See also Ruth Keim, interview by Susannah Brody, April 4, 2008, CCQDP. Several historians have noted the fragility of symbolic messages and the difficulty of reading messages. Ricky Clark, "The Needlework of an American Lady: Social History in Quilts," in Lasansky, *Heart of Pennsylvania . . . Symposium*, p. 65; Barbara Brackman, "Rocky Road to Analysis: Interpreting Quilt Patterns," *Uncoverings* 25 (2004): 1–9.

55. Johnson interview. Author's meetings with Friendship Quilters and Calico Cutters. The foundation that fostered these efforts makes no bones about its approach, stating prominently on the homepage of its web site: "This foundation is not about politics. It's about people." (http://www.qovf.org).

56. Johnson interview; Voorhees interview.

57. Brown interview.

58. Gray interview.

59. Benson, *Drema's Quilt*. Eva Unger Grudin explores this genre in *Stitching Memories: African American Story Quilts* (Willamstown, Mass.: Williams College Museum of Art, 1989).

60. Author's conversation with Ellen Endslow, August 15, 2008; Sleichter interview; Gray interview.

61. Smoker interview.

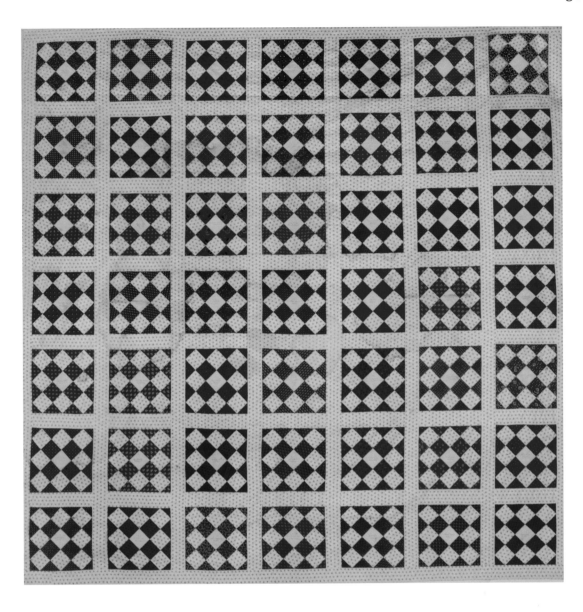

Friendship Quilt, 1843
Believed to be made by Amy Ann Marshall. Family names on the quilt include Marshall, Matlack,
Preston, Taylor, Smedley, James, Ashbridge, Hoopes, and Hicks from East Goshen, Westtown,
Thornbury, East Marlborough, West Bradford and Willistown.
Cotton top; cotton back; 100 ½" x 100 ½"
Courtesy of Rachel Neville

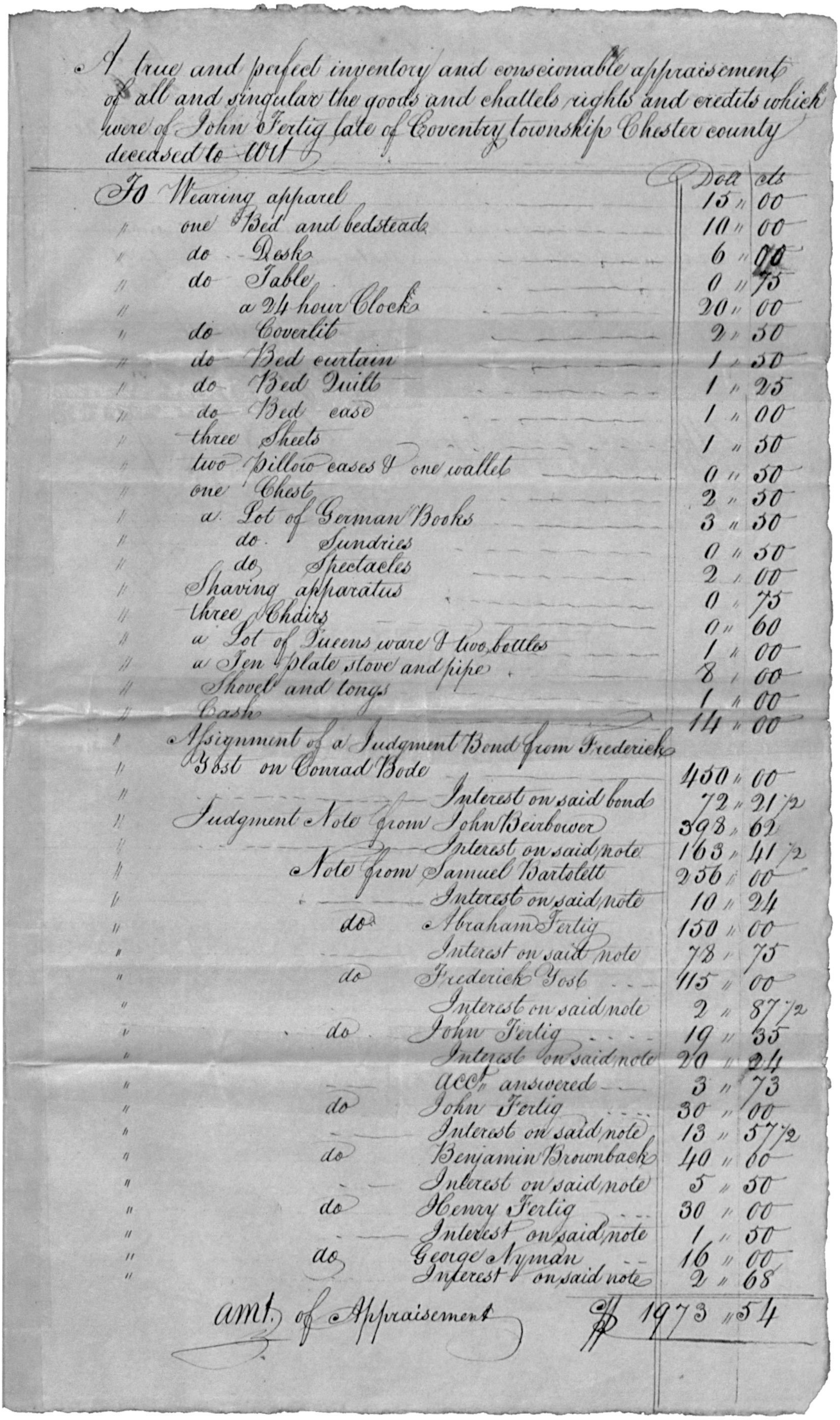

A true and perfect inventory and conscionable appraisement
of all and singular the goods and chattels rights and credits which
were of John Fertig late of Coventry township Chester county
deceased to Wit

		Doll	cts
To Wearing apparel		15	00
" one Bed and bedstead		10	00
" do Desk		6	00
" do Table		0	75
" a 24 hour Clock		20	00
" do Coverlit		2	50
" do Bed curtain		1	50
" do Bed Quilt		1	25
" do Bed case		1	00
" three Sheets		1	50
" two Pillow cases & one wallet		0	50
" one Chest		2	50
" a Lot of German Books		3	50
" do Sundries		0	50
" do Spectacles		2	00
" Shaving apparatus		0	75
" three Chairs		0	60
" a Lot of Queens ware & two bottles		1	00
" a Ten plate stove and pipe		8	00
" Shovel and tongs		1	00
" Cash		14	00
" Assignment of a Judgment Bond from Frederick			
" Yost on Conrad Bode		450	00
" Interest on said bond		72	21½
" Judgment Note from John Beirbower		398	62
" Interest on said note		163	41½
" Note from Samuel Bartolett		256	00
" Interest on said note		10	24
" do Abraham Fertig		150	00
" Interest on said note		78	75
" do Frederick Yost		115	00
" Interest on said note		2	87½
" do John Fertig		19	35
" Interest on said note		20	24
" Acct answered		3	73
" do John Fertig		30	00
" Interest on said note		13	57½
" do Benjamin Brownback		40	00
" Interest on said note		5	50
" do Henry Fertig		30	00
" Interest on said note		1	50
" do George Nyman		16	00
" Interest on said note		2	68
Amt of Appraisement		$ 1973	54

Fig. 1. Estate Inventory, John Fertig, 1831
Register of Wills
Chester County Archives, West Chester, PA

Patricia J. Keller

Taking Inventory:
Quilts and Quiltmaking in Chester County, Pennsylvania, 1725–1860

The history of quilts and home quiltmaking in Chester County, Pennsylvania, offers fruitful ground for researchers. Until quite recently many quilt historians have assumed that early British immigrants brought a longstanding tradition of home quiltmaking to the region, and that quiltmaking was an enduring household craft among rural British Pennsylvanians from settlement onward.[1] Because quiltmaking was not a Continental household textile tradition, it has been widely supposed that rural Pennsylvania Germans in southeast Pennsylvania "adopted the quilting and associated piecing and appliqué work of their English neighbors" by the mid-nineteenth century. Among other conditions, this model of cultural transmission presumes a large number of British Pennsylvanians engaged in home quiltmaking well before quilts were added to Pennsylvania German bedding.[2] Yet investigations into the belongings of Chester County's early householders lead us to quite different conclusions: only a handful of eighteenth-century residents, whether of British or German descent, had any bedquilts at all.[3]

To gain a broader perspective on the history of quilts and quiltmaking in Chester County during the eighteenth and nineteenth centuries, I examined a sample of Chester County estate inventories filed between 1725 and 1859 (fig. 1). I looked specifically at inventories from four of the county's rural townships and its two urban centers, and then considered that data in conjunction with information gathered during the Chester County

Quilt Documentation Project.[4]

Estate inventories (also known as "probate inventories" or "household inventories") are detailed listings of the personal property belonging to an individual at the time of his or her death, assembled to help settle an estate.[5] Household inventories document the presence (or absence) in decedent households of various items such as chairs, tables, beds and bedding, kitchen equipment, farming tools, livestock, and crops harvested or in the ground. For our purposes, the inventories reveal much information about different kinds of furnishing textiles (including bedquilts), unworked cloth, unprocessed and processed textile fibers, and spun yarn found in the home (fig. 2.1 – 2.5). They also list tools used to act upon textiles (quilting frames, sewing machines), yarns (weavers' stocking and garter looms), and fibers (spinning wheels, reels, cards) the appraisers encountered as they worked their way from garret to cellar—and through the estate's various outbuildings.

Inventories also supply the economic values ascribed to these items by the appraisers—men selected by the estate administrator(s) or executor(s) for their expertise in such matters. Careful reading of estate inventories and a systematic sorting of the appraisers' notations allows us to discern changes in the presence and values of household furnishing textiles and tools used for textile-related work. Structuring this information provides opportunities to observe

2.2

Fig. 2.1. Finished bedding, unworked linen cloth, and skeins of linen tow yarn.
Courtesy of Patricia Keller and Kory Berrett

Fig. 2.2. Flax prepared for spinning or storage.
Chester County Historical Society

2.3

2.1

2.4

2.5

Fig. 2.3. Wool Cards, mid-1800s
Chester County Historical Society

Fig. 2.4. Flax Spinning Wheel, early 1800s
Chester County Historical Society

Fig. 2.5. Sewing Basket, late 1800s,
Gift of Lela S. Walker.
Pin Cushion, mid-1800s,
Gift of Francis D. and Deborah H. Brinton.
Turkey-red Print Swatches, 1840s
Chester County Historical Society

patterns of continuity and change in the types of textiles in use in households and the organization and extent of household textile production.

Each estate inventory provides a glimpse of an assemblage of personal property collected and edited by its owner over an often-long lifetime. In the eighteenth and nineteenth centuries individuals acquired and released personal property in numerous ways—including purchase or barter, multiple marriages, the receipt or giving of gifts, inheritance, loss by fire, the liquidation of material assets to repay creditors, and advancements to children by parents, to name just a few. Items listed in any inventory may have been acquired by the household twenty or more years or only a few days prior to the inventory process.[6] For our purposes, the value of studying inventories lies in determining the patterns of presence or absence of items over time, and in following changes in descriptive information, including assigned monetary values provided by the appraisers.

The inventories examined for this study come from locations selected to reflect the county's cultural and economic diversity and offer perspective on change and continuity over this 135-year period. One of Pennsylvania's three original counties, Chester County was populated predominantly by persons of English ancestry, although a significant number of immigrants were of Scots Irish, Welsh, and of Germanic descent (table 1, map 1).[7] On the whole, the county was a predominantly rural and agricultural region, but it also was home to artisans and laborers, many of whom likewise "tilled some land and pastured some cows."[8] The towns of Chester and, later, West Chester were notable urban exceptions, and they served the county successively as centers for governance, commerce, and society.[9] Each of the rural townships—Nottingham, Coventry, Tredyffrin, and Uwchlan—fall within the geographic boundaries that define Chester County today. However in this study I observed the geographic boundaries of each one as established at their founding in the early decades of the eighteenth century. I consulted each estate inventory on file for decedents residing in all four townships during six ten-year periods: 1725–1734, 1750–1759, 1775–1784, 1800–1809, 1825–1834, and 1850–1859 as well as those from the town of Chester in the years 1725–1734, 1750–1759, and

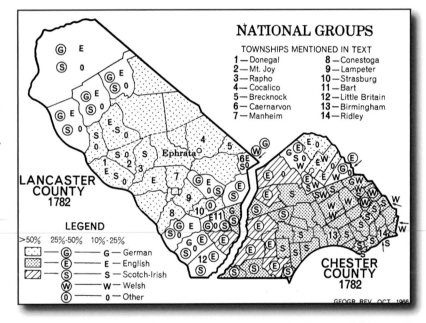

NATIONAL GROUPS

TOWNSHIPS MENTIONED IN TEXT

1 — Donegal   8 — Conestoga
2 — Mt. Joy   9 — Lampeter
3 — Rapho   10 — Strasburg
4 — Cocalico   11 — Bart
5 — Brecknock   12 — Little Britain
6 — Caernarvon   13 — Birmingham
7 — Manheim   14 — Ridley

LANCASTER COUNTY 1782

CHESTER COUNTY 1782

LEGEND

>50%   25%-50%   10%-25%

G — German
E — English
S — Scotch-Irish
W — Welsh
0 — Other

GEOGR REV OCT 1966

Table 1: National groups in Chester County, 1730–1782

	1730	1759	1782
English	67%	59%	63%
Welsh	17%	8%	7%
Scots Irish, Scots, Irish	12%	23%	19%
German-speaking	2%	5%	8%
Other and unassigned	2%	5%	3%
Approximate total population of county	10,025	24,500	34,500

Source: James T. Lemon, "The Agricultural Practices of National Groups in Eighteenth-Century Southeastern Pennsylvania," Geographical Review 56, no. 4 (October 1966): 469.

Note: Lemon arrived at these percentages by doing surname analyses of the 1782 tax lists published in Pennsylvania Archives and the 1730 and 1759 manuscript lists of returns and assessments in the Chester County Historical Society library. Undifferentiable names, such as Smith and Brown that could be either German or English, he placed in the unassigned category.

(Top) Map 1. Source: James T. Lemon, "The Agricultural Practices of National Groups in Eighteenth-Century Southeastern Pennsylvania," *Geographical Review*, vol. 56, no. 4 (Oct. 1966), fig. 5, p. 486. Image used with permission.

Table 2. Number of estate inventories filed in each of the six decades

	1725–1734	1750–1759	1775–1784	1800–1809	1825–1834	1850–1859	Total
Nottingham Township (50+% English, 25–50% Scots Irish in 1730)[a]	15	44	48	69	145	165	486
Tredyffrin Township (50+% Welsh, 10–25% English in 1730)[a]	1	9	19	36	31	33	129
Uwchlan Township (50%+ Welsh, 10–25% English in 1730)[a]	4	12	29	14	40	40	139
Coventry Township (50+% German, 25–50% English in 1730)[a]	2	n.d.	12	43	63	78	198
Chester	8	13	25				46
Borough of West Chester				10	32	83	125
Total	30	78	133	172	311	399	1,123

Source: Inventories, Chester County Archives, Chester County, Pennsylvania.
Note: Township boundaries for all decades are those of original organization.

[a]The 1730s ethnicity percentages are based on James T. Lemon, The Best Poor Man's Country: A Geographical Study of Early Southeastern Pennsylvania (Baltimore: Johns Hopkins Press, 1972), fig. 24. Lemon's fig. 26 indicates that by 1782 the ethnic composition three townships had shifted: English and Scots Iris residents were evenly numbered in Nottingham Township; English residents comprised 50% or more of Tredyffrin Township's population, with Welsh and German residents comprising 10–25% each; and approximately 50% of Uwchlan township's population was English, with Welsh and Scots Irish being about 25 each. The percentage of Germanic residents in Coventry Township remained steady.

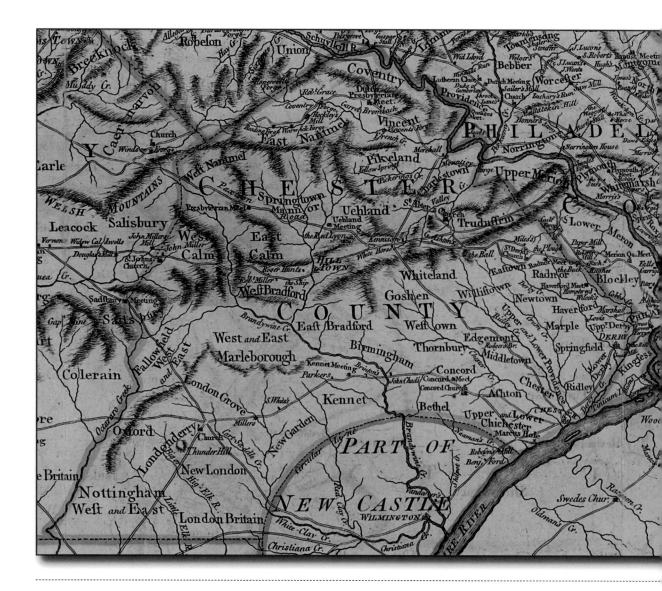

Map 2. Detail taken from "A Map of Pennsylvania . . . Laid down From Actual Surveys, and Chiefly from the late Map of W. Scull Published in 1770," in William Faden, *The North American Atlas* (London: the author, 1777). Original full sized map from which this image is derived is in the collection of the Library of Congress.

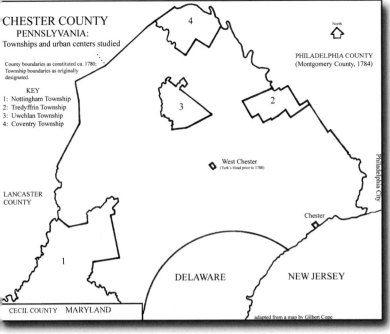

CHESTER COUNTY
PENNSYLVANIA:
Townships and urban centers studied

County boundaries as constituted ca. 1780;
Township boundaries as originally
designated.

KEY
1: Nottingham Township
2: Tredyffrin Township
3: Uwchlan Township
4: Coventry Township

North

PHILADELPHIA COUNTY
(Montgomery County, 1784)

West Chester
(Turk's Head prior to 1788)

Philadelphia City

LANCASTER
COUNTY

Chester

CECIL COUNTY   MARYLAND

DELAWARE   NEW JERSEY

adapted from a map by Gilbert Cope

the 1725–1734 period. The decedents' personal estates in this decade ranged from a modest £22-16-8 (that of Richard Osborn of Nottingham Township in 1726) to a substantial £409-7-9 (that of merchant John Baldwin of Chester in 1732).[11]

The small size of this group of early inventories—just twenty-five—makes it risky for us to conclude that no householders in the county had any quilted bedcoverings in the early eighteenth century. Even if we were to examine each inventory filed for every Chester County decedent, we still would not know about quilted bedcovers that had been acquired and worn out through daily use, nor would we know of any that had been sold, traded, or given away as gifts during a particular individual's lifetime. Yet the total absence of bedquilts among these inventories is itself a kind of evidence, suggesting bedquilt ownership was not widespread among rural or urban households in this early period.

What many of the households did have were spinning wheels, essential tools for transforming processed textile fiber into hand-spun yarns for knitting or weaving. Most Pennsylvania spinners produced yarns for cloth intended for household consumption, rather than for exchange in markets, although a small proportion worked at their craft for board, wages, or store credit.[12] Of these same 25 inventories, 17 listed one or more spinning wheels: 16 of the households owned "little" wheels, intended for spinning flax; 3 households owned

1775–1785, while it served as county seat, and those from the borough of West Chester from 1800–1809, 1825–1834, and 1850–1859, after it became seat of county government (table 2; maps 2 & 3).

More than three-quarters of the 1,123 inventories in the sample contain itemized listings of household furnishings, including specific kinds of table and bedding textiles, spinning wheels, processed and unprocessed textile fibers, fiber-processing tools, thread, and yarn.[10] Data presented in the rest of this essay is drawn from that informative subset (table 3).

Information from this sample of Chester County estate inventories reveals much about the use and production of quilted bedcoverings in Chester County households over several generations' lifetimes. Bedquilts do not appear in any of the inventories listing household goods in

Table 3. Estate inventories itemizing household goods

	1725–1734	1750–1759	1775–1784	1800–1809	1825–1834	1850–1859	Total
Nottingham Township	10	34	40	60	113	118	375
Tredyffrin Township	1	7	16	30	26	24	104
Uwchlan Township	4	11	23	10	31	28	107
Coventry Township	2	n.d.	11	41	54	62	170
Chester	8	8	22				38
Borough of West Chester				5	26	56	87
Total	25	60	112	146	250	288	881

Source: Inventories, Chester County Archives, Chester County, Pennsylvania.

Note: Township boundaries for all decades are those of original organization.

(Top) Map 3. Map of Chester County showing selected towns, four townships and subsequent subdivisions. For details about dates for land divisions, refer to endnotes, page 77.

Table 4: Spinning wheel ownership in all sampled regions

	1725–1734	1750–1759	1775–1784	1800–1809	1825–1834	1850–1859
Inventories itemizing household goods	25	60	112	146	250	288
Listing spinning wheel(s)	17 (68%)	43 (72%)	78 (70%)	105 (72%)	162 (65%)	56 (19%)
Listing flax wheel(s)	16 (94%)	39 (91%)	70 (90%)	94 (90%)	143 (88%)	52 (93%)
Listing wool wheel(s)	3 (18%)	19 (44%)	45 (58%)	51 (49%)	63 (39%)	10 (18%)
Listing both flax and wool wheel(s)	2 (12%)	15 (35%)	37 (47%)	40 (38%)	44 (27%)	6 (11%)

Source: Inventories, Chester County Archives, West Chester, Pennsylvania. See table 3 for sampled regions.

"long" or "big" wheels for spinning wool; and 2 households owned both kinds of spinning wheels (table 4).

A quarter of a century later the picture had begun to change. During the 1750–1759 decade, 60 estate inventories listed household goods. As in the previous group the decedents were economically diverse: inventoried personal property ranged from £14-18-6 for the estate of yeoman William Armstrong of Londonderry Township (carved from Nottingham Township in 1734), to £1641-9-10 for that of Justice Caleb Cowpland of Chester.[13] Eleven of the 60 inventories listed one or more bedquilts (table 5). Five of these households were in the town of Chester; 5 were in Nottingham Township, and 1 was in Tredyffrin Township. The surnames of 10 indicate British ancestry: Backhouse, Boyd, Cowpland, Hamilton, Lea, McComons, Morgan, Rich, Robinson, and Welsh. The 11th decedent, William Melchior, was very likely of German descent.[14]

Of the 11 households with bedquilts, 5 had just one; 4 owned two, 1 had three, and 1 listed four. Appraisers labeled five quilts as "old." The inventory that included four bedquilts, none of which was described as old, was that of Sarah Robinson of Chester, the only female decedent in this group.[15]

Robinson left personal property totaling £173-12-6, a middling amount by the standards of her

time and place, but a significant personal estate for a woman of the 1750s.[16] Appraisers arranged the list of items in her household in room-by-room order, an aspect that permits us to understand how her house was furnished and used. In "the front room upstairs" the appraisers noted "one Bed, Bedsted, hangings, Quilt, Blankets, 2 Sheets, 2 pillows & Boulster," which they assigned a combined value of £5-0-0, and "one feather bed, bedsted 2 Blanketts, 2 Sheets, 1 Quilt 2 pillows & one Boulster" worth £3-0-0. In "the Middle Room" they encountered the most costly constellation of sleeping appointments: "one bed bedstead, 2 Sheets, 2 Blanketts, 2 Pillows, Curtains and Window Curtains & Boulster & quilt" valued together at £13-5-0. In "the back room" on the second floor they found "one bedsted and Counterpane" valued at £1-10-0, and "one bed and bedstead, one pair of Sheets, quilt, Blanketts, two pillows & boulster" appraised together at £8-0-0. In each case the aggregate values for the bedding assemblages suggest that the completely dressed beds were costly—and, by implication, important—household furnishings. This is especially evident in comparison with a much less sumptuous bedding assemblage in "the Garrett" of her house: "one Chaff bed, B'sted, 2 Rugs, a blankett and a Sacking bottom" which the assessors valued at £1-10-0. Bedsteads, beds, and bedding accounted for nearly a fifth of the value of Sarah

Table 5: Bedquilt ownership in all sampled regions

	1725–1734	1750–1759	1775–1784	1800–1809	1825–1834	1850–1859
Inventories itemizing household goods	25	60	112	146	250	288
Number listing bedquilt (s)	0	11	5	20	62	73
Percentage listing bedquilts	0%	18%	4%	14%	25%	25%

Source: Inventories, Chester County Archives, Chester County, Pennsylvania. See table 3 for sampled regions.

Robinson's personal property, a considerable and significant allocation of resources. The identification in Robinson's inventory of a first floor "Common Room" furnished with tables, chairs, accessories to drinking spirits and dining, and a bell (to call for service), suggests that the home was a small boardinghouse, with a relatively genteel standard of amenity, operated by the widow as a source of income.[17]

Although appraisers did not set an individual value for any of Sarah Robinson's four quilts, their probable worth may be deduced from appraised bedquilts listed in two other Chester estate inventories in this decade. Thomas Morgan's 1756 estate inventory included a bedquilt valued at 18 shillings, and in 1758 Justice Cowpland's bedquilt was valued at 10 shillings.[18] If each of Robinson's was worth just 10 shillings, then the combined value of all four quilts would have been £2, a handsome amount. To lend perspective: 10 shillings was 1½ pence more than the average male laborer in Philadelphia earned for three days' work in 1754.[19]

The appraisers did not identify the fabrics or designs of the quilts owned by Sarah Robinson, Thomas Morgan, and Caleb Cowpland. However, extant eighteenth-century quilts from nearby Philadelphia and descriptive inventory data from Philadelphia households provide guidance. Appraisers' notes there suggest most bedquilts in Philadelphia at midcentury were expensive, high quality, imported or locally made bedcoverings worked up by professional artisans from costly textiles such as silk, worsted calimanco, and printed or colored cotton calicoes and chintz.[20] Thus the quilts noted within inventories for 1750s estates in the town of Chester and Chester County's more rural townships were also likely of the same type, a type known today as "whole cloth" quilts—quilts whose surfaces are made up of lengths of a single fabric sewn together lengthwise. The decorative aspects of these quilts were lodged in the sumptuous textiles of which they were comprised and in the delicate hand-stitched quilting patterns that became apparent as daylight and candlelight played across their sculpted surfaces.

Such costly quilts were items of "inconspicuous consumption," which, like gleaming silver tea wares, were seen only by persons welcomed to private rooms within a home's interior.[21] There these costly goods strategically yet silently identified their owners as persons of affluence, discernment, and genteel sensibilities.[22] But unlike silver with its metal's intrinsic worth, bedquilts did not retain value in the face of wear or changing fashion; their presence in a home indicated an owner's ability and willingness to spend a substantial sum on an elegant yet ephemeral object without concern for preserving original investment. A bedquilt in this era was an asset of another kind: a tangible investment made to generate social capital.

The sample compiled a quarter of a century later (1775–1784) is nearly double the size of the previous one, but a smaller proportion of households owned quilts. Just 5 (4%) of 112 estates listing household goods had one or more bedquilts: 3 from the town of Chester, 1 from Oxford Township (formerly within Nottingham Township) and 1 in Uwchlan Township.[23] The values of the decedents' personal goods ranged from £314-15-0 to £2,014-16-8, though Revolution-

Fig. 3. Whole Cloth Quilt, circa 1774 – 1783
Linen top; linen back; 86" x 77"
Gift of Clara P. Garrett, Chester County Historical Society, 1987.857

era inflation complicates comparisons: for example, values assigned to a single bedquilt range from 15 shillings in 1777 to 10 shillings in 1782 to £2-10-0 in 1784.[24] All 5 owners had surnames of British derivation: Hayes, Cowpland, Salkeld, Owen, and Shaw.

In nearby Philadelphia the market for imported bedquilts had declined at midcentury. Since estate inventories document personal property obtained and edited over a lifetime, it is unsurprising that inventories listing quilts in the 1775–1784 decade were compiled for decedents whose age and assets suggest they had acquired fashionable imported or commissioned bedquilts some years earlier as signals of personal wealth and taste. When bedquilts fell from fashion these same people likely removed those bed coverings from the best bedchambers to less important rooms as bedding for children or servants. Others, finding their imported quilts passé, likely passed them along to new owners or offered them for sale—thus removing them from the household and the eventual inventory process.[25]

Inventory data also indicate a change in home textile production. Nearly the same proportion of inventoried households owned spinning wheels in the years 1750–1759 (72%) and 1775–1784 (70%) as in the earliest decade sampled.[26] However, an increasing proportion of households had added wool wheels to their assemblages of fiber processing tools by the mid-1780s (see table 4). The larger number of households with wool wheels suggests the production of woolen yarn had intensified in the intervening decades.[27]

This pattern changed little for the 1800–1809 decade, as 72% (105) of 146 inventories listing household goods specified one or more spinning wheels.[28] A new item also appears: "Cotton wheels" used for spinning cotton fiber into yarn are noted in four inventories, all from Coventry Township. These same households also had one or more flax wheels, and one had two wool wheels, a cotton wheel, and three flax wheels.[29]

About the same time imported bedquilts fell from fashion, home quiltmaking rose in popularity as a stylish needlework craft among women from leading families in the mid-Atlantic region's urban centers.[30] Using expensive imported silks and other fine goods these women took up quiltmaking to demonstrate their gentility, refined taste, and

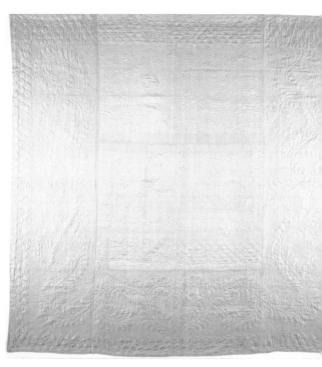

competency in the needle arts. Their quilts symbolized each maker's (and by extension her family's) wealth and leisure time, as such needlework projects were both costly and labor intensive, far beyond the financial reach of most.[31]

The inventory evidence in the three eighteenth century samples makes it quite clear that British immigrants did not bring with them a tradition of home quiltmaking when they sailed from England to Pennsylvania. However, at least one extant bedquilt provides evidence that some women in Chester County had adopted quiltmaking as a home textile craft late in the third quarter of the eighteenth century (fig. 3). Passed down through several generations of the Garrett family of Chester County, whose members first settled in the region in the late 1600s, this linen whole cloth quilt ornamented with block-stamped designs on its face and filled with carded wool is attributed to Susanna Lewis Garrett (1743–1821), wife of weaver/farmer Samuel Garrett (1742–1812) of Willistown Township, adjacent to Tredyffrin Township.[32] Susanna Garrett, possibly with the assistance of her mother, Susanna Johns Lewis, likely made the politically charged bedcovering in the early 1770s.[33] Susanna Garrett's ability to conceptualize her quilt's politically communicative aspects provides eloquent evidence that she—and likely many other Chester County residents—were fluent in the visual language of textiles typically used by women of leisure when making bedquilts

Fig. 4. Silk-Faced Quilt, late 1700s
Reportedly made in part from the 1773 wedding petticoat of Mary Davis Ashbridge.
Silk top; cotton and wool back; 105" x 107 ¾"
Gift of Pennell T. and William W. Phillips, Chester County Historical Society, Q20

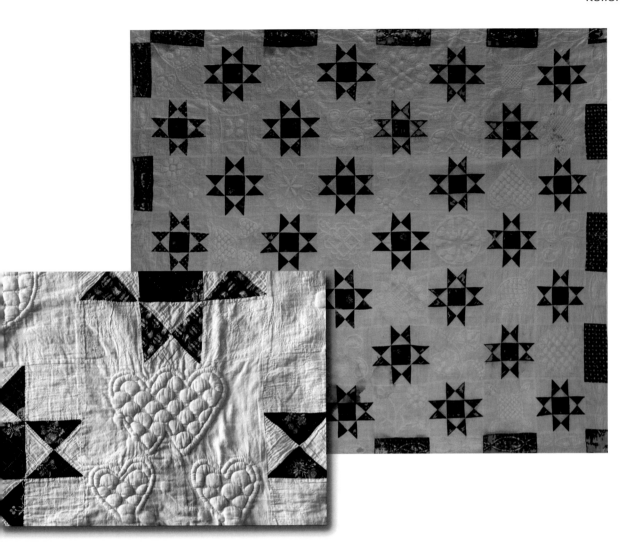

(Top) Fig. 5.1 & 5.2. Pieced Quilt and detail, Eight-Point Star (fragment), 1790 – 1830. Possibly descended from the Wallace family of Highland Township; embellished with stuffed work. Cotton top; cotton, linen back; 90 ½" x 80 ¾" Courtesy of Barbara Huston

Fig. 6.1 & 6.2. Pieced and Appliquéd Quilt and detail, 1810 Probably made by Barbara Walter Gundaker (Gundacker) of Lancaster; embellished with stuffed work. Cotton top; cotton back; 122" x 122" Courtesy of the Heritage Center of Lancaster County

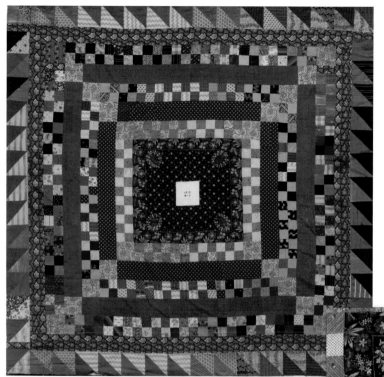

backed and quilted to blend with the petticoat's stitched design. In the colonial era Philadelphia merchants offered imported silk-faced quilted petticoats, generally announcing the arrival of a new supply in newspaper advertisements. Such petticoats became an important part of stylish attire in the early 1770s: the decoratively stitched petticoats made of elegant and costly fabrics were framed by the fashionable divided skirts of women's gowns.

By the 1770s, American women of means adopted the mode of making bedquilt tops of "patchwork," defined in

in the years immediately preceding the American Revolution. She inverted the norm of crafting quilts from fine imported fabric by instead choosing cloth woven of yarns handspun from flax very likely grown nearby; the cloth may have been woven in Pennsylvania, perhaps by Susanna's weaver husband. The choice of "homespun" linen cloth silently but unmistakably spoke of her family's support of domestic American manufactures, nonimportation, and nonconsumption. This quilt's probable date of production and its materials' communicative implications also suggest some Chester County women participated in home quiltmaking as a fashionable pastime at least by 1770 and perhaps earlier.[34]

Quilts made in Chester County in the later eighteenth or very early nineteenth century are now quite rare. One such quilt incorporating in its center pieces taken from a quilted silk-faced petticoat reportedly was assembled by a descendant of Mary Davis of Haverford who, tradition holds, wore the petticoat on the day of her marriage in 1773 to fellow Quaker Joshua Ashbridge of Goshen, Chester County (fig. 4).[35] Sometime between 1790 and 1810 the quiltmaker detached the petticoat skirt, cut it into two equal size pieces, sewed them together, and joined them to a wide silk border of a coordinated hue, which she then

1786 as "Work made by sewing small pieces of different colours interchangeably together."[36] Extant examples demonstrate that women of British and of Germanic ancestry created patchwork bedquilts in Chester County in the late eighteenth and early nineteenth century. A patchwork quilt thought to date from the period 1790–1820, now likely reduced from its original size, is among the earliest bedquilts brought to any of the Chester County Quilt Documentation Project events, its maker being an as-yet-unidentified ancestor of the county's extended Humphrey/Scott/Best/Wilson/ Wallace families (fig. 5.1 & 5.2).[37] Comprised of cotton fabric and filling, the quilt has a block-style format elaborately embellished by stuffed work. Its pieced (or patchwork) blocks are made from printed and plain cotton fabrics stitched together to form eight-pointed stars; these alternate with blocks of plain

Fig. 7.1. Framed Center Quilt Top, 1812
Made by Margaret (Hanna) Gordon (1776 – 1868) of East Fallowfield Township.
Cotton; 106" x 106"
Courtesy of Margaret Chalfant

Fig. 7.2. Detail of Framed Center Quilt Top showing appliquéd linen handkerchief with cross stitched "MG 1812."

bric ornamented by cotton-filled stuffed work
gures, whose designs vary from block to block
d include renderings of floral sprays, grapes, and
neapples. These embellishments are strikingly
milar in design to stuffed work elements
rnamenting a quilt made in the borough of
ncaster that dates from 1810 and that is likely to
ve been made by Barbara Walter Gundaker
Gundacker), wife of prominent merchant Michael
undaker (fig. 6.1 & 6.2).[38]

Whether Barbara Gundaker and the
nidentified Chester County quiltmaker belonged
the same extended family remains speculative;
owever, their quilts suggest that they both may
ve participated in a regional social network

ig. 8.1 & 8.2. Framed Center Quilt and detail, circa 1820
rom the Acker or Laubaugh Families, possibly of Uwchlan or Pikeland Townships.
Cotton top; cotton back; 100" x 100"
Courtesy of The State Museum of Pennsylvania, The Pennsylvania Historical and
Museum Commission, 98.60.1

through which each of them gained access to the source for their similar stuffed-work motifs.

Some early nineteenth-century quilts made in Chester County display pieces of printed cotton fabrics arranged in concentric frames around a central square. One surviving quilt top (a quilt's presentation side without filling, backing, or quilting) composed in this layout features a printed handkerchief as its central square (fig. 7.1 & 7.2). Whipstitched to the center of the handkerchief is a plain cream-colored cloth square embroidered "1812" and initials "MG" in silk, making it the focal point for the entire design. The reputed maker, Margaret Hanna Gordon (1776–1868), and her husband William Gordon (1768–1823) lived in East Fallowfield Township.[39]

A completed cotton quilt of framed center construction reportedly made by a Pennsylvania German woman living in Chester County circa 1810–1830 is in the collection of the State Museum of Pennsylvania (fig. 8.1 & 8.2). The quilt is attributed to an unidentified member of the intermarried Acker and Laubaugh families. Conrad Acker (1741–1815), a first-generation Pennsylvania German, in 1771 settled on a farm in Uwchlan Township with his wife Barbara Rubel (1744–1825). Johannes Laubaugh (1728–1808), born in Dorning, in the German state of Hesse, arrived in Pennsylvania about 1750, and with his wife Anna Catharina (née Schumeny, 1733–1798) settled in Pikeland Township, adjoining Uwchlan Township. The intermarriages began in the next generation.[40]

If some women in Chester County adopted home quiltmaking by at least 1770, and if the practice increased in popularity during the first half of the nineteenth century, evidence of this should begin to appear in estate inventories early in the nineteenth century.[41] Indeed, the inventories taken between 1800–1809 reveal an uptick in the numbers and proportions of estates with bedquilts. Of 146 inventories that itemized household goods

in those ten years, 20 (14%) included quilted bedcovers, with 9 households listing one quilt, and the other 11 listing two or more. David Howard of Tredyffrin Township had six bedquilts, valued together at nearly $16.[42] Most of the quilts in this decade received an appraisal valuation of between $1 and $3, the higher figure being for "1 new Beadquilt" in the 1801 inventory of Christian Trea in Uwchlan Township, and "one Bed Quilt" owned by the late James Jackson of West Chester in 1808.[43] One decedent among the twenty, Frederick Landis was of Germanic ancestry; all other surnames in the group are of English, Irish, Scots Irish, and Welsh derivation.[44] Thus, in the aggregate the inventory data reveal that demographically proportionate numbers of Chester County residents of British (95%) and Germanic (5%) ancestry had simultaneously adopted home quiltmaking in the latter part of the eighteenth century.[45]

Inventories compiled twenty-five and fifty year later reveal an increase in the proportion of estates listing quilted bedcovers. Sixty-three (25%) of the 250 itemized inventories in the 1825–1834 decade listed one or more quilts, nearly double the proportion of that in the preceding group. Forty-nine decedents owned two or more quilts; 16 of them owned between five and ten quilts. Most quilts that were individually valued were appraised at about $1.00, though quilt values in the sample ranged widely, from 25¢ for Sarah Speakman's "Bec quilt much worn" in 1833, to $5.00 each for the "3 Calico bed quilts" in Joseph Strawbridge's 1829 estate, to $5.75 for the "one Quilt" left by John Mackey in 1825.[46]

In the 1825–1834 group, as in the 1800–1809 group, the vast majority (90%) of quilt owners had surnames of British derivation. The Germanic surnames were Abraham, Conrad, Fertig, Maurer, Setzler, and Stiteler.[47]

Table 6. Percentage of bedquilt owners, 1800–1859 (relative to number of inventories itemizing household goods)			
	1800–1809	1825–1834	1850–1859
Borough of West Chester	20% of 5	42% of 26	30% of 56
Nottingham, Tredyffrin, & Uwchlan Townships combined	17% of 100	27% of 170	24% of 170
Coventry Township	5% of 41	9% of 54	24% of 62
Total	14% of 146	25% of 250	25% of 288

Source: Inventories, Chester County Archives, West Chester, Pennsylvania.

Note: Township boundaries for all decades are those of original organization.

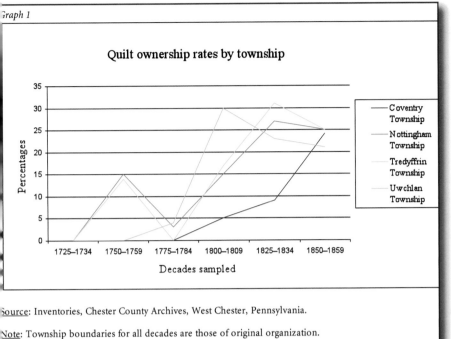

Graph 1

Quilt ownership rates by township

Source: Inventories, Chester County Archives, West Chester, Pennsylvania.

Note: Township boundaries for all decades are those of original organization.

Germanic households in the late 1700s and first years of the 1800s, the nineteenth-century quiltmaking trajectory of women in sampled British-dominated townships varied distinctly from that of quiltmaking women residing in Germanic Coventry Township. The craft initially gained favor more rapidly in the three townships dominated by British residents; only about 1820 did the Pennsylvania German inhabitants of Coventry Township follow suit (table 6). After 1800 in Uwchlan Township and after 1820 in Nottingham and Tredyffrin Townships, quilts and home quiltmaking declined in popularity; concurrently, home quiltmaking and quilt ownership intensified in Coventry Township (graph 1).

Although surviving quilts and manuscript evidence proves that some women in Pennsylvania stitched patchwork quilts as early as the 1770s, the first mention of "patchwork" quilts appears in the Chester County inventory sample from the 1850s.[50] In 1852 appraisers valued a "Lot of patchwork" at 50¢ when compiling the listings for Christian Beary's Coventry Township estate. Susanna Rinewalt's 1852 inventory, also from Coventry Township, included, "a lot of patchwork" valued at 25¢, "a cradle quilt, & an unfinished quilt" worth 35¢, and "a sewing basket & Patchwork" appraised at 25¢. "Bed quilt part made," listed in the 1852 inventory of Richard Strode's West Chester estate, was assigned a worth of $1.00, a rather high valuation given that many completed (and thus usable) bedquilts in this decade were similarly valued at $1.00, including the "new Calico quilt" that had belonged to Betsey Mercer in 1856.[51]

The slight decrease in the proportion of households with spinning wheels in the 1825–1834 [ ]t hints at a decline in the home spinning of yarns [s]ee table 4). Only 65% (162) of the households had [s]ome kind of spinning wheel, a 7% decline.[48] [f]ibers of flax or wool were listed in 35% of the [i]nventories that included spinning wheels; none of [th]ese households listed any fibers of cotton or [h]emp.

The proportion of bedquilt owners remained [u]nchanged in the 1850s. Of 288 inventories in [w]hich appraisers itemized household goods, 73 [(]25%) listed quilted bedcoverings. Most households [w]ith quilts had two or more; four owned more [th]an a dozen, and one possessed eighteen. The [v]alues assigned ranged from 25¢ to $3.00 for [in]dividual quilts in several inventories.[49] Owners [w]ith Germanic surnames—Acker, Bealer, Grubb, [H]offecker, Rinewalt, Root, Shafer, Shaner, Snell, [a]nd Souders—remained distinctly in the minority [(]10 out of 73), but proportionally had risen to 14%.

Inventory data provides insights about the [d]emographics and timing for the adoption of [h]ome quiltmaking among residents of rural [C]hester County. The proportion of bedquilt [o]wning decedents whose inventoried households [w]ere located in townships dominated by residents [o]f British ancestry (Nottingham, Uwchlan, and [T]redyffrin) stands in contrast to those who lived in [t]he township dominated by German-speaking [r]esidents (Coventry). While home quiltmaking [a]ppears to have been adopted by some British and

A relatively large proportion of West Chester estate inventories listed quilted bedcoverings after 1800 (see table 6). This crossroads village (formerly called Turks Head) had become the county seat in 1786. (Three years later the state legislature reduced the size of the county by creating Delaware County from the easternmost townships.) In 1800 West Chester's population stood at about 350; by 1820 its residents numbered about 530, most of whom were of British extraction and many of whom were Quaker.[52]

Why a relatively high proportion of West Chester decedents owned bedquilts is open to speculation. Personal wealth and social position may have been contributing factors. Of the 29 nineteenth-century decedents whose inventories listed quilts (finished or part-made), 16 were in the top two wealth quintiles (based upon the value of inventoried personal property, or personalty). The appraised personal property of these individuals ranged in value between $2,550.42 and $54,289.84. Women accounted for 7 of the 13 quiltowners in the lower three quintiles, having personalty ranging from $118.00 to $2,021.78; at least 3 of the 7 were widows. Because a woman's social position depended to a great extent on her father's or husband's wealth and occupation—information usually not included in an estate inventory or will—it is often hard to discern what these women's position may have been within West Chester society.

Biographical information provides some insights. Research into the lives of the 30 decedent women of West Chester in the 1850s suggests that the town attracted single women and widows, some of whom had previously lived on farms in the surrounding townships.[53] Such is the case of Betsey Baily (1771–1856), who married Jesse Mercer (1766–1837) before the London Grove Meeting in November 1790. They resided on his 250-acre farm in Westtown Township, Chester County, and attended Birmingham Meeting with their children. A few years after Jesse Mercer's death, the couple's daughter and son-in-law moved into the family homestead. By 1847 Betsey Mercer, then age seventy-six, resided in West Chester. She had considerable resources at her disposal, having inherited a cash legacy from her uncle Samuel Painter and the inalienable ownership of the household goods in her husband's estate. At her death nine years later her personal estate was valued at $3,129.48; all but $62.48 of it in cash or investments. The few items she owned included a bedstead with sacking bottom, bedclothing, a bureau, a "drum and pipe" for heat, a basin and pitcher and a tray and shaving glass, a rocking chair and stool, a chest with more bedclothes and some table linens, a black trunk filled with china ware and table furniture, a looking glass, and a Bible. Her extensive store of bedclothes included "2 quilts & 2 Comforts" valued at $2.50, "5 sheets & 3 pair pillow cases" at $2.00; "2 Coverlets" at $3.00, and "2 Blankets" at $3.00. In addition, there were 2 other quilts among Betsey's things—a "Silk Bed Quilt" valued at $3.00, and a "new calico bed-quilt" valued at $1.00—both of which Betsey had set apart in her will, specifically identifying them as legacies for granddaughters Hannah M. Darlington and Irene Darlington,

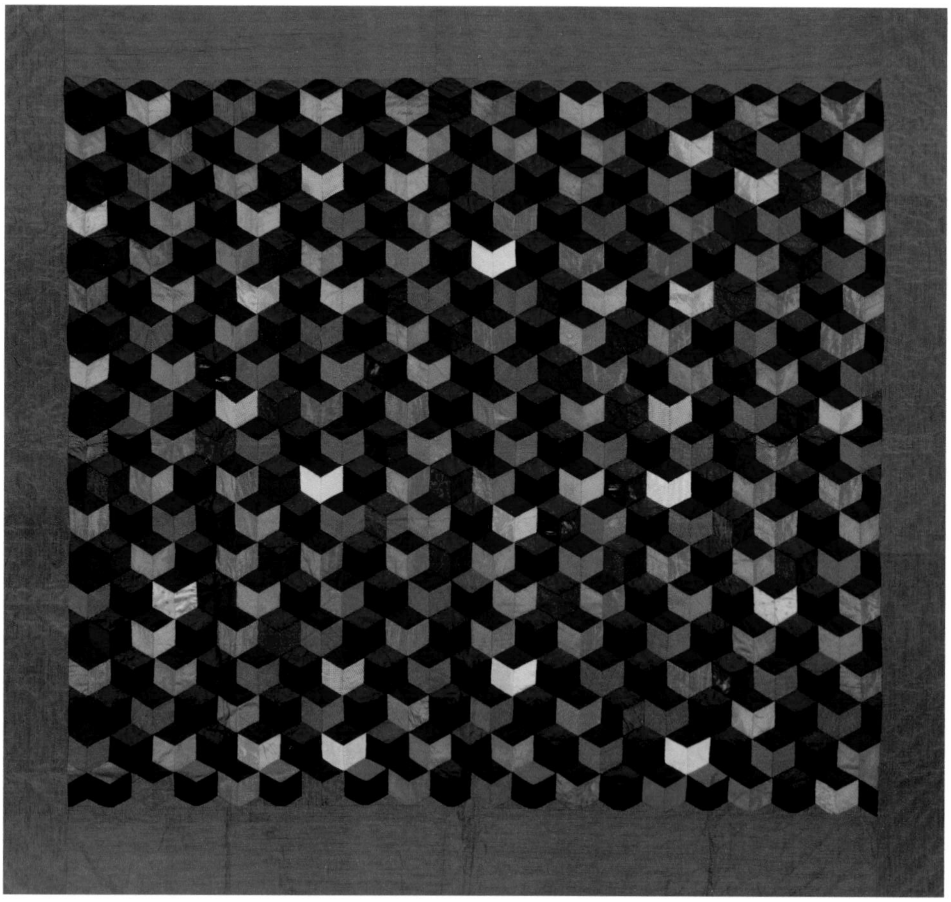

Fig. 9. Tumbling Block Quilt, 1850 – 1875
Descended in the Scattergood family of Chester County and may have been made by Lydia Eldridge Scattergood (1843 – 1884) of East Goshen Township or by Lydia Ann (Hoopes) Davis (1829 – 1893) of West Caln Township.
Silk top; cotton back; 90" x 90"
Courtesy of Margaret Chalfant

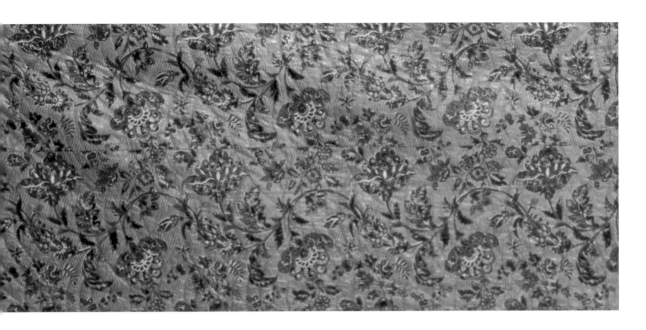

children of Betsey's second-eldest daughter, Sarah.[54]

We can only guess what Betsey's "Silk Bed Quilt" and "new calico bed-quilt" looked like, though clues exist among prescriptive household literature and surviving nineteenth-century quilts. The silk quilt may have dated from Betsey's own girlhood, or her mother's, but equally possible it may have been a pieced silk quilt made in the first half of the nineteenth century (fig. 9). Quilts of pieced silks were favored by Delaware Valley Quakers long before silks used in the "crazy" quilt style came into vogue in the late nineteenth century.[55] Her "new calico bed-quilt" may have been made in the whole-cloth style suggested in Eliza Leslie's housekeeping guide, the first Philadelphia edition of which had appeared in 1840. Leslie advised: "Quilts are now made entirely of the same sort of dark calico or furniture chintz; the breadths being run together in straight seams, stuffed with cotton, lined with plain white or buff-dyed muslin, and quilted simply in diamonds, shells, or waves."[56] Such is the construction of a whole-cloth quilt made in Chester County about 1830 from lengths of colorful polished chintz. Created by an as-yet-unidentified quiltmaker, this bedquilt was constructed with a plain muslin backing; the quilting is executed in an overall "clamshell" pattern of the sort described by Miss Leslie (fig. 10).

According to Eliza Leslie, the fashion in quilted bedcoverings had by 1840 turned the visual focus away from handwork, supplanting hand-stitchery and pieced or appliquéd designs with figures machine-replicated on the printed surfaces of furniture chintz or calico.[57] However, in rural Chester County townships some women's engagement with quiltmaking followed a different path. Though some county quiltmakers embraced the "new" fashion for whole-cloth dark calico or furniture chintz bedquilts, surviving quilts attest that many quiltmakers persisted in producing quilts that showcased handwork in their finely quilted pieced or appliquéd compositions. The custom Leslie described, "of buying new calico, to cut into various ingenious figures, for what was called handsome patch-work" as well as the use in quiltmaking of cutaway scraps of new cloth left from home dressmaking endured as popular and meaningful activities among some women in Chester County in the 1840s, 1850s, and many decades later. The quilting on these textiles is often quite detailed, with many featuring multiple quilting designs including scrolling feathers, vines with flowers and foliage, twisted chains, and much, much more—a far cry from Leslie's advice that the designs for quilting fashionable new bedclothes be limited simply to "diamonds, shells or waves."[58]

Some Chester County bedquilts were created and exchanged specifically to establish and maintain systems of sociality.[59] Many quilts were (and continue to be) sewn expressly for circulation as gifts to mark occasions and relationships. In the minds of the giver and recipient, these quilts are stand-ins, or metonyms, for the quiltmaker and/or giver, conceptually taking on the social form of persons. In this way the quilt's maker or giver

Fig. 10. Whole Cloth Quilt detail, 1825 – 1835
Glazed cotton top; cotton back; 110 ¼" x 108 ½"
Gift of Mrs. F. von Ceban and Mrs. Emily N.
Hamersley, Chester County Historical Society, Q71

remains conceptually associated with the gift quilt as long as memory of the gift exchange continues to be part of the object's context.

Among quilts of this type are numbers of block-style signature quilts produced in the second and third quarters of the nineteenth century by individuals or groups of Chester County quiltmakers. A popular fabric palette among the county's nineteenth-century pieced or appliquéd signature quilts featured patterned turkey-red cotton calicos set off by plain white cotton cloth; turkey-red printed cottons were also frequently combined with solid white fabric and figured green cottons. Other color combinations also existed (fig. 11). These colorful inscribed textiles gained popularity, especially among the county's Quaker residents, who made many documented signature quilts, and whose sect not coincidentally assiduously recorded and preserved detailed genealogical and related information concerning its members.[60] The signatures on these quilts act as the social beings and voices of those whose names appear, and their collective presence gives an account of the named individuals' membership in communities connected by social ties such as affinity, kinship, and organizational membership.[61]

Fig. 11. Friendship Quilt, 1847
Made by Martha Thomas Lewis (1825 – 1912) of Newtown Square, Delaware County, PA with names of family and friends in Willistown, Birmingham and other Chester County locations.
Cotton top; cotton back; 92" x 91"
Gift of Joann H. Lewis, Chester County Historical Society, 2008.25.1

Table 7. Percentage of spinning wheel owners in rural townships, 1800–1859 (relative to number of inventories itemizing household goods)

	1800–1809	1825–1834	1850–1859
Nottingham, Tredyffrin, & Uwchlan Townships combined	72% of 100	66% of 170	19% of 170
Coventry Township	78% of 41	72% of 54	27% of 62
Total	74% of 141	67% of 224	22% of 232

Source: Inventories, Chester County Archives, West Chester, Pennsylvania.

Note: Township boundaries for all decades are those of original organization.

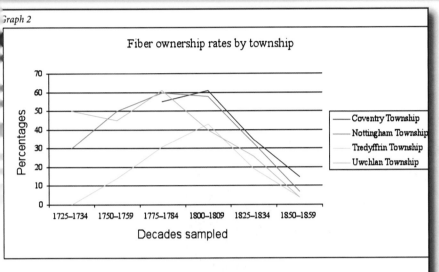

Graph 2

Source: Inventories, Chester County Archives, West Chester, Pennsylvania.

Note: Township boundaries for all decades are those of original organization.

The inscription of names as part of a quilt's embellishment irrevocably seals and makes visible relationships linking quilt, quiltmaker (or giver) and recipient in a manner that outlasts the context of living memory.

Though a quarter of the households inventoried in the 1850s included one or more bedquilts, far fewer had spinning wheels. In the face of industrialized textile manufacture, hand-spinning and hand-loom weaving no longer served most families' economic ends. Of 288 inventories that itemized household goods only 56 (19%) listed any kind of spinning wheel (see table 4). Just 9 (16%) of the households with wheels also possessed flax or wool fiber, suggesting that by midcentury some households retained spinning wheels for reasons more symbolic than practical.[62]

Households in Germanic Coventry Township appear to have practiced hand spinning somewhat more intensively and relinquished it a bit more slowly than households in the rural British townships studied (table 7).[63] Textile fiber ownership rates track in a similar manner; in each

of the three nineteenth-century decades studied, Coventry Township inventories show higher fiber ownership rates than those in the other three townships (graph 2).[64]

As a whole, the weight of evidence in estate inventories during this century and a half and the evidence presented by quilts themselves throws considerable doubt on the long-standing assumption that rural Pennsylvania German women learned the skills of quiltmaking "from their English neighbors." Signs of home quiltmaking appear at the same time in the inventories of all four rural Chester County townships included in this study (seen in the strong uptick between 1775–1784 and 1800–1809 in graph 2). Thus some other source of social or cultural influence simultaneously animated some of these British and Germanic women to invest labor and economic resources in home quiltmaking.

Initially the late-eighteenth-century home quiltmaking efforts correlate with an increase in the numbers of households owning hand-spinning equipment, a finding that in turn correlates with Revolutionary-era fervor for domestic manufactures and the politics and privations of nonimportation. After 1800, however, the popularity of quiltmaking waxed as the traditional tasks of household textile production waned, although residents of the primarily Germanic Coventry Township made the shift a bit more slowly than did the residents of primarily-British areas in the study.[65]

The chronological profile of the quilts brought to the Chester County Quilt Documentation days correlates with the story of home quiltmaking revealed in the sample of eighteenth- and nineteenth-century estate inventories. Estate records indicate that few bedquilts were owned by eighteenth-century residents of Chester County, and today eighteenth-century quilts are exceedingly rare, as are county quilts from the earliest decades of the nineteenth century. As the nineteenth century progressed, an increasing proportion of estate inventories list quilts; larger numbers of quilts from the 1840s and the years beyond are found today (and comprise the clear majority of quilts brought to county documentation days). Inventory data and extant quilts separately and together support the conclusion that home quiltmaking simultaneously became a household textile craft among Chester County residents of British as well as German descent, and that home quiltmaking was not a textile tradition brought to the New World by either group of immigrants.

The industrialization of textile production was the determinative context within which some women appropriated quiltmaking as a household textile craft.[66] Inexpensive cloth and yarn from the mills eliminated households' economic incentive for producing hand-spun yarn to be woven into cloth by local craftsmen. Mechanized spinning forever disrupted an ancient gendered domestic craft tradition and extinguished an important source of women's social identity and economic authority, arguably producing profound cultural dislocation in traditional communities across the American countryside. Communities reacted to the disruption occasioned by dismantling such core structures by symbolically reasserting the compromised tradition.[67] In Chester County as elsewhere in rural nineteenth-century Pennsylvania some women sought to restore cultural balance in the wake of this disruption by reinventing quiltmaking as an everyday household craft. Cut to pieces and rejoined, cloth from the mills was re-rendered by women's hands into new textiles that the mills could not produce. Quiltmakers working in the pieced or appliqué tradition re-established women's critical transformational role in the production of significant cultural material, and thereby symbolically restored cultural order.[68]

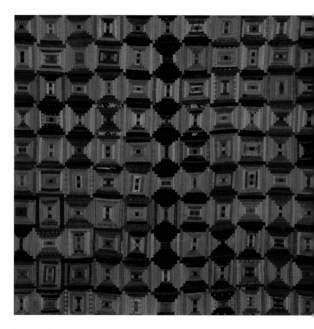

Endnotes

Patricia J. Keller is an independent curator and consultant for museums, historical societies and historic house museums. She is a member of the Department of History at Millersville University and currently a Research Associate with the McNeil Center for Early American Studies, University of Pennsylvania.

The author acknowledges with gratitude the considerable assistance provided by Clifford C. Parker, Archivist, Chester County Archives, and Ellen E. Endslow, Director of Collections, Chester County Historical Society, in support of this essay's preparation, and Catherine E. Hutchins's remarkable editorial skill.

1. By the late 20th century, historians of Pennsylvania's quilted bedding textiles reached a revisionist consensus concerning the history of quiltmaking by rural Pennsylvania German women. Instead of being an imported Continental bedding tradition, as earlier authors had thought, these historians claimed Pennsylvania German women learned this textile craft in the first half of the 19th century "from their English neighbors," whom, they believed, brought the tradition of home quiltmaking to Pennsylvania in the earliest years of settlement. For example, Jeannette Lasansky, "Quilts in the Dowry," in *Bits and Pieces: Textile Tradition*, ed. Jeannette Lasansky (Lewisburg, Pa.: Oral Traditions Project of the Union County Historical Society, 1991), 51, states that among Pennsylvania British settlers and their descendants, "'English' ... estate inventories ... demonstrated that quilts had always been a major bedding component—in America as well as in the

Courthouse Steps, 1870 – 1900
Maker possibly from the Pusey family of Chester County
Cotton, wool, silk top; cotton back; 79 ½" x 82"
Courtesy of Ann Pusey Heess Lee

British Isles;" yet in the notes Lasansky does not cite evidence to support her assertion. For additional discussion on this point, see Patricia J. Keller, "The Quilts of Lancaster County, Pennsylvania: Production, Context, and Meaning, 1750–1884" (Ph.D. diss., University of Delaware, 2007), 122–24.

2. Patricia T. Herr, "Iwwerich un Ender: Those Small Pieced, Appliqued, and Quilted Objects in the Pennsylvania German Household," as cited in Lasansky, *Bits and Pieces*, 27. This model of cultural transmission also relies upon social emulation, ethnicity, and geographic proximity.

3. Adrienne D. Hood, "Organization and Extent of Textile Manufacture in Rural Pennsylvania: A Case Study of Chester County," (Ph.D. diss., University of California, San Diego, 1988), table 4.5, p. 226, examined 100 Chester County inventories ("the first twenty inventories" filed in 1718, 1737, 1757, 1776, and 1795). The inventories from 1718 and 1737 listed no quilts (0%); just 1 estate among 20 (5%) included a bedquilt in each of the 1757 and 1776 samples, and just 2 among 20 (10%) in the 1795 sample. Margaret B. Schiffer, *Chester County, Pennsylvania Inventories: 1684–1850* (Exton, Pa.: Schiffer Publishing, 1974), reported on the contents of 10,788 inventories filed for Chester County decedents in the years 1684–1849. She located only 18 quilt-owning decedents in the 18th century and just 50 such decedents during the entire 165-year period; however, she collected data only on inventory references that included descriptive information about selected household furnishings (so she included, for example, "Calicoe bed quilt" or "Linsy Woolsy Blankit" but excluded a listing of "bedquilt" or "blanket"), a critical methodological limitation.

Quilted bedcoverings, called "quilts" today, were frequently labeled "bedquilts" or "bed quilts" in Pennsylvania's 18th- and 19th-century estate documents. This term distinguishes quilted bedding from quilted petticoats, garments also colloquially known as "quilts." Care with interpreting the word "quilt" is advised when mining inventories for evidence of bedquilt use or ownership. A "quilt" listed in an estate inventory amidst or adjacent to items of women's apparel likely signifies a quilted petticoat, but a "quilt" noted among other bedclothes or household furnishing textiles is likely a bedquilt.

4. Townships in this study were evaluated and selected on the basis of their geographic location within Chester County, their date of organization, settlement patterns, and the denominations of their earliest religious organizations or faith communities, with care taken to select a sample representative of the county's ethnic, economic, and religious diversity, from a range of geographic locations. Townships that were partitioned in 1789 to form Delaware County were excluded from consideration, as were inventories from the borough of

Chester after that 1789 division. The Chester County Archives facility in West Chester, Pennsylvania (hereafter cited as CCA), is the public repository for Chester County's 18th- and 19th-century estate records. This study included all of the inventories on file in the CCA for the geographic areas and years I selected for study. A project of the Chester County Historical Society (hereafter cited as CCHS), the Chester County Quilt Documentation Project consisted of 9 public quilt documentation events held in 2002 and 2003 at locations throughout the county, all funded by the Pennsylvania Historical and Museum Commission. The historical society has continued to document quilts and has held 5 additional documentation days since 2003.

5. The use of estate inventories in the study of social and economic history has limitations. For critical discussions about the use of estate inventories as primary evidence for historical reconstruction, see Kevin M. Sweeney, "Furniture and the Domestic Environment in Wethersfield, Connecticut, 1639–1800," *Connecticut Antiquarian* 36, no. 2 (1984): 10–39, reprinted in *Material Life in America, 1600–1860*, ed. Robert Blair St. George (Boston: Northeastern University Press, 1988), 261–63; Kevin M. Sweeney, "Using Tax Lists to Detect Biases in Probate Inventories," and Anna L. Hawley, "The Meaning of Absence: Household Inventories in Surry County, Virginia, 1690–1715," both in Peter Benes et al., *Early American Probate Inventories* (Boston: Boston University, 1988), 32–41 & 23–31, respectively. For an analysis of the system that governed entry into probate in Sturbridge, Mass., prior to 1850, see Holly Izard, "Random or Systematic? An Evaluation of the Probate Process," *Winterthur Portfolio* 32, nos. 2/3 (Summer/Autumn 1997): 147–67. For cautionary advice about estate inventories from southeast Pennsylvania, see Keller, "Quilts of Lancaster County," 338–52.

6. Inventories are best interpreted in concert with the decedent's will, if one was written. In Lancaster and Philadelphia counties during the 18th and 19th centuries, appraisers might choose to list or choose to ignore bequeathed property when compiling an estate inventory; additionally, personal property distributed to satisfy a widow's claims might be excluded from the estate inventory. See Keller, "Quilts of Lancaster County," 340–43, 346–48.

7. James T. Lemon, *The Best Poor Man's Country: A Geographical Study of Early Southeastern Pennsylvania* (Baltimore: Johns Hopkins Press, 1972), 42–70, a benchmark study, provides a nuanced analysis and visual representation of settlement patterns by both national origin and religious orientation.

8. Lemon, *Best Poor Man's Country*, 9.

9. The town and borough of Chester was originally known as Upland, a settlement founded in 1644 by Swedish immigrants. William Penn renamed the town Chester shortly after landing at Upland aboard the Welcome in 1682. Chester served as Chester County's center of government and commerce until 1786. It became the seat of the newly formed Delaware County in 1789 but ceded that status to Media in 1851. For the history of Chester, see Henry Graham Ashmead, *History of Delaware County, Pennsylvania* (Philadelphia: L. H. Everts, 1884), 20–22, 435.

10. Inventories that did not itemize household goods still listed other kinds of personal property belonging to the decedents' estates, including one or several of the following categories of property: financial instruments, livestock, crops in the ground or elsewhere, farm or other capital equipment, rents, interest, or legacies due to the deceased.

11. Median estate value for this group = £100-2-2. Inventory of Richard Osborn, 1726 (file 223); inventory and will of John Baldwin, 1732 (file 426), CCA.

12. Adrienne D. Hood, *The Weaver's Craft: Cloth, Commerce and Industry in Early Pennsylvania* (Philadelphia: University of Pennsylvania Press, 2003) describes the system of household textile production in Chester County in the 18th and early 19th centuries, at which time hand-spinners were characteristically female and the weavers were all trained males. See also, Adrienne D. Hood, "The Material World of Cloth: Production and Use in Eighteenth-Century Rural Pennsylvania," *William and Mary Quarterly*, 3d ser., 53, no. 1 (January 1996): 43–66. Most fiber spun in Chester County households was flax or wool; occasionally inventories list small quantities of hemp fiber, which could be worked up into a durable cloth. Lucy Simler, "The Landless Worker: An Index of Economic and Social Change in Chester County, Pennsylvania, 1750–1820," *Pennsylvania Magazine of History & Biography* 114, no. 2 (April 1990): 182–83, offers evidence that, between 1790 and 1796, 25 women and girls came to live and spin at the home of Hannah and Edward Darlington in Chester County.

13. Will and inventory, William Armstrong, 1753 (file 1496); administration bond and inventory, Caleb Cowpland, 1757 (file 1687) & 1758 (file 1714), CCA. Armstrong identified himself as a "yeoman" in his will; Cowpland identified himself with the title "Esq." in his will; "Esquire" was used to identify Cowpland in the administration bond. Median estate value for this group = £60-11-6.

14. Ralph Beaver Strassburger, *Pennsylvania German Pioneers* (Norristown: Pennsylvania German Society, 1934), lists "Melchior," "Melchier," and "Melcher" among the surnames of male immigrants whose names appear on passenger lists of ships arriving in Philadelphia 1730–1753.

15. Inventory, Sarah Robinson, 1754 (file 1523), CCA.

16. Women's estate inventories are considerably fewer in number than men's. Legal restrictions on married women's rights to control property and incur personal debt created few instances that necessitated an inventory to settle a woman's final affairs. Laws of coverture prohibited most married women from controlling property, incurring debts in their own names, or engaging in legal actions. For an overview of inheritance law in Pennsylvania and its ramifications for widows and other women, see Carole Shammas, Marylynn Salmon, and Michel Dahlin, *Inheritance in America from Colonial Times to the Present* (New Brunswick: Rutgers University Press, 1987), 83–101; for a discussion of women and the laws of coverture, see Marylynn Salmon, *Women and the Law of Property in Early America* (Chapel Hill: University of North Carolina Press, 1986).

17. Inventory, Sarah Robinson, 1754 (file 1523), CCA. For a discussion of travelers' accommodations, see Bernard L. Herman, *Town House: Architecture and Material Life in the Early American City, 1780–1830* (Chapel Hill: University of North Carolina Press, 2005), 235, 231–59.

18. Inventory, Thomas Morgan, 1756 (file 1643, CCA), contained a single line that listed "1 Bed Bedsteads & Curtains 8£ bed Quilt 18/ & 8 Blankets 3£." His personalty totaled £521-1-4 ½. Cowpland's initial 1757 inventory (file 1687, CCA) listed "Five coverlids, a bed quilt and bedtick" valued together at £8-5-0. Appraisers were called in 1758 (file 1714, CCA) to again evaluate Cowpland's personalty, at which time they itemized: "one Bedquilt" and set the value at 10 s.

19. Based on the "Indices of Laborers' Wages" appearing in Billy G. Smith, "Struggles of the 'Lower Sort': The Lives of Philadelphia's Laboring People, 1750 to 1800," (Ph.D. diss., University of California, Los Angeles, 1981), tables 3–8, p. 103.

20. Susan Prendergast Schoelwer, "Form, Function, and Meaning in the Use of Fabric Furnishings: A Philadelphia Case Study, 1700–1775," *Winterthur Portfolio* 14, no. 1 (Spring 1979): 39–40, 84, 86–87, found in her study of colonial Philadelphia city and county inventories that "most quilts used in colonial Philadelphia were quite clearly expensive, high-quality, imported or professionally made goods—symbols of status and cosmopolitan taste," and she added that home quiltmaking became an activity of leisured and affluent Philadelphia women only after the mid-18th century.

In England the first quilted bedcoverings had been luxurious and costly imports from the East that were affordable only to members of the aristocracy, gentry, and merchant families of the 16th and 17th centuries; see Dorothy Osler, *Traditional British Quilts* (London: B. T. Batsford, 1987), 83; Margaret Renner Lidz, "The Mystery of Seventeenth-Century Quilts," *Antiques* 154, no. 6 (December 1998): 834–43. By the early 1700s quiltmaking had become well-integrated into England's professional needle crafts, and by the 1730s professional needleworkers, upholsters, and outworkers turned out ready-made quilted bedcoverings for customers in both Europe and the New World. In Philadelphia numerous newspaper advertisements announced the availability of imported wares, among them that of February 3, 1737, in the Pennsylvania Gazette: shipmaster John Stedman had just arrived with a stock of "Blankets, Quilts, [and] Cotton Counterpains" plus other "goods from Europe, very cheap" and "direct from London." During most of the colonial period quilted bedcoverings were the bailiwick of skilled professional artisans on either side of the Atlantic basin: in 1722 John Housman, "Upholsterer, in Market Street, Philadelphia," advertised his plans to depart for England and promoted the sale of his remaining stock, "consisting chiefly in standing Beds, Feather-Beds, Quilts, Blankets, Stuffs for Curtains, Chairs, Looking-glasses, Couches &c." (*American Weekly Mercury*, June 28, 1722).

21. In his landmark study, *Rural Household Inventories: Establishing the Names, Uses and Furnishings of Rooms in the Colonial New England Home, 1675–1775* (Boston: Society for the Preservation of New England Antiquities,1964), Abbott Lowell Cummings provided evidence from Boston and Suffolk County, Mass., inventories that substantiates dining and tea-taking as activities considered suited to the well-appointed New England bedchamber in the 18th century.

22. Virginia Postrel, "Inconspicuous Consumption: A New Theory of the Leisure Class," The Atlantic.Com (July/August 2008), http://www.theatlantic.com/doc/200807/consumption, writes about 21st-century consumer behavior; her model also provides a framework for considering consumption and deployment of consumer goods in the early modern era. The Atlantic mercantile trade network brought early 18th-century American colonists a "stunning range" of choice among imported fabrics with which to make clothes and household furnishings. The newly available and changing vocabularies of color, design, texture, weight, and drape required Americans to quickly attain a kind of visual literacy in the language of fashionable textiles. Timothy H. Breen, *The Marketplace of Revolution: How Consumer Politics Shaped American Independence* (New York: Oxford University Press, 2004), 158–59. No one conversant in the language of things could miss the implications of an elegant bedquilt atop an ample featherbed and bedding in the home of a gentleman, yeoman, or gentlewoman. Although quilts' softness, warmth, and cushioning properties suggest they were purchased or made to enhance physical comfort, in the 18th century people acquired consumer goods less often for that reason than to serve as displays of gentility; see John E. Crowley, *The Invention of Comfort: Sensibilities and Design in Early Modern Britain and Early America* (Baltimore: Johns Hopkins University Press, 2001), esp. 142–49.

23. Oxford Township was created from Londonderry Township (until 1734 part of Nottingham Township) in 1754; in 1797 Upper Oxford Township and Lower Oxford Township were created from its subdivision.

24. Inventory, John Salkeld, 1777 (file 3037); inventory, Margaret Hayes, 1782 (file 3444), and inventory, Jane Owen, 1784 (file 3613), all CCA. Median estate value for this group = £306-9-6. Inflation (the devaluation of money in relation to the goods and services it will buy) was steepest in 1778, 1779, & 1780; see Anne Bezanson, *Prices and Inflation during the American Revolution: Pennsylvania, 1770–1790* (Philadelphia: University of Pennsylvania Press, 1951). This sample is too small to discern any urban bias in the values assigned.

25. The *Pennsylvania Gazette* commenced publication in Philadelphia in 1728. Between January 27, 1737, and September 20, 1750, the newspaper carried 18 different advertisements (some printed in multiple issues) placed by 15 vendors announcing the availability of newly imported bedquilts. After 1750 vendors no longer mention imported bedquilts in their advertisements. Due to their expense when new, used textiles formed part of the Philadelphia-area second-hand market. For example, on July 14, 1763, the *Pennsylvania Gazette* included the following notice: "To be SOLD very Reasonable, A VALUABLE English Silk Damask Bed and Window Curtains, with Feather Bed, Satin Quilt, &c., has been some Time in use, Enquire of Plunket Fleeson, in Chestnut street."

26. Of 60 estate inventories listing household goods in the years 1750–1759, spinning wheels are specified in 6 of 8 households in the town of Chester, 28 of 34 households in Nottingham Township, 2 of 7 in Tredyffrin Township, and 7 of 11 in Uwchlan Township. No household inventories are on file for Coventry Township estates for these years, and only 2 for the 1725–1734 decade. Of 112 inventories in the 1775–1784 itemized group, spinning wheels are listed in 13 of 22 households in Chester, 28 of 40 in Nottingham Township, 10 of 16 in Tredyffrin Township, 16 of 23 in Uwchlan Township, and 8 of 11 in Coventry Township.

27. In the 1750–1759 decade, wool wheels are listed in 3 of 8 estates in Chester, 10 of 34 in Nottingham Township, 4 of 11 in Uwchlan Township, and in 2 of 7 Tredyffrin Township estates. Of 112 inventories itemizing household goods in the next period (1775–1784), wool wheels appear in 6 of 22 listings in Chester, 4 of 11 in Coventry Township, 20 of 40 in Nottingham Township, 6 of 16 in Tredyffrin Township, and 9 of 23 households in Uwchlan Township.

28. Of 146 inventories for 1800–1809 itemizing household goods, spinning wheels are found in 32 of 41 Coventry Township estates, 48 of 60 Nottingham Township estates, 16 of 30 Tredyffrin Township estates, 8 of 10 Uwchlan Township estates, and 1 of 5 estates in the borough of West Chester. By this decade the town of Chester was no longer part of Chester County.

29. Cotton wheels appear in the Coventry Township inventories of Ann Beary, 1804 (file 5125); Abraham Brower, 1805 (file 5326); Jacob Rinewalt, 1809 (file 5593), and Catharine Coulter, 1808 (file 5466), all in CCA.

30. Schoelwer, "Form, Function, and Meaning," 39–40; Lynne Bassett and Jack Larkin, *Northern Comfort: New England's Early Quilts, 1780–1850* (Nashville: Rutledge Hill Press, 1998), 11; Jane Nylander, "Quilt," *The Great River: Art and Society of the Connecticut Valley, 1635–1820* (Hartford: Wadsworth Atheneum, 1985), 378, as quoted in Linda Welters and Margaret T. Ordoñez, eds., *Down By the Old Mill Stream: Quilts in Rhode Island* (Kent: Kent State University Press, 2000), 15.

31. For a discussion of sampler-making as a form of needlework that afforded social status and created social capital, see Jennifer Catherine Van Horn, "Samplers, Social Capital, and the Formation of Feminine Identities: The Embroidery Work of Leah Galligher and Her Students, Lancaster, Pennsylvania, 1798–1802" (M.A. thesis, University of Delaware, 2002), and the subsequent article, Jennifer Van Horn, "Samplers, Gentility, and the Middling Sort," *Winterthur Portfolio* 40, no. 4 (Winter 2006): 219–48.

32. The attribution is based on the author's research. Willistown Township was organized in 1704, and, like Tredyffrin Township, was part of the "Welsh tract," a large land area in Chester County originally surveyed for Welsh settlement. Roughly half of Willistown Township's western border adjoins Tredyffrin Township.

33. Patricia J. Keller, "Quilt By Association: Gender, Political Discourse, and Homespun Rhetoric in Pre-Revolutionary Chester County, Pennsylvania," paper presented for the "Object Lessons in Early America" panel at the joint Thirteenth Annual Omohundro Institute Conference and Fifth Biennial Society of Early Americanists Conference, June 2007.

34. Evidence argues that the circumstance prompting the production of this bedquilt is the formation by the first Continental Congress of the Continental Association of 1774, a pan-colonial effort at influencing British administrative policy through a coordinated, locally enforced program of colonial nonimportation, nonconsumption, and, eventually, nonexportation.

35. Mary Davis (1746–1796) was the daughter of Lewis Davis of Haverford, a community that in 1773 lay within Chester County's geographic boundaries. Joshua Ashbridge (1746–1820) was the son of George Ashbridge and Jane Hoopes. Davis and Ashbridge were married November 4, 1773, and resided at the groom's family homestead in Goshen, Chester County; the wedding is recorded in the minutes of the Chester Monthly Meeting.

36. Samuel Johnson, *A Dictionary of the English Language: In Which the Words Are Deduced from Their Originals, Explained in Their Different Meanings* (8th ed.; London, 1786). According to textile historian Lynne Bassett, in the 18th century "patchwork" referred to "a pieced mosaic design created by the repetition of a single geometrical shape, such as a square or hexagon." She writes: "The art of making patchwork quilts came to America from England where it had a history dating back at least to the beginning of the eighteenth century" (Bassett and Larkin, *Northern Comfort*, 27). The history of quiltmaking as a home textile craft in the British Isles is incomplete. British quilt historians Tina Fenwick Smith and Dorothy Osler, "The 1718 Silk Patchwork Coverlet: Introduction," *Quilt Studies: the Journal of the British Quilt Study Group*, nos. 4/5 (2002/03): 24–25, note that "eighteenth century quilting had two clear strands in Britain—professional quilting and domestic quilting," adding that more research is required to develop a nuanced history of each branch.

37. Quilt 97F, documentation file, CCQDP, and author's conversation with the current owner, May 2008.

38. Attribution based on the author's research; see Keller, "Quilts of Lancaster County," 236–41. Previously this quilt has been attributed to Gundaker's daughter, Ann Margaret Gundaker; see Patricia T. Herr, *Quilting Traditions: Pieces from the Past* (Lancaster, Pa.: Schiffer Publishing, 2000), 24–25. Preliminary genealogical research has not revealed any kinship relationships linking the Gundakers with the Chester County family line through which this quilt passed to its present owner.

39. Margaret Hanna was the daughter of John Hanna and his wife Abigail Wilson (ca. 1739–ca. 1833; daughter of Thomas Wilson, b. ca. 1710, of Newlin Township, Chester County). The quilt top descended from Margaret Hanna Gordon through the Gordon, Pyle, and Barnard families to its current owner.

40. See J. Smith Futhey and Gilbert Cope, *History of Chester County, Pennsylvania* (Philadelphia: Louis H. Everts, 1881), 461, 627; and genealogical charts and information at http://www.geocities.com/byronic106/acker.html, and http://www.geocities.com/byronic106/german.html. Futhey and Cope's 1881 brief biographies of Acker and Laubaugh differ in detail from that published on the internet by professional historian Douglas Harper, an Acker descendant.

41. Quilts made between 1750 and 1775 would most probably appear in inventories taken from about 1790 through the 1820s, provided the quilt was not passed to another household.

42. David Howard's 1802 estate inventory (file 4920), CCA, listed 6 quilts valued at £6-0-0; equal to $15.96 when converted to Pennsylvania currency ($1.00 = £0-7-). Howard's total personal property was valued at $1,298.97; in terms of inventoried personalty, he was among that township's wealthiest decedents in the 1800–1809 set. Eleven of the 20 inventories with quilts (55%) were among those with the highest dollar amounts of appraised personal property for their township. Currency conversion rate from *Kimber's Almanac, for the Year of Our Lord 1805: Particularly Adapted to the Use of Friends* (Philadelphia: by the author), n.p.

43. Inventory, Christian Treat, 1801 (file 4881), CCA, lists "1 Old Beadquilt" 10 s., and "1 new Beadquilt" 22 s. 6 d. ($1.33 and $3.00 in Pa. currency); see also inventory, James Jackson, 1808 (file 5510), CCA.

44. Frederick Landis was born in 1738 or 1739 in Heppenheim, near Altzey, Hesse, Germany; he immigrated at age 10 to Pennsylvania. A deed records the purchase of 150 acres of land in Easttown Township, Chester County, by "Frederick Landus" a "Yeoman" then a resident of Philadelphia County. He and his wife Elizabeth had five children, one of whom they named Frederick. Frederick Landis, Sr., died intestate in Chester County in 1803. He owned a tract of land on the edge of Tredyffrin and Easttown Townships. His household inventory, valued at a total of £554-0-0, lists five beds with bedding and bedsteads, and additional sheets and bed cases, but no bedquilts are specifically mentioned. Frederick Landis, Jr., remained in Chester County, but his brothers Philip and Jacob migrated to Ohio. See inventory, Frederick Landis, Sr., 1803 (file 4985), CCA; http://archiver.rootsweb.ancestry.com/th/read/LANDIS/2006-05/1147174367; and http://archiver.rootsweb.ancestry.com/th/read/PA-OLD-CHESTER/2008-04/1207683813. Surnames of quilt-owning decedents in the 1800–1809 decade include Baker, Criswell, Evans, Garrett, Gwin, Hayes, Hood, Howard, Jackson, Kennedy, Landis, Llewellyn, Patterson, Pollock, Pugh, Robeson, Rutherford, Treat, Walters, and Wilson.

45. Lemon, "Agricultural Practices," 469, table 1, pegs British (English, Welsh, Irish, Scots, and Scots Irish) residents of Chester County at 96% of the population in 1730, 90% in 1759, and 89% in 1782. For the same years German-speaking residents constituted 2%, 5%, and 8%, respectively.

46. Thomas Williams's 1825 estate (file 7699) included "1 unfinished Bed quilt old stuf" at 75¢ and "1 unfinished Bed quilt new stuf" at $1.25; Susanna Baily's 1827 inventory (file 8173) listed 50¢ worth of "Calico for Bed Quilts." See also the inventories of Sarah Speakman, 1833 (file 8955), Joseph Strawbridge, 1829 (file 8368), John Mackey, 1825 (file 7741), all in CCA.

47. Inventories of Hannah Abraham, 1832 (file 8905), Joseph Conrad, 1833 (file 8964), John Fertig, 1831 (file 8592), Peter Maurer, 1833 (file 8973), Philip Setzler, 1828 (file 8277), and Eve Stiteler, 1828 (file 8199), all in CCA.

48. In addition to the specific wheels itemized in table 4, decedents in the 1825–34 decade owned cotton wheels (3 estates), both flax and cotton wheels (2 estates), and both cotton and wool wheels (1 estate).

49. Inventory, Robert P. Wilkinson, 1856 (file 12983, CCA) listed "18 bed quilts & Chest" valued at $18.00. The inventory of Elizabeth Price, 1856 (file 12847, CCA), lists 8 quilts, including "1 Silk Quilt" valued at $3.00.

50. For example, in 1778 Sarah (Sally) Burd Yeates of Lancaster Borough arranged for her mother and sisters to quilt her patchwork quilt top at the Burd family's home near Carlisle, Pennsylvania; see Sarah Shippen Burd to Sarah Burd Yeates, 1778, Jasper Yeates Family Papers, MG 127, box 1, correspondence, folder 8, Pennsylvania State Archives, Harrisburg. See Keller, "Quilts of Lancaster County," 231–32. Schiffer, Chester County Inventories, 11–12, found 1 "patch work" quilt in the London Grove Township inventory of Hannah Cope's estate (1824) and a "Red patch work" quilt in the West Goshen Township inventory of George Given's household goods (1825).

51. Inventories of Richard Strode, 1852 (file 12149); Christian Beary, 1852 (file 11998), and Susanna Rinewalt 1852 (file 12,058), all in CCA. The "calico quilt" in Betsey Mercer's West Chester estate inventory valued at $1.00 was identified by the decedent in her May 1847 will as "my new calico bed-quilt;" Will and Inventory, Betsey Mercer, 1847, 1856 (file 13013), CCA.

52. Lemon, *Best Poor Man's Country*, fig. 36, & pp. 130–31. West Chester attained Borough status in 1799. The 1807 Pennsylvania Septennial Census includes 124 names for West Chester taxables; those associated with leading families of Quaker faith include Darlington, Garrett, Guest, Hannum, Hoopes, and Sharpless.

53. Inventories are on file for 41 female decedents of West Chester in the 1850s; 30 of these list household goods, and of these, 13 owned one or more quilts. Widows among the 13 include Esther Painter (1757–1854), Betsey Mercer (1771–1856), Mary Hoopes (d. 1850), Rebecca Carpenter (d. 1850), and Ann Talley (d. 1858). Two other women, Mary Hemphill (ca. 1776–1852) and Phebe Ann Woolley (1818–1856), never married. Among the estates settled for West Chester decedents in the 1825 and 1834 group, just one quilt-owning household was that of a woman: Phebe Warner (d. 1826), a widow. None of the inventories for female decedents in the 1800–1809 group lists quilts.

54. Betsey (Betty) Baily was a daughter of Isaac Baily (1743–1826) and his wife Lydia Gilpin Painter (1746–1829). Hannah M. Darlington (b. 1833) and Irene Darlington (b. 1834 were children of Betsey's daughter Sarah Mercer (1804–1873) and her husband Isaac G. Darlington, who owned a farm in East Bradford Township. Genealogy reconstructed from Gilbert Cope, comp., *Genealogy of the Baily Family of Bromham, Wiltshire, England, and More Particularly of the Descendants of Joel Baily, Who Came from Bromham about 1682 and Settled in Chester County, Pa.* (Lancaster, Pa.: Wickersham, 1912). Appraisals of "comforts" or "comfortables" first appear in 1825; the items are listed in one or more inventories compiled for every sampled year thereafter. Descriptive information about comforts is scant, though occasionally "old," "new," "light," "dark," or "cotton" comforts are noted. One appraiser recorded "striped," "brown," and "check" comfortables; another recorded a "calico" comfortable.

55. Patricia J. Keller, *"Of the Best Sort, but Plain": Quaker Quilts from the Delaware Valley, 1760–1890* (Chadds Ford, Pa.: Brandywine River Museum, 1996), 19–20.

56. Eliza Leslie, *The House Book: Or, a Manual of Domestic Economy for Town and Country* (5th ed.; Philadelphia, 1841), 311. Leslie's book quickly became a best seller, and within a year of its initial 1840 publication had gone through several editions. For biographical notes on Leslie see http://digital.lib.msu.edu/projects/cookbooks/html/authors/author_leslie.html. Surviving quilts show that Chester County quiltmakers continued to produce pieced or patchwork quilts many years after Leslie pronounced such quilts "obsolete."

57. Though the quilts Eliza Leslie described were of the whole-cloth type, the simple quilting designs she advocated conceptually inverted the design and visual focus of elaborately quilted solid-color whole-cloth quilts stitched from silk and other costly stuffs in the 17th and 18th centuries. On 17th-century whole-cloth quilts, see Lidz, "Mystery of Seventeenth-Century Quilts," 834–43.

58. Leslie, *House Book*, 311.

59. See Marilyn Strathern, *The Gender of the Gift: Problems with Women and Problems with Society in Melanesia* (Berkeley: University of California Press, 1988), 134. Such quilts are produced with the intention of circulation as objects within social and familial systems of gift exchange. These quilts become social beings, and are inseparable conceptually from their maker(s)/giver(s) as long as direct or indirect memory of the exchange persists.

60. On signature quilts, see Linda Otto Lipsett, *Remember Me: Women and Their Friendship Quilts* (San Francisco: Quilt Digest Press, 1985). Some signature quilts were made as presentation gifts to mark special occasions; others document friendship and family networks. My observations of 19th-century Pennsylvania estate inventories are that appraisers identified signature quilts as "album quilts," probably because they are of a sort with the book-style signature albums popular at roughly the same time. However, Jessica Nicoll, *Quilted for Friends: Delaware Valley Signature Quilts, 1840–1855* (Winterthur, Del.: Henry Francis du Pont Winterthur Museum, 1986), n.p., differentiated an "album quilt" from a "friendship quilt," and termed both as distinct types of "signature quilts." The fashion for stitching signature quilts seems to have originated in the mid-Atlantic region and was undoubtedly fueled at least in part by the 1830s development of indelible ink suited for use on textiles.

61. See Bernard Herman's essay elsewhere in this volume for additional discussion of signature quilts and voice.

62. For discussion of the spinning wheel as productive/reproductive symbol, mnemonic object, and political emblem, see Keller, "Quilts of Lancaster County," 290–94; as icon, see Christopher Monkhouse, "The Spinning Wheel as Artifact, Symbol and Source of Design," in *Victorian Furniture: Essays from a Victorian Society Autumn Symposium*, ed. Kenneth L. Ames, published as Nineteenth Century 8, nos 3–4 (1982): 155–172; and Beverly Gordon, "Spinning Wheels, Samplers, and the Modern Priscilla: The Images and Paradoxes of Colonial Revival Needlework," *Winterthur Portfolio* 33, nos. 2/3 (Summer/Autumn 1998):163–94.

63. This is consistent with patterns of spinning wheel and textile fiber ownership in the same time periods in Lancaster County's Cocalico valley and Drumore Township (as originally defined). For specifics, see Keller, "Quilts of Lancaster County," chaps. 1 & 2.

64. Of the 41 inventories in predominantly Germanic Coventry Township in the 1800–1809 decade, 61% specified some kind of textile fiber; in the 1825–1834 years, the percentage dropped to 46%, and in 1850–1859 fell to 15%. Among a combined total of 100 inventories taken in the largely British townships of Nottingham, Uwchlan, and Tredyffrin in the 1800–1809 decade, 52% listed textile fibers; for 1825–1834 the percentage fell to 29%; by 1850–1859 it dropped to 6%.

65. The same is true for quiltmaking and spinning wheel ownership in Lancaster County's Cocalico valley and Drumore Township households inventoried in the 18th and 19th centuries.

66. For an extended discussion of the underlying factors motivating quilt production and ownership among 19th-century women in rural Lancaster County, see Keller, "Quilts of Lancaster County."

67. On compensatory cultural behavior in communities, see Anthony P. Cohen, *The Symbolic Construction of Community* (New York: Routledge, 1989), 39–96.

68. For a detailed exploration of this interpretive proposition, see Keller, "Quilts of Lancaster County," 287–305.

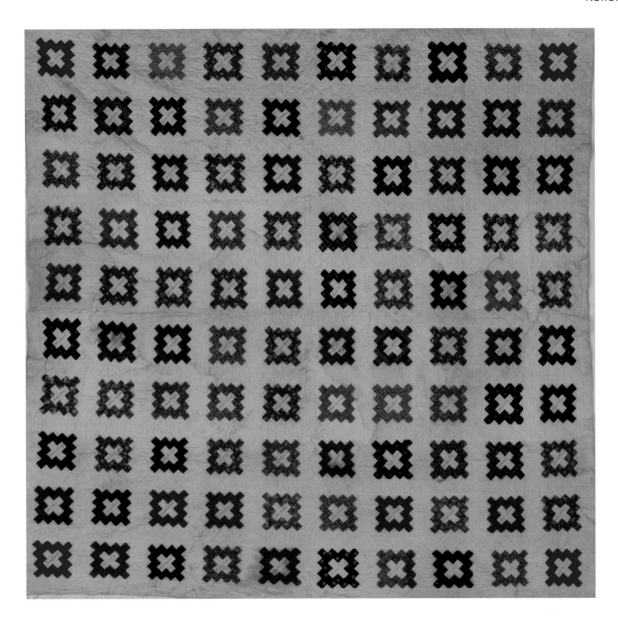

Map 3 - According to "Table of Chester County Townships," (West Chester: Chester County Historical Society, n.d.), Nottingham Township (organized in 1715) was divided into East Nottingham Township (1717; divided 1857 to form Elk Township) and West Nottingham Township (1717), Londonderry Township (1734; divided to form Penn Township in 1817), and Oxford Township (1754; divided into Upper and Lower Oxford Townships in 1797); Oxford Borough was created from parts of Lower Oxford and East Nottingham townships (1833), as was the Borough of Hopewell (1853.) Tredyffrin Township was organized ca.1707. Uwchlan Township (organized 1717) was divided in 1758 into Upper and Lower Uwchlan Townships. Coventry Township (organized 1724) was in 1841 divided to form North and South Coventry Townships.   East Coventry Township was taken in 1844 from a part of North Coventry. Chester (formerly Upland, now in Delaware County), served as Chester County's original seat of jurisprudence. State legislation in 1784 mandated construction of new facilities for county administration sited within 1.5 miles of Goshen Township's Turk's Head Tavern; in 1786 West Chester became county seat, gaining Borough status in 1799.

Chimney Sweep, 1840 – 1870
Cotton top; cotton back; 96" x 85 ¾"
Courtesy of Barbara Zorn

Fig. 1. Chester County quilts made of cotton.

Adrienne D. Hood

Cloth and Color:
Fabrics in Chester County Quilts

Cotton and color epitomize the fabrics of quilts over the two hundred and fifty year history of their presence in Chester County homes (fig. 1). Makers also used silks and wools and later rayon and synthetics, but mostly they opted for the wide array of plain and printed cottons that were increasingly available in the nineteenth century. The factors that determined the selection of the cloth are complex and suggest a fascinating multilayered narrative. At this point it is possible only to peel back some of these layers and to suggest the many avenues of detailed research that remain to be pursued on both the quilts in the database constructed during the recent documentation project and any future undertakings of this nature. This could take many years of historical research—delving into the vast collection of diaries, letters, newspaper clippings, and business records held at the Chester County Historical Society and its archives, and moving outward to the rich trove of material at Hagley and Winterthur Museums and into neighboring counties and states—because the story of Chester County quilts moves from local to regional to national and indeed to global contexts. Far from an insular rural community, Chester County residents engaged broadly in the social, commercial, and industrial worlds of the eighteenth, nineteenth, and twentieth centuries. An exploration of some of those worlds shows how the fabrics of the quilts can open up new perspectives on these important objects.

Quilts are prompts for memories of all kinds.

Some observers may look at a quilt and recall a rural past when the pace of life was slower than it is today or may recollect family members or a community long since vanished. The sewing skills awe us and leave us nostalgic for the shared conviviality of the sociable gatherings where the quilt was assembled. Indeed, nostalgia is a powerful component of the memories evoked by quilts, but embedded in these colorful bedcoverings are also historical clues to a world beyond the household.[1] For example the fabrics of quilts might reveal the intimacies of personal relationships—swatches collected from the garment of a sibling, a parent, or friend. Or they may highlight a family's economic status—scraps that were accumulated carefully over time, or conversely, new yardage bought especially for a project. Moreover, the way the pieces of cloth were assembled can indicate an individual's artistic sensibilities—some quilters created their own unique designs while others carefully followed printed patterns or the instructions in a kit.

But the textiles also tell a story that goes beyond the intimate and local to include the wider world of national and international economies, changing modes of production, and an expanding consumer culture. While it is often difficult to identify the individual women who created the quilts, taken as group, the fabrics from which these bedcoverings were made provide a narrative of a county that was deeply engaged in the wider world of fashion and change, largely through the women who lived there—surprising, perhaps, because

GRAND
PRIZE
WINNER
Sears
NATIONAL
QUILTING CONTEST
∧
A CENTURY
OF PROGRESS
CHICAGO
1933

Feathered Star

*Now Available—This Famous Design and Complete Outfit
for Making Quilt Tops*

Chosen as Grand Prize Winner from more than 15,000 entries! A quilt
that surpasses anything we've ever seen for beauty of design and fine
needlework! The original was on display in the Sears, Roebuck Building
all during A Century of Progress Exposition. Miss Margaret Rogers
Caden, its maker, was awarded the Grand National Prize of $1000.00
and $250.00 in regional prizes.

This original prize winning quilt was made entirely from Sears Fast Color
Cottons in two shades of green combined with a green and yellow print.
Border is a plain green to match the star. The beautiful feathered design
is made with cotton padding, outlined with hundreds of tiny stitches.

Answering thousands of requests for this pattern, we're now offering a
complete outfit for making a similar quilt top, size about 72x90 inches.
This includes the proper assortment of plain and printed "80 square"
cotton patches in box with illustration and instructions for making. Not
Prepaid. Shipping weight, 2 pounds.

25A5799—Complete Outfit..$3.25
25A47201—Perforated Quilting Pattern for above. Shpg. wt., 2 oz....25c

today we tend to think of quilts as the product of undervalued domestic production, poverty, and necessity.

A 1934 pamphlet, published by Sears Roebuck to capitalize on the prize-winning quilts exhibited in Chicago's Century of Progress International Exposition the previous year, captures, and indeed may have even helped to perpetuate, the common notion that "in the pioneer days of early America quilt-making became a necessity, unrestricted to class. . . . The scrap-bag won an honored place in every home. Many of the old quilts, because of the varied materials and unrelated color combination, could lay claim to beauty only because of their fine quilting" (fig. 2).[2] Today we admire these old bedcoverings partly because of our impression that they were made by women who created something functional yet attractive out of carefully saved snippets of old clothing and household textiles. As Karin Gedge points out elsewhere in this volume, Chester County women took pride in "making something from nothing." In fact, argues Gedge in another version of her essay, the "less work Americans do at home, the more they seem to admire the time and work that their ancestors expended to house, feed, and clothe their families." In our present society marked by planned obsolescence and disposable commodities, it is easy to romanticize an era that valued people's ability to recycle old goods into new and useful things,

---

Fig. 2. Sears Roebuck Pamphlet, 1934
This pamphlet highlights the prize winning quilts in Chicago's
Century of Progress International Exposition held the previous year.
Courtesy of Hagley Museum and Library, Wilmington, DE

the harvest, when the seasonal farming routines slowed down, there was ample time to make things to barter or frequently to sell—barrels, shoes, furniture, or cloth—which in turn meant they had money to purchase goods they needed or, more to the point, wanted. Textiles, among the commodities in largest demand, could be obtained from local weavers, but these were limited in quantity, quality, and variety by the fiber produced (wool and flax were grown locally but cotton and silk had to be imported) and by the fact that there were only a few weavers in each township (never more than 10% of the population had looms to make cloth), most of whom worked part time. Europe, however, and England in particular, was producing an increasing array of manufactured goods, and the American colonies with their expanding population provided the perfect market, which urban merchants, country stores, and wandering peddlers serviced (fig. 3). In addition, as British trade with Asia grew, Chinese and East Indian goods were commodities sought by Europeans and Americans alike. This was an era of expanding global trade and increasing manufacturing, and with it, or perhaps because of it, mounting demand for newly fashionable and available products. Chester County residents, including the many Quakers among them, participated in this growing consumer culture, much of which is evident in the quilts they bought and made.

Few Chester County households counted bedquilts among their belongings in the eighteenth century, as Keller's research demonstrates, though this began to change in the postrevolutionary era. Most people who owned them tended to belong to the top echelons of society, and it is likely that the majority of these quilts were imported rather than locally made, though very few from this period survive and none turned up in the Chester County Quilt Documentation Project (CCQDP). Nevertheless, quilted clothing of all sorts, especially women's petticoats, was in such demand that an extensive ready-made industry grew up in Britain. Skilled seamstresses, some working in their own homes, but many lodged in centralized workshops, quilted the fabric on large frames, after which it was made into petticoats before being warehoused for distribution throughout England and to the

hereby allowing them to attain a degree of self-sufficiency. While the perception that rural Chester County households in the eighteenth and nineteenth centuries were somehow able to provide for most of their material needs locally is not altogether wrong, it is a notion that needs some correction. In order to understand the evolution of quilts and quilting in the county, it is helpful to look back to the eighteenth century to consider the importance of cloth to the first generations of residents.

From the earliest days of settlement, Chester County was involved in a global marketplace.[3] As Patricia Keller shows in her essay, this was an ethnically diverse region, attracting colonists of Welsh, English, Scots-Irish, Swiss, and German ancestry from areas of Europe that were making the transition from agriculture to manufacturing. As a result, many of the early Chester County farmers arrived in the colony with craft skills that allowed them to maximize the profits from the very productive land on which they settled. After

Fig. 3. Assigned Estates, 1834 #1, Jacob Wesler, Jr.
Chester County Court of Common Pleas
Courtesy of Chester County Archives, West Chester, PA

American colonies. Expensive silk petticoats had wool batting for warmth and usually had a linen or wool backing; the less expensive ones were made from worsted wool (a hard-spun, smooth, lustrous yarn), perhaps in dark blue or red.[4] Some of the elite women in Chester County may have followed the practice of their New England counterparts by quilting their own petticoats, which would have been more highly ornamented than those mass-produced in England. Whether the petticoats were imported or locally made garments that may have been later refashioned into bedquilts, they were status symbols that reinforced the social, economic, and cultural position of the owners (fig. 4).[5]

An examination of eighteenth-century newspapers, in which merchants regularly advertised imported cloth for sale, shows that there was a variety of imported quilts and quiltings offered for purchase in Pennsylvania and available to Chester County consumers during the middle decades of the eighteenth century, among them: the "quilted [petti] coats" already discussed; "quilts;" "bedquilts;" "fine quilted humhums [a coarse, open-weave Indian cotton, likely a printed calico];" "turkey quilt petticoats;" "cotton counterpains;" "flower'd Italian counterpains;" "Troy wall quilting;" "French quilt for ladies under petticoats;" "white Dutch quilts;" and "French quilts."[6] Those who could afford it and were eager to follow the latest fashions acquired such commodities.[7] Imported or highly worked clothing and textiles were costly, however, so when Philadelphia silk dyer Michael Brown began advertising in 1735 that among other things he could clean or dye "Gentlemens Imbroidered Wastcoats, Quilted [petti] Coats and Bed Quilts . . . all to as much perfection as in London," he likely received a lot of business from both urban and rural people who wanted to maintain their investments. Not only did the ownership of expensive clothing and textiles reinforce one's position in society, so too did the ability to keep them clean. Brown's services as a cleaner and dyer proved satisfactory, as the business was still operating in 1755, though by then his wife (or daughter), Sarah Brown, had taken it over.[8]

All the quilted textiles imported before the 1770s were stitched by hand, and most were whole cloth rather than small pieces sewn together. The earliest were made in India of colorful cotton cloth known as "chintz" or "calico." The meanings of

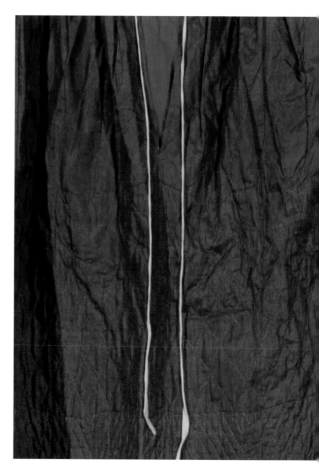

these words have changed over time, as textile historian Florence Montgomery has noted, but both originated in seventeenth-century India:

> Calico comes from Calicut, a port on the west coast of Malabar, south of Madras, where textiles were collected for shipment by the East India Company. The name was applied to Indian cotton cloth, whether coarse or fine, woven with colored stripes or checks, painted or printed. Chintz, from the Hindi word chint, meaning variegated, was applied in the Indian trade either to printed or painted calicoes. Today calico generally refers to cottons with printed, small-scale conventionalized patterns, especially dress goods. Chintz is defined in the Oxford English Dictionary as "cotton cloths fast-printed with designs of flowers, etc. in a number of colours, generally not less than five and usually glazed," and, one might add, especially suited to furnishings.[9]

Fig. 4. Petticoat, 1810 – 1840
The silk fabric in this petticoat would have indicated the status of its wearer but the quality of the quilting suggests it may have been imported ready-made from England. Descended through the Sharpless family of West Grove. Silk with cotton lining
Courtesy of Ruth Smedley Thompson

development of patchwork in the English-speaking world. According to John Irwin and Betty Brett, authors of the seminal *Origins of Chintz*, when new

n the first half of the eighteenth century, chintz nd calico fabrics, and quilts made of these textiles n both India and Britain, were imported regularly o Pennsylvania, and even the poorer sorts were vearing the fashionable commodity. By this time oo, European textile manufacturers had begun to rint cottons, though they were unable to replicate ie vibrancy of color and design of the Indian loth. In 1721 a runaway servant girl was described s wearing "a Petticoat of stamped Calico in a dark tamp," and merchants were selling quantities of alicoes and chintz, some "with fine large bed atterns."[10] East Indian cottons gained quick opularity with the British and North Americans ecause the exotic, colorful, floral designs were nlike anything available from European nanufacturers. Moreover, they were easy to wash nd did not fade (fig. 5.1 & 5.2). The foundation of ie British textile industry was wool, and nanufacturers were so threatened by the demand or these brightly hued cotton fabrics that in 1721, fter a series of unsuccessful deterrents, the overnment banned all dress and furnishing ottons from England. These attempts at rohibition may well have been the catalyst for the

Indian cottons became hard to obtain, some people cut up worn chintz and reassembled the pieces to create new bedcovers and curtains made of patchwork and appliqué.[11] Rather than eliminate the demand for printed cotton cloth the various proscriptions ultimately stimulated the development of English manufactures that competed with the Indian imports.[12] The long-term result of this action had profound implications for the economies of England and, ultimately, the United States, which are documented and reflected in the quilts made by Chester County women.

Until the last third of the eighteenth century, most Chester County quilts, like those in other parts of America, were whole cloth quilts made out of solid-colored wool fabric or colorful printed Indian or European cotton. Though many would have been purchased, it does not mean that there was no local quilting. The skill was among the favorable assets listed in a young servant girl advertised for sale in 1747 who was "fit for town or country business, can spin, sew, make gowns, quilt, etc."[13] By the end of the eighteenth century, evidence of the impending nineteenth-century quilting explosion appeared.

In January 1777 John Bray and Edward Stroud announced in the *Pennsylvania Evening Post* that they had recovered "a parcel of WEARING

ig. 5.1 & 5.2. Banyan and detail, 1745 – 1816
his illustrates the variety of vibrant colorfast hues in the imported Indian cottons.
: belonged to William Buckley. Indian cotton chintz with a 17" x 24" repeat
;ift of Mrs. C. Padgett Hodson; Chester County Historical Society, 1990.500

APPAREL' apparently stolen by Eleanor Clark. Among the goods were a lot of textiles including "a patchwork counterp[a]in." Two years later, on March 2, 1779, Mary Stock of Philadelphia advertised for goods that had been stolen from her the night before, including "one green quilt," and some "brown durant [a glazed woolen cloth] ready for quilting," and "one patch-work counterpane."[14] The idea of cutting up worn fabric and reusing the remaining good pieces made a lot of sense in North America given that cloth was hard to come by. The patchwork trend that seems to have begun in early eighteenth-century England had taken root in Pennsylvania by the time of the American Revolution, if not sooner (fig. 6). By that time as well, a textile revolution was occurring in the Atlantic world.

As eighteenth-century consumer demand for stylish clothing and household textiles grew, traditional modes of production had to change in order to keep up with it. The only way hand weaving and spinning could expand was to bring more people into the labor force or to increase people's hours of work, but both technology and the availability of raw materials limited output. Wool from sheep was abundant in Britain and available in America, but it had to be cleaned and carded—brushed to align the fibers before spinning—requiring a minimum of six people working to provide enough fiber for a spinner. Flax grew well in Ireland and Pennsylvania, but it was extremely labor intensive to cultivate and process, and it was difficult to dye. Silk fiber must be reeled from the cocoons of silk worms, and it took a great deal of expertise to keep the worms alive and a lot of skillful labor to reel the filaments in quantity. As a result both Chinese and European silk was always a luxury good. Cotton did not grow in Europe because the plant needed a warmer climate, and until late in the eighteenth century it remained difficult to extract and card the fiber economically. Nevertheless, British manufacturers obtained cotton from the east through the Levant Company as well as from the British West Indies in the seventeenth and early eighteenth centuries, and the French began cultivating cotton in New Orleans in the 1720s.[15]

Cloth output was further hindered by the fact that it took approximately 6 to 10 spinners to provide enough yarn to keep one weaver

occupied—a situation that changed with the 1738 invention of the fly-shuttle loom, which speeded up the weaving process but required the production of more yarn.[16] Many of the bottlenecks cleared in the second half of the eighteenth century with a series of pivotal inventions in carding, spinning, and weaving and the application of first water then steam power to the new machines.[17] While this new technology hugely expanded cloth output, the evolution of the cotton gin was of utmost importance in paving the way for the explosion of cotton fabrics that became available in the nineteenth century.

Before the American Revolution cotton was not an important commodity in the thirteen British colonies—indigo and tobacco were more so. As a new nation, however, encouragement for domestic manufacturing became an essential component of economic policy, and American-grown cotton for use both at home and as an export was crucial. By the early 1790s the initiative

Fig. 6. Broderie Perse Appliqué Quilt, 1800 – 1840 Showing pieces from a larger imported chintz bedcovering that was cut up and reused in a "patchwork" quilt.
Cotton top; cotton back; 76" x 47 ⅜"
Chester County Historical Society, Q175

ore fruit. Close to half a million pounds of American cotton was shipped to British factories and provided the raw material for three newly established spinning mills in Rhode Island, New Jersey, and South Carolina. Output like this was possible due to the warm climate of the southern states and the availability of enslaved laborers to cultivate the crop. In addition, Americans had been refining a ginning technology that allowed an efficient removal of cotton seed from the fiber, which took a big step forward in 1794 when Eli Whitney came up with a different kind of gin. The result was an even greater expansion of the southern cotton culture and the slave system of labor on which both nineteenth-century British and American manufacturing came to depend.[18]

Emergent eighteenth-century consumer demand provided the catalyst for expanding textile output and the fashion for printed cottons pushed the Europeans to develop new ways of manufacturing this kind of cloth. The history of fabric printing is a long, involved one that went hand in hand with improvements in the other branches of textile production. It centered on discovering the complex chemical secrets of Indian dyeing and learning how to apply the color to cotton cloth in multi-hued designs that did not fade. By the late seventeenth century Europeans had begun to print cottons using wooden blocks, some with metal inserts for more clearly defined outlines, and they had discovered how to use the fixing agents or mordants (chemicals that allowed color to penetrate the cloth) crucial to the India dyers, though a stable indigo blue remained elusive.[19] Fifty years later British printers mastered the technique of producing fast blues and reds

Fig. 7. Pieced quilt made from scraps of cotton with a red and white background of Pillar Prints and Toiles de Jouy, 1790 – 1800. Made by Eliza Newhard Evans Walton (1870 – 1943) and her mother, Elizabeth Bartholomew Evans, of Charlestown. Cotton top; cotton back; 89 ½" x 83"
Courtesy of Esther Grealey Wise

(using the roots of the madder plant), and in combination with the establishment of design schools, they were able to manufacture elegant printed chintzes. Around this time, too, woodblocks were replaced by copperplates that allowed a larger surface to be printed with more finely etched designs, though only a single color could be used. Jouy, France, became particularly famous for printing these monochrome cottons, and *toiles de Jouy* evolved into a generic name, even for those made in England. These *toiles* were fashionable for over fifty years, and some show up in Chester County quilts (fig. 7).

There were several other important developments in the late eighteenth century that transformed the textile printing industry. One was the discovery of the chemical chlorine as a bleaching agent that removed the need for the large tracts of land on which to sun-bleach lengths of fabric for months at a time. Effective bleaching was also an important component in the ability to create turkey red, a bright, colorfast scarlet that originated in the Mideast. French dyers were the first to learn the secrets of this complicated dye, but by 1790 turkey-red fabric had become an important product of the Scottish textile industry and remained popular until the end of the nineteenth century. Turkey red was just the beginning of a new array of colors that began to appear in 1810 as dyers successfully experimented with how to chemically alter the traditional dyestuffs of indigo, madder, cochineal (red), and quercitron (yellow).[20]

One invention that capitalized on all the late eighteenth-century improvements in fabric production and dye technology was patented by Thomas Bell of Scotland in 1783. Instead of flat copperplates to print a design on cloth, Bell employed engraved copper cylinders that could print with up to six colors, replacing the labor of about forty hand-block printers. The earliest fabrics created using this technology were for women's dresses in a single color with small overall designs. But by 1810, Manchester mills had gained enough experience to begin to manufacture the larger scale prints desirable for furnishing fabrics.[21] Ten years later Scotland, with its with developing production of turkey-red fabrics, and Lancaster, with its large cotton weaving mills fed by fiber from the United States, were positioned to provide cheap colorful cloths in demand by a growing middle class in England and in North America. As a result of the increased concentration of textile manufacturers, many smaller, local British firms could no longer compete, and some knowledgeable printers moved to North America where they saw a potential market for their talents and products.

In the Philadelphia region, a number of calico printers—the best known and documented of whom is John Hewson—advertised their skills to local consumers. Over the course of almost half a century (1774–1820s) Hewson, along with a series of partners and later his son, printed designs on linen and on cotton imported from India. A surviving bedcover made by Hewson, according to Florence Montgomery, is "technically remarkable for its [pre 1800] date in America, and is comparable to some of the most handsome English furnishing fabrics of the same period." Other remnants of his printed fabrics survive as patchwork and appliqué in several quilts, following the British tradition of reusing remnants of expensive textiles.[22] Hewson, much like his British counterparts, printed quantities of cloth for sale, but most other calico printers in the region who tried to make a go of it in the late eighteenth century tended to work on a custom-order basis. For example, in 1787 Robert Taylor advertised to "merchants, traders, and the public in general that he has fitted up the Bleachfield in Lower Merion Township," where he would "carry on the Printing and Bleaching branches the same as in Britain." Local merchants and traders could examine Taylor's patterns and choose those they thought would be attractive to their customers. Even individual "Farmers and Mechanics" could bring their homemade cloth directly to him to be printed to order as he had several designated places in the region where people could look at the pattern books and drop off their cloth. Taylor also bleached linen and bleached and dyed yarn.[23] Many of these fledgling industries did not last, but Chester County residents might well have taken some of their own locally made linen cloth to printers like Taylor.

The population in the Philadelphia region participated in the changes in the textile manufacture as both consumers and producers. Throughout the eighteenth century Chester County weavers had operated on a custom-order basis, using flax and wool grown and usually spun by their local clientele. The output was small and consisted of functional clothing and household textiles, such as coarse and fine linen and linsey (a blend of wool and linen) that was plain, checked, or striped; linen sacks and bedticking; drugget (a coarse fabric with a wool weft and cotton or linen warp); wool blankets, carpets, and coverlets.[24] Wool continued to be a major component of the local economy, and for over a century local weavers turned it into serviceable cloth for clothing and bedding. Indeed, many of the first textile mills in the county carded, spun, and eventually wove the wool into cloth.

Given the importance of wool manufacture, it is intriguing that there are so few documented woolen quilts in Chester County, suggesting perhaps that cotton was preferred for beauty over warmth. This seems surprising because in nineteenth-century Ontario, for example, women made a lot of quilts, stuffed with wool, from pieces of homespun wool fabric, sometimes lined with an old blanket (fig. 8). While the climate of rural Ontario was colder, Pennsylvania too, experienced its share of wintery weather as indicated by many nineteenth-century diary entries that often began with a description of the day's conditions. For example, on March 4, 1864, eighteen-year-old Jennie Sellers of Pocopson Township noted that it was "storming, snowing in the morning," and on

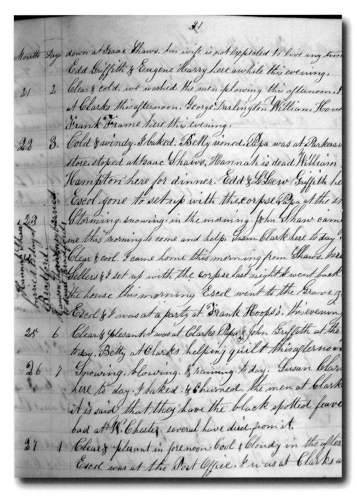

Fig. 8. Pieced Woolen Homespun Quilt made in Canada, 1865 – 1870
Originally belonged to Elizabeth McLean Harrison of Ontario, Canada. Flannel, wool top; cotton back
Courtesy of the Royal Ontario Museum, Gift of Mrs. James T. Burt-Gerrans, 948.157

Fig. 9. Diary of Jennie Sellers, March 25, 1865
Possibly from Pocopson Township.
Chester County Historical Society Library, mss 3500

the 7th it was "snowing, blowing and raining today." The females of Sellers's household took advantage of the bad weather that week to complete indoor chores like ironing, baking, and churning. It was ideal weather for quilting too, and Sellers commented on the fact that seventy-six-year-old Betty Brown spent an afternoon at their tenant's house to help quilt (fig. 9).[25] One might expect to find some warm, woolen quilts among those documented by the Historical Society since 2002; however, the very few wool quilts brought in date from the late nineteenth century and especially from the 1930s. The crazy quilt made in Elkdale by the Nieweg family is such an example. Devised as a project to keep a boy busy while he recovered from rheumatic fever, the quilt is dated 1934. According to the family history, the fabric is from old children's clothing, much of it belonging to his siblings (fig. 10).

That so few wool utility quilts turned up during the documentation project deserves further comment given the early local manufacture of wool and Chester County's climate. Generally quilts made from woolen fabrics are plainer and more functional than those constructed of colorful cottons or elegant silks, so they may have been used until they wore out. And unless they were lovingly embellished, like the Bucks County quilts made by Lily Althouse Loos in the 1890s, on which she embroidered a different array of flowers in each block, for example, they may not have been cherished and handed down in families (fig.11) Even if they do survive, wool quilts are often deemed too plain to be worthy of historical

Fig. 10. Crazy Quilt, 1934
Made by Ella Weir Crowl Nieweg (1890 – 1965) of Elkdale.
Cotton top; cotton, wool back; 80 ½" x 75 ¾"
Courtesy of Beatrice Thomas / Denise Rash

documentation. Historian Jeanette Lasansky heard from Pennsylvania quilters who were born early in the twentieth century that heavy wool bedcoverings, known as "comforts," or "comfortables," or "haps," some quilted and others tufted, were common until homes were better heated (fig. 12).[26] It is also possible that wool utility quilts were not produced in quantity in Chester County during the first half of the nineteenth century because local wool was woven into blankets and decorative wool coverlets, the latter of which may have been preferred over quilts for warmth and beauty. Many coverlet weavers had ceased production by the mid nineteenth century, by which time heating systems had been improved. Further research might also shed light on whether ethnic traditions or location in the county were factors, affecting decisions to use wool cloth in quilts.

It is relevant to note that Chester County resembles neighboring New Jersey—both regions seem to have had a tradition of wool whole-cloth quilts used by wealthier families until the end of the eighteenth century. In the late nineteenth century wool quilts reappear but as utilitarian bedcoverings, some of which may have been made from precut samples of men's suiting fabric.

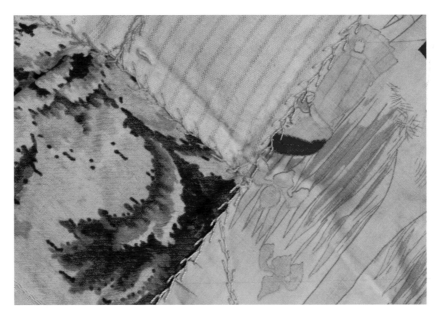

Fig. 11. Embroidered Block Quilt, 1900 – 1930
Made by Lilly Althouse Loos (1870s – 1958), Shartlesville, Berks County, PA.
Wool top; rayon back; 66 ⅜" x 66 ½"
Courtesy of Barbara Crocker

Fig. 12. Detail of Crazy Quilt, 1930 – 1940
Heavy, tied quilts like this were often referred to as "comforts," or "comfortables." Made by Louisa Emerick Byerly, Northumberland County, PA.
Cotton top; cotton back; 82" x 82"
Courtesy of Sally Moore

According to quilt historian Barbara Brackman, "[a]fter the Civil War, with the rise of inexpensive domestic wool, a new style developed for wool pieced quilts in the Log Cabin pattern and its variations like the Pineapple." In fact, one of the earliest nineteenth-century wool quilts in the CCQPD was constructed in a light and dark variation of the Log Cabin design from a variety of colorful printed wool dress fabrics that closely resemble the cotton prints from the period (fig. 13). It seems, however, that at least for the first two thirds of the nineteenth-century Chester County quilters, like their counterparts elsewhere, used cotton as the fabric of choice.[27]

By 1810 cotton had transformed the nature of local production in Chester County, as it had in Manchester, England, and in New England, where Samuel Slater had established one of the earliest and best-known American cotton spinning mills in 1794. Weavers in the region who had previously woven mostly locally grown fiber began to substitute cheaper, mill-spun cotton yarn for labor-intensive and difficult-to-process flax. For the first time since he began his account books in the mid 1780s, for example, Joseph Eldridge, a weaver living in East Goshen Township, noted in the back of one of them in 1810 that he had received "A Packet of Cotton yarn from Providence R.I. Manufacturing Company." A few years later he and his cohorts could buy it locally because, according to the 1820 Census of Manufactures, there were fourteen textile mills in the County, six of which were cotton-

Fig. 13. Log Cabin, 1850
Made from printed wool and silk that resemble the cotton dress fabrics of the period.
Made by Mary M. Shields (early 1800 – 1894) of Coatesville.
Wool and silk top; cotton back; 86 ¼″ x 84 ¼″
Courtesy of Mary Larsen

spinning mills (though they did not yet make cloth). Many of these small enterprises also advertised that they produced carded cotton "of various qualities for Bed Quilts and Comfortables."[28]

One mill is of particular interest because a rare sample book from 1828 survives. Samuel Dickey built the first structure of what became Hopewell Cotton Works in Oxford Township in 1809 to spin the southern cotton that came through the ports of Philadelphia and Wilmington in 300-pound bales. Over time he and his brothers moved and expanded the operation. By the 1820s they were producing more than one hundred varieties of cloth in checks, plaids, and stripes that were mostly blue and white and some with red and brown; the majority was woven in simple plain weave with a few twills. These textiles would have been for everyday clothing—a former schoolboy of the period recalled that "the blue and white cotton, striped and cross-barred, for coat and pantaloons, gave us a rather more modern appearance than those who depended on the spinning wheel and the flax and wool manufactured at home."[29] Fabrics like these were in common use throughout the century—they were durable, did not show dirt, and were easy to wash. Such cottons are so generic that today it is difficult to identify where they were made, but it is easy to imagine the blue and white checks from a worn apron, skirt, or jacket saved and used later by a quiltmaker in Oxford or a nearby township (fig. 14). Many of the early American mills had difficulty competing with the flut of cotton goods manufactured in Manchester, England, however. When the trade embargo was lifted after the War of 1812, the British resumed trade, flooding the American market with cheap cotton wares, and many fledgling mills went under.

In 1830, Chester County residents could buy locally all the European fabrics they needed and could afford. Retailers stocked textiles of all kinds including wools and linens and even velvet and silk, but often printed cottons far exceeded everything else in their inventories, unlike in the eighteenth century where the reverse had been true.[30] Among the textiles listed in the assigned estate of storekeeper Jacob Wesler of Schuylkill County in 1834, for example, were huge arrays of chintzes in plain, green, red, yellow, purple, and black (see Fig. 3). The colors referred to the background on which the designs, mostly floral, were printed; the plain, green and yellow were the cheapest (at 7¢ and 8¢ cents a yard) and comprised the largest quantities, followed by red at 10¢ a yard, and brown purple and black each at 11¢. Wesler also had more than 500 yards of calico in various colors with "darks" predominating followed by green, "light," red, white, and yellow; calicoes were generally more expensive than the chintzes. In addition, he had dark, light, and red ginghams, fabrics where the color was woven into the cloth similar to that produced at Hopewell Works, so it could have been made locally.[31] All of this cloth was available for garments or household textiles and some undoubtedly ended up in quilts.

Early in the nineteenth century white quilts became fashionable, probably in response to the elegant corded quilts made of white silk and linen that had been produced in eighteenth-century France. Shipped through the port of Marseilles to England and then to the colonies, the "French quilts" advertised for sale in 1754 may well have been this type.[32] By 1763 British textile manufacturers had registered a patent for "'weaving together two, three and four pieces of single cloth so that they will

Fig. 14. Sample Book, Hopewell Cotton Works, 1828
Showing the blue and white checked cottons made by early American cotton mills and common throughout the nineteenth century next to a Pineapple Quilt Block, 1800s made with similar fabrics.
Sample Book, Gift of Thomas E. Gillian; Quilt block, Chester County Historical Society

appear as if stitched together.'" It was "a new method of weaving and quilting in the loom ... in imitation of the common manner of quilting as of India, French and Marseilles quilting."[33] The early loom-woven quilts were all white, and came to be known as "Marseilles quilts." By 1785 Pennsylvania merchants were selling "Elegant Marseilles bedquilts, Loom quilting, corded and plain quiltings," commodities that enjoyed an enduring popularity well into the next century; in 1819 the West Chester–based firm of Townsend and Sharpless continued to advertise "Marseilles Bed Quilts" and "Counterpanes" for sale.[34] According to textile historian Sally Garoutte, Marseilles quilts are easy to recognize; all are "made of white cotton, having a fine-woven face cloth, a coarser back cloth, and a heavy unspun roving as a stuffing layer."[35]

Whether inspired by the earlier French quilts, or the English machine-made imitations, Chester County quilters made their own all white quilts, some of them stuffed. In 1816 Sidney Lewis Passmore, a Quaker from Chester County, embroidered the date in her beautiful white-work quilt.[36] With its central medallion, flowers and meandering vines it resembled the loom-woven quilts she may have seen around her. She also may well have used white English calico that she purchased nearby (fig. 15). Although not whole cloth, another early example that turned up in the documentation project had beautiful stuffed motifs combined with patchwork. It may represent a transition from the fashion for pure white quilts to include the use of some of the early dark calico similar to that listed in Jacob Wesler's inventory (fig. 16). White quilts were elegant testaments of taste, skill and wealth as they required yards of new fabric, a great deal of time and expertise to make, and they had to be kept clean. Colored calico and chintz however, provided a lot more options for making distinctive yet

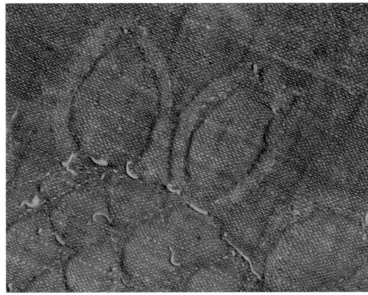

practical bedcoverings.

The expansion of color chemistry and printing technology that began in the eighteenth century continued in the nineteenth century. Before 1830 and more likely before 1860, quilters in Chester County used fabric imported from Europe. Early in the century some of the quilts were whole cloth using chintz with dark backgrounds in exotic pseudo-Asian designs and later fanciful birds and palm trees with classical architectural features; remnants of such fabric can be found in pieced quilts. Textile historian Stuart Robinson lamented what he saw as the post-1835 deterioration of design among the British manufacturers, attributing it to the introduction of "a most unpleasant solid green and a very ugly Russell brown in place of the old softer colors." And there

-----

(Top) Fig. 15. Whole Cloth Quilt, 1816
Descended from Sidney Lewis Passmore of Kennett Square. Cotton top; linen back; 102" x 102". Courtesy of Kennett Underground Railroad Center, Gift of Lucille Sharpless Koenig

Fig. 16. Nine-Patch, 1790 – 1830
Detail of the back of a brown and white quilt showing a stuffed flower. See page 61 for overall image. Possibly descended from the Wallace family of Highland Township. Cotton top; cotton and linen back; 90 ½" x 80 ¾" Courtesy of Barbara Huston

new CLOTH STORE" in West Chester where he had just received "a general assortment of British Goods," among them ginghams, calicoes, silk shawls, plaid silks, and India muslins. Still in business in 1830, Everhart announced for sale textiles that he had imported directly from Canton among them "Super black and coloured Sattins," as well as fabrics he had bought in Philadelphia, including a "splendid assortment of French and British Goods, among which are the most fashionable and cheapest goods [he had ever sold] cloths, cassimeres and silks." He claimed, furthermore, that he would sell them at both

was a growing tendency to overcrowd designs with a proliferation of irrelevant and random units often totally unrelated to the main pattern."(fig. 17) Part of the problem too, he argued, was that as their economic plight worsened, calico printers became less interested in printing quality goods for the high-end market and catered instead to consumer demands for ever cheaper and cheaper cottons."[37] This was a predicament that influential people recognized at the time and among the steps taken to remedy the situation was the publication of design journals such as the *Journal of Design and Manufactures* published in London between 1849 and 1852. The editors included actual fabric swatches and commented on the quality of the design in phrases like "especially frightful," or "delicate and pretty" (fig. 18).[38] Interestingly, it is clear from this journal that calico printers blatantly copied designs produced by their European counterparts.

Whether well designed or not, the English printed cottons were readily and locally available to the residents of Chester County. In 1817 William Everhart advertised that he had opened "a

CALICO,

Printed by Nelson Knowles and Co., Manchester.

Manufactured principally for Spain and Portugal, and a clever specimen of executive skill; attractive for its purpose. Upon this and other goods prepared for foreign markets, we shall have some extended comments to make hereafter.

(Top) Fig. 17. Whole Cloth Partridge Pattern showing the overcrowded designs, fanciful birds and brownish colors introduced in the 1830s. Descended in the Rakestraw family. Cotton top; cotton back; 96 ½" x 98 ½" Gift of Maereta Hershey, Chester County Historical Society, Q80

Fig. 18. *Journal of Design and Manufactures*, March 1850. Journals like this aimed to improve the design of English Printed textiles. Courtesy of Hagley Museum and Library, Wilmington, DE

retail and wholesale rates so they were "well worth the attention of country merchants."[39] In 1861 Everhart's store was still in business, and young Quaker Jennie Sellers of Pocopson commented regularly in her diary on the fabric and clothing she purchased there. In April 1861 she noted that "papa got me a new dress today at Everharts store in W. Chester;" in November 1862 she "got stuff for a winter cloak; it is a Black Cloth. Gave one dollar and a half;" in November 1863 she "got a new dress of calico. Gave 22cts a yard;" and in July 1864 "Papa was at W. Chester got some muslin got me a new dress. Gave 56cts a yard. 12 yds." Both rural and urban Chester County residents could buy the "most fashionable" imported textiles to wear and for furnishing their homes, some of which would have ended up in quilts.

Everhart was not just selling cottons. The silk goods he mentions would have appealed to the well-to-do consumers in the county, including the Quakers. One fascinating and attractive quilt top brought in during the documentation days was made of silk in a tumbling block pattern and attributed to Mary Roberts of Schuylkill Township. Along with the quilt came two bonnets, her photograph, and one of her journals that covers the years from 1845 (when she was sixty years old) to 1854. In addition, the information handed down with her needlework was that she made the quilt top from the material used in Quaker bonnets: when the two are viewed side by side the story seems plausible (fig. 19). Roberts was a quilter and regularly noted her quilt-related activities in her journal. On one occasion she went with Mary Ann Rossiter and Elizabeth Rapp to "John Rapp's to a quilting;" on another "William, Susan, & Benjm Roberts come to see us, took dinner and tea—we finished our quilting;" on December 21, 1846, she noted "Clear and cold—began to quilt a petticoat for Patience Thomas," and on February 14, 1848, she "laid out a quilt [and] Jane Davis came here this afternoon to learn to knit suspenders."[40] Quilting was a social occasion for Mary Roberts, especially in the winter months, and

she may also have enjoyed traveling to West Chester or Philadelphia to select and purchase the silk for her bonnets and quilts. That this particular quilt top remained unfinished suggests that she

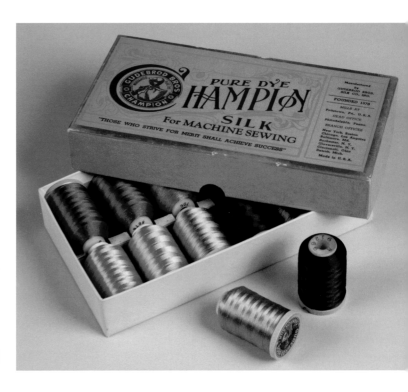

(Top) Fig. 19. Detail showing the silk Quaker bonnet and Tumbling Block Quilt Top with the same fabric, 1850 – 1880. Descended from the Roberts family of Tredyffrin or Schuylkill Townships.
Silk; 78" x 70 ½"
Courtesy of Susann E. Welsh

Fig. 20. Pure Dye Champion Silk for Machine Sewing, Gudebrod Bros. Silk Co. Inc., 1870 – 1950. One mill is located in Pottstown. Gift of Marie Ludwick, Chester County Historical Society, 2005.33.6

information about the latter, the fabric used for both was likely imported, but the thread could well have been made in Philadelphia (fig. 20).[42]

For the first half of the nineteenth century, with the exception of some simple calicos, most quilters would have bought imported textiles—turkey reds from Glasgow, and a variety of green, yellow, and blue prints from Manchester. A quilt like that made by Sara Rhoads is indicative of the large variety of cotton prints available to quilters at midcentury (fig. 21). But a lot changed for American manufacturing around 1860. The Civil War cut off cotton shipments to Britain, creating what became known in Manchester, England, as "the cotton famine." In addition, declines in the British silk industry prompted many skilled workers to emigrate, and a number relocated to Patterson, New Jersey. At the same time New England and Philadelphia were becoming important cotton-printing centers. With the development of a synthetic purple in 1868, by British chemist William Henry Perkin, a new class of aniline dyes opened up limitless design possibilities (fig. 22). Add to that the recently invented sewing machine that was becoming popular in American homes, developments in sewing thread, and changes in retail merchandising, especially mail-order catalogues,

egan it late in her life. The silks she chose for it re strikingly comparable to those in a similarly atterned multi-colored quilt top at the Historical ociety.[41] Though there is little specific

---

ig. 22. *Dockham's American Trade Reports nd Directories: Textile Manufacture and Dry ioods Trade*, 1878. In the late nineteenth entury both aniline and natural dyes were eing used by cotton printers. Courtesy of lagley Museum and Library, Wilmington, DE

(Top) Fig. 21. Charm Quilt detail, 1850s
Shows the large variety of printed cottons available to Pennsylvania quilters in the middle of the nineteenth century. Made by Sara Rhoads, Pine Forge, Berks County, PA. Cotton top, cotton back; 77" x 75 ½"
Courtesy of Geri Dulis

and it is little wonder that the second half of the nineteenth century was a time of major quilt production throughout North America. The fabrics in the Chester County quilts from this period reflect their proximity to the Patterson silk mills and Eddystone Manufacturing Company, a major cotton printworks near Philadelphia (fig. 23). They are also a testament to the evolving design expertise within the American textile industry.

Prior to the 1870s, American cotton printers copied and purchased designs from European manufacturers, which has made it difficult for textile historians to pin down the origin of many of the mid-nineteenth-century cottons. Gradually, however, factory owners began to recognize that in order to capture the American market they needed a better understanding of the relationship between fashion and design in promoting and selling their textiles. As textile historian Diane Fagan Affleck noted, "the production of printed cotton textiles required manufacturers to perfectly blend artistic ideas with complex technical processes." To this end in the 1870s textile firms led the way in establishing design schools, first in New England and shortly thereafter in Philadelphia. Ultimately, the designers working for the cotton printers were more concerned with creating goods that sold and were less worried about setting fashion trends or dictating good taste. Many mills produced over 1,000 patterns each year for dresses, shirtings, and furnishings (drapery, upholstery, bedding, etc.), so consumers had a huge array of printed cottons from which to choose.[43] To create the designs and

keep track of their progress through the system, some firms, including Eddystone Manufacturing Company, used watercolor renderings that were pasted into large volumes, indicating when or if it was produced, what color combinations might work, and when it was taken "offline" (fig. 24).

Eddystone Manufacturing Company, situated along Chester Creek in the southwest corner of Ridley Township, became one of the nation's largest cotton manufactories in the late nineteenth century (fig. 25). Ultimately known as Eddystone Village, the factory covered over seventeen acres and employed hundreds of people, more than half of whom were foreign born—mostly English and French.[44] Fire insurance drawings done for the owners, William Simpson and Sons in 1885, illustrate what was involved in cotton printing: in one building the printing rollers were engraved and stored and the colors were developed; the fabric was bleached in another, and far away from

(Top) Fig. 23. Detail of Crazy Quilt, 1887 Made of silks that may have come from a Patterson, NJ silk factory. Descended in the Wells family of Charlestown, Kimberton and West Chester. Silk top; cotton back; 78 ¾" x 78" Courtesy of Patricia Patterson

Fig. 24. Eddystone Printworks Engraving Book for Dress Goods, 1916 – 17, showing some of the designs for dress fabrics. Courtesy of Hagley Museum and Library, Wilimington, DE

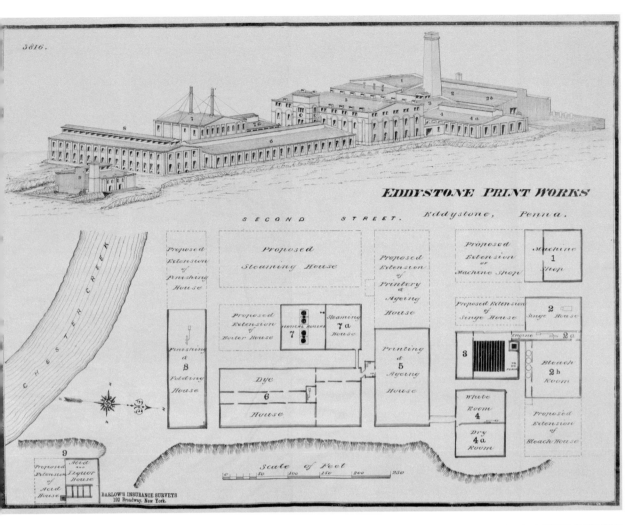

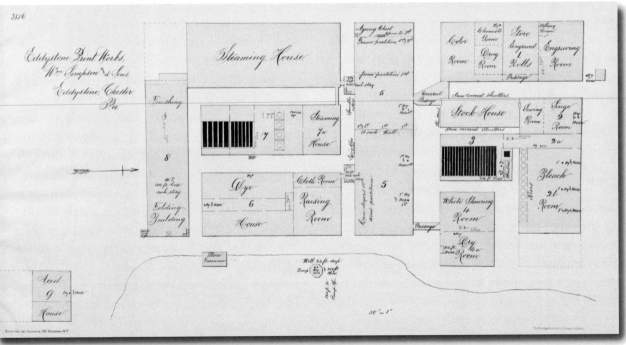

(Top) Fig. 25.1. Eddystone Print Works architectural elevation with proposed extensions, 1870s; and (Below) Fig. 25.2. Eddystone Print Works detailed extensions, 1870s. Wm. Simpson and Sons, Eddystone, Chester, Delaware County, PA, Barlow Insurance Survey. Courtesy of Joseph Downs Manuscript Collection, Winterthur Museum and Library, Winterthur, DE

that was the dye house; the finishing and folding processes were housed together. The drawings also suggest that the company was expanding, with proposed extensions of each building sketched in.[45] In the late nineteenth century Eddystone relied on twenty-two printing machines to produce about 24,000 pieces of fabric a week. Its specialty at that time was "Mourning and Fancy Prints," and the company capitalized on the fact that it had won an award in 1869 from the American Institute in New York for "Superior Cambric Prints," by highlighting that on its labels.[46]

Some turn-of-the-century Eddystone pattern books with swatches of dress cottons survive.[47] Although many of the designs and colors are generic polka dots, stripes, and other small motifs, some of their black and white designs are distinctive enough to be recognizable in quilts that arrived during the documentation days in Chester County. They provide sufficient proof that many late nineteenth-century quiltmakers used fabrics manufactured in Pennsylvania (figs. 26, 27).

The 1891 diary entries of Ella Swayne of Kennett Square encapsulate some of the changes that affected Chester County quilters on the cusp of a new century.[48] Mail-order shopping was newly available, and so were store deliveries. John Wannamaker's Department Store in Philadelphia sent new quilting frames to Ella's sister-in-law Hannah, which arrived on February 12, 1891. A few weeks later, on March 7, Ella and Hannah "worked at her under-waists today." And "Wanamakers delivery wagon brought the cotton wadding for our last quilt this afternoon." Obviously prolific quilters, two days later Ella recorded with satisfaction that since the new frame's arrival less than a month earlier, she and Hanna had "quilted the fifth and last quilt today." Skipping ahead sixteen years, Swayne remained involved in quilting, but this time by helping to collect fabric for a young man, Zakariah Kane, to quilt. Her entry for January 7, 1907, is indicative of all the different ways quilters acquired fabric for their quilts: "Miss R brought some calico for Zakariah Kane to make patchwork quilt, Amanda from Mrs Hall's was here on Saturday to ask for pieces for him, so Miss R thought she would get some new. Annie had some pieces of her dresses for him & Amanda came for all in the afternoon." Zakariah was lucky to have these ladies looking out for him

with the result that he received a quantity of brand new fabric, perhaps some unused scraps from a sewing project, and a few pieces that were cut out from old dresses.

In 1929 Eddystone Manufacturing Company merged with Joseph Bancroft and Sons, another local cotton manufacturer, and the new venture changed direction completely as they began to make synthetic fabrics, beginning with a line of rayon goods in the 1930s. Because it is slippery, rayon is not a fabric of choice for quilters, but it dyes and drapes well, making it a good substitute for silk. One quilt that family members thought was made of silk, is actually rayon (fig. 28). Helen McCuskey, who lived in Mount Carmel, pieced it together and during the winter of 1944, her mother Frances, her sister Constance von Wening, and the occasional neighbor or relative stopped by to quilt it. The sisters liked to travel and clearly had a sense of style as attested to by several photographs that accompany the quilt, and the lovely bedcovering reflects this. The blocks are made of rayon fabric with large dots while the sashing is pieced from a

Fig. 26. Ascot Percale Sample Book, Eddystone Manufacturing, 1910, showing some of the popular black and white printed cottons that appear in some Chester County quilts. Courtesy of Hagley Museum and Library, Wilmington, DE

Fig. 27. Nine-Patch detail, probably early 20th century, showing some of the printed cottons that may have been made at the Eddystone Printworks. Cotton top; cotton back; 73 ¾" x 71" Gift of Betty and Leighton Haney, Chester County Historical Society, 2007.65.1

(Top) Fig. 28. Twenty-Five Patch detail, 1930 Made by Helen McCuskey Pryzblinski (b. 1907) of Berwyn and assisted by Frances McCuskey, Constance Von Wening and Mrs. Ruginis. Rayon top; rayon back; 85" x 89". Courtesy of Dorothy Lammer. See quilt on page 156.

series of prints with oriental motifs that appear to be different colorways of the same design, which intimates that they were samples, perhaps from a factory like Bancroft and Sons, rather than fabrics from old dresses or sewing projects. The quilt is handsome enough to use for special occasions and adorned the bed on Sundays only.

The invention of rayon and its use in quilts in some ways marks the end of an era in quiltmaking, at least as far as the fabric used to make them is concerned. For the remainder of the twentieth century, how quilters acquired and selected their textiles is addressed in the oral histories collected during the documentation project and in Karin Gedge's essay in this volume. Throughout the eighteenth, nineteenth and early twentieth centuries however, a wide range of factors at the local, national, and international levels had influenced the production and distribution of fabrics that appear in local quilts. Trade with the East brought new textiles into European and American homes and spurred the development of innovative technologies in Europe with which to manufacture comparable cloth that could meet consumer demand for the popular colorful cottons. Political change resulted in growing American manufacturing as the postrevolutionary era ushered in a desire to be independent of British goods. The residents of Chester County participated in these trends as both fashionable consumers and as textile manufacturers, all of which is reflected in quilt fabrics. Although details of many of the quilts made in the county may have been lost over time, the surviving quilts offer tantalizing hints about each maker's thoughts, her rationale for making them, and her connection to the wider world of production, trade, distribution, and fashion.

Endnotes

Adrienne D. Hood is a Professor and Associate Chair in the Department of History at the University of Toronto. Formerly a Curator in the Textile Department at the Royal Ontario Museum, she is the author of The Weaver's Craft: Cloth, Commerce, and Industry in Early Pennsylvania *(Philadelphia: University of Pennsylvania Press, 2003) and* Fashioning Fabric: The Arts of Spinning and Weaving in Early Canada *(Halifax: James Lorimer & Co., 2007)*

1. For a discussion about how to study various aspects of quilts see Patricia J. Keller, "Methodology and Meaning: Strategies for Quilt Study," *Quilt Journal* 2, no. 1 (1993): 1–4.

2. *Sears Century of Progress in Quilt Making* (Chicago: Sears, Roebuck, 1934), 4.

3. The following discussion is taken from Adrienne D. Hood, *The Weaver's Craft: Cloth, Commerce, and Industry in Early Pennsylvania* (Philadelphia: University of Pennsylvania Press, 2003).

4. Beverly Lemire, *Dress, Culture, and Commerce: The English Clothing Trade before the Factory, 1660–1800* (New York: St. Martin's Press, 1997), 67–68, notes that the worsted wool petticoats have not survived in as large a number as those of silk, partly due to the fact that they were less valued and either used until they were worn out or recycled into quilts, as was the case with an indigo blue petticoat in the Royal Ontario Museum. A similar fate befell two quilted petticoats that were part of this documentation project.

5. Marla R Miller, *The Needle's Eye: Women and Work in the Age of Revolution* (Amherst: University of Massachusetts Press, 2006), 102.

(Top) Block Quilt, early 1900s
Unknown Chester County maker.
Cotton top; cotton back; 35 ½" x 35 ½"
Courtesy of Jane Brigman

American Weekly Mercury, June 7–14, 1722; *American Weekly Mercury*, October 20–27, 1737; *Pennsylvania Gazette*, January 27, 1743; August 13, 1748; August 4, 1748; March 29, 1748; May 2, 1754. The definition of "humhum" is from the online Oxford English Dictionary. It is unclear what the term "Troy Wall Quilting" describes.

Karin Calvert, "The Function of Fashion in Eighteenth-Century America," in *Of Consuming Interests: The Style of Life in the Eighteenth Century*, ed. Cary Carson, Ronald Hoffman, and Peter J. Albert (Charlottesville: University Press of Virginia for the United States Capitol Historical Society, 1994), 252–83.

American Weekly Mercury, December 18–23, 1735; *Pennsylvania Gazette*, November 6, 1755. Artisans such as Brown often had a drop-ff point for country people to leave their goods for cleaning, a service likely used by his Chester County customers.

Florence M. Montgomery, *Printed Textiles: English and American Cottons and Linens, 1700–1850* (New York: Viking Press, 1970), 13.

10. *American Weekly Mercury*, August 21–28, 1740; *American Weekly Mercury*, May 11–18, 1738. Possibly the stamped calico petticoat was of British manufacture, not Indian.

1. John Irwin and Katharine B. Brett, *Origins of Chintz: With a Catalogue of Indo-European Cotton-Paintings in the Victoria and Albert Museum, London, and the Royal Ontario Museum, Toronto* (London: H.M.S.O, 1970), 26. See Schnuppe von Gwinne, *The History of the Patchwork Quilt: Origins, Traditions and Symbols of the Textile Art* (West Chester, Pa.: Schiffer, 1988), 67, for a detail of a British patchwork bed curtain from 1708.

2. Beverly Lemire, *Fashion Favourite: The Cotton Trade and the Consumer in Britain, 1660–1800* (Oxford: Oxford University Press, Pasold Research Fund, 1991), 41–42.

3. *Pennsylvania Gazette*, August 13, 1747.

4. *Pennsylvania Evening Post*, January 29, 1777; *Pennsylvania Packet, or the General Advertiser*, March 2, 1779.

5. Angela Lakwete, *Inventing the Cotton Gin: Machine and Myth in Antebellum America* (Baltimore: Johns Hopkins University Press, 2003), 24–26.

6. The fly shuttle, a spring-loaded mechanism, automatically and speedily carried the weft across the warp. It allowed wide cloth to be woven by one person (previously it took two—one person threw the shuttle to another who caught it; otherwise the width of cloth was determined by the span of a weavers arms as he threw the shuttle with one hand and caught it with the other).

17. For a succinct summary of the 18th-century textile inventions, see Victor S. Clark, *History of Manufactures in the United States*, vol. 1 1607–1860 (New York: Peter Smith, 1949), 422–37.

18. Lakwete, *Inventing the Cotton Gin*, 45–46; Ronald Bailey, "The Other Side of Slavery: Black Labor, Cotton, and Textile Industrialization in Great Britain and the United States," *Agricultural History* 68, no. 2 (Spring 1994): 35–50. Lakwete argues that Whitney's gin, though using a different technology than the roller gin, was not a major invention but represented a continuation of a process that had been evolving for a long time. According to Bailey, in 1860 American slave-grown cotton supplied 88% of the cotton used in the British textile industry.

19. Stuart Robinson, *A History of Printed Textiles* (Cambridge: M.I.T. Press, 1969), 15, and Jeremy Elwell Adamson, *Calico and Chintz: Antique Quilts from the Collection of Patricia S. Smith* (Washington, D.C: Renwick Gallery, National Museum of American Art, Smithsonian Institution, 1997), 17.

20. Robert Chenciner, *Madder Red: A History of Luxury and Trade; Plant Dyes and Pigments in World Commerce and Art* (Richmond: Curzon, 2000), chap. 11: "The Secret Recipes of Turkey Red." Robinson, *History of Printed Textiles*, 22.

21. Robinson, *History of Printed Textiles*, 26–27.

22. Montgomery, *Printed Textiles*, 98; Florence Harvey Pettit, *America's Printed & Painted Fabrics, 1600–1900* (New York: Hastings House, 1970), 169–71, has images of these quilts using his fabrics; Linda Eaton, *Quilts in a Material World: Selections from the Winterthur Collection* (New York, Abrams /Winterthur Museum, 2007), 94, 97, provides excellent images of a Hewson printed counterpane and a quilt that has appliqué designs made with Hewson's fabric.

23. *North-American Intelligencer*, April 4, 1787. Taylor placed the same ad in a number of local newspapers.

24. Hood, *Weaver's Craft*, 116–17.

25. Jennie Sellers, diaries, Diary Collection, Chester County Historical Society (hereafter CCHS).

26. Jeannette Lasansky, *In the Heart of Pennsylvania: Nineteenth- & Twentieth-Century Quiltmaking Traditions* (Lewisburg, Pa.: Oral Traditions Project of the Union County Historical Society, 1985), 27.

27. Rachel Cochran, ed., *New Jersey Quilts, 1777 to 1950* (Paducah, Ky.: American Quilter's Society, 1992), 16; Barbara Brackman, *Clues in the Calico a Guide to Identifying and Dating Antique Quilts* (McLean, Va.: EPM Publications, 1989). Brackman noted that "once the craze for calico quilts began in the 1840s, wool fabric faded in importance. Not a single wool quilt appeared in the database [that she created] between 1840 and 1865." She went on to say, however, that there are some undated wool quilts that could be from those years, but they are varied in style and "seem more a matter of personal whim than fashion" (p. 45).

28. Eldridge account book, ms. 3788, CCHS. *Poulson's American Daily Advertiser*, October 2, 1819.

29. Sample Book, 1828, Hopewell Cotton Works, CCHS. John Bradley, *The Dickey Family and the Growth of Oxford and Hopewell* (Elkton, Md.: privately printed, 1990) 8–10; Hood, *The Weaver's Craft*, 148.

30. For examples of the variety of fabrics in the 18th centuries, see the probate inventory files for the following estates: Nathaniel Newlin, 1729 (file 352); Thomas Morgan, 1757 (file 1643); John Trimble, 1772 (file 2711); George Ashbridge 1773 (file 2758), all in Chester County Archives, West Chester, Pa.

31. Jacob Wersler, 1834/5, Assigned Estates, #1, Chester County Archives

32. *Pennsylvania Gazette*, May 2, 1754.

33. As quoted in Sally Garoutte, "Marseilles Quilts and Their Woven Offspring," *Uncoverings*, 3 (1982): 119.

34. *Pennsylvania Packet and Daily Advertiser*, October 13, 1785; *Village Record*, April 28, 1819.

35. Garoutte, "Marseilles Quilts," 126.

36. It is likely, although not certain, that Passmore made this quilt.

37. Robinson, *History of Printed Textiles*, 24.

38. Six volumes of the *Journal of Design and Manufactures* are in the Library at Hagley Museum and Library, Greenville, Delaware.

39. Everhart advertisements, clippings file C&DF (10/29/1817) & AR (6/29/1830), CCHS.

40. Entries of September 3, 1845, January 23, 1846, Mary Roberts journal, private collection.

41. The only information that accompanies this artifact is that it was from the second half of the 19th century (document file, 00/69 Q103, CCHS); further research might connect the two pieces.

42. Jacqueline Field, Marjorie Senechal, and Madelyn Shaw, *American Silk, 1830–1930: Entrepreneurs and Artifacts* (Lubbock: Texas Tech University Press, 2007), 42, lists the American silk manufacturers in 1843 and what they were making. The three in Philadelphia made sewing silk, trimmings, and ribbons.

43. Diane L. Fagan Affleck, *Just New from the Mills: Printed Cottons in America* (North Andover, Mass.:, Museum of American Textile History, 1987), 21, 24, 25, 32, 39, 29.

44. Information taken from the Historical Society of Delaware County website: http://www.delawarecountypahistory.com/eddystonebo ough.html.

45. Fire insurance records for Williams and Sons, ms. 637, box 4, folder 3, Joseph Downs Manuscript Collection, Winterthur Museum and Library, Winterthur, Del.

46. Affleck, *Just New from the Mills*, p.88.

47. Ascot Percale Book, ca. 1906, Eddystone Company records, Hagley Library.

48. Ella Swayne diary, CCHS.

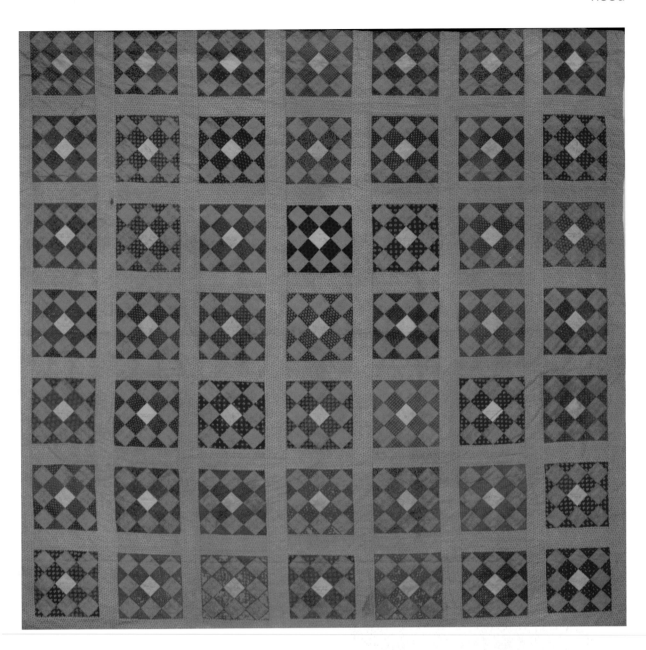

Friendship Quilt, 1840s
Descended through the men of the James family. Includes family names of James, Marshall, Hoopes, and others of East Goshen, West Bradford, Thornbury and Westtown. Aaron James, a potter from Westtown is also included. It was probably owned early on by Hunt James.
Cotton top; cotton back; 108 ½" x 101"
Courtesy of Francis Marshall James, III

Chester County Friendship Quilts with turkey-red prints, mid-1800s.

Dawn Heefner

Another Piece of the Pennsylvania Quilt Puzzle

Since the early 1990s, Joanie Pigford, of Taos, New Mexico, has kept a tally of quilt documentation projects across America and the books that came from them. Her current list stretches over both sides of a 13-inch page, small type listing titles, authors, year, and publisher. Alabama, Alaska, Arizona, it begins, and on it goes down the page with columns also listing how many quilts were documented in each project, plus how many documentation days. At the bottom of the page appear the listings for Ohio and then Oklahoma…. On the top of the reverse side sits a veritable feast: a dozen books from Pennsylvania!

The Pennsylvania books present nearly 13,200 quilts—more than from any other state. Yet those volumes only represent about two dozen of the state's more than five dozen counties. Now, with the publication you are reading, we can begin to fill in the blank on another county—Chester County.

Our sampling is similar to other county projects. In York County 1,500 quilts were documented in about eighteen months. Even more have been seen since, as there now is a yearly documentation day held by the York County Heritage Trust. In the northwestern nine counties, 1,000 quilts were documented. Another 2,000 were surveyed in seven northcentral counties during the Oral Traditions Project in 1984, with an additional 1,500 emerging from eight more counties during the second phase of that project. About 700 quilts were brought into projects held in each of three other counties: Adams, Monroe, and Berks; 1,800 came through the door in Lancaster County's project.

The idea for a major community quilt documentation began in 1980, with Bruce Mann, a thirty-six-year-old quilt dealer in Kentucky. Mann was concerned that Kentucky quilts were being sold and taken elsewhere, and he wanted to document the existing ones to "preserve for posterity what remains of our early quilt heritage."[1] Mann died in a traffic accident before the Kentucky Quilt Project began; however, he laid the groundwork for what we do today. He had opened Pandora's Box, and inside were tens of thousands of quilts, all across America, waiting to be discovered.

Shelly Zegart, who co-founded the Kentucky Project and has played about every role possible with quilts (historian, appraiser, collector, dealer, lecturer, and author), terms the quilt project movement "the largest grassroots phenomenon in the last half of the twentieth century." "Look how it has changed how we see quilts," says Zegart. "Documentations have totally changed the dynamics of how families value their quilts."[2] Families often come in knowing very little about their quilts, uncertain whether these have a place in their twenty-first century lives. Those same families often leave with broad smiles, knowing much more about their quilts and how they connect the limbs of the family tree.

Zegart also says documentations have "cracked the nut open, to make quilts worthy of true scholarship."[3] She notes that each successive project raises the level of scholarship for future ones. The 1981 data collection form filled one side of one page; the 2007 version required eight double-sided pages to record just one aspect: the physical characteristics, such as size, type of fabrics, quilting patterns.

Both the expected levels of scholarship and presentation have risen over the years. Some states, such as Texas and Virginia have held second rounds of documentation and even published second books. The first Virginia book, *Virginia Quilts*, published in 1987, ran 40 pages; the second, *Quilts of Virginia, 1607–1899*, published in 2006, filled 168 pages with a much more detailed text and many more images. As Hazel Carter, a key member of both projects, puts it, "We learned that pictures were important to readers."[4]

Noted quilt historian and author Merikay Waldvogel believes quilt search projects have contributed to the continued existence of many quilts. "I feel like I have had an input on the preservation of quilts and quilt stories. That would not have happened if the documentations had not started when they did."[5] She believes that the community projects, largely organized and staffed with quiltmakers, collectors, and independent scholars, vastly enriched the knowledge of professional institutions. She cites her own experience, beginning as a quilt collector and independent scholar, moving on to co-direct the Tennessee Quilt Project. She has also authored numerous books, including *Soft Covers for Hard Times: Quilts of the Depression, Patchwork Souvenirs: Quilts of the 1933 World's Fair*, and *Southern Quilts: Surviving Relics of the Civil War*. In addition, she has served with many quilt organizations and has consulted with museums, including the International Quilt Study Center in Lincoln, Nebraska, and the Mint Craft and Design Museum in Charlotte, North Carolina.

Speaking of those institutions, she says, "At the outset, their collections contained very little information about the individual quilts, and they asked me (and others) to 'authenticate' the quilts. The more information you provide the staff, the more excited they become about their holdings. This excitement gets transformed into more quilt-centered public events, more exhibits, more accurate quilt caption cards, etc."[6] And this enthusiasm ripples throughout the community.

Katy Christopherson, a consultant to the Kentucky Quilt Project, points out another of those ripples: the proliferation of reproduction fabrics, patchwork patterns, and quilting designs based on those seen in antique quilts. Fabric designers are continually searching for fresh inspirations for new fabric lines, drawing on the "harvests" from these projects. Within the past year, reproductions from the York County efforts made their way to stores, and a line based on quilts in the Lancaster Quilt and Textile Museum was recently released. Through these, many modern-day quiltmakers form connections with their foremothers.

The genre of "quilt scholar" itself is a major outgrowth of the quilt project movement. It has led to the creation of organizations such as the American Quilt Study Group and the Alliance for American Quilts, both dedicated to revealing and preserving the stories of quilts. They are also vital networking vehicles for both professional and independent scholars. In each project, dozens of volunteers enter as quiltmakers and finish being able to identify quilt types, fabrics, and techniques that set the quilts in their locality apart.

I confess I am a "serial documenter," having taken part in projects in Chester, York, and Franklin counties in Pennsylvania as well as those in Kent County, Maryland, and the entire state of Delaware. Out of these projects and other quilt study, I became the first appraiser in Pennsylvania certified by the American Quilter's Society and an officer with the American Quilt Study Group. I have probably seen 5,000 quilts over the past dozen years on documentation or appraisal days. Yet I can't wait to see the next one opened up on the table. Will I, or another of the volunteer documenters, be observant enough, insightful enough to read the clues that quilt presents? Will I offer the owners information to help them better value the quilt, the maker, and her life so many years ago?

For me, and I imagine for most quilt historians the thrill is in making connections, in reading the unspoken language these patchwork puzzles present.

We documenters are practicing a form of forensic science, with each search project adding vital information to recreate the "body" of quiltmaking (figs. 1, 2, 3). Preconceived notions are perpetually being verified—or dashed to smithereens. Merikay Waldvogel, speaking of the Tennessee project, recalls, "We were surprised to see so many red and green appliqué quilts here, and so

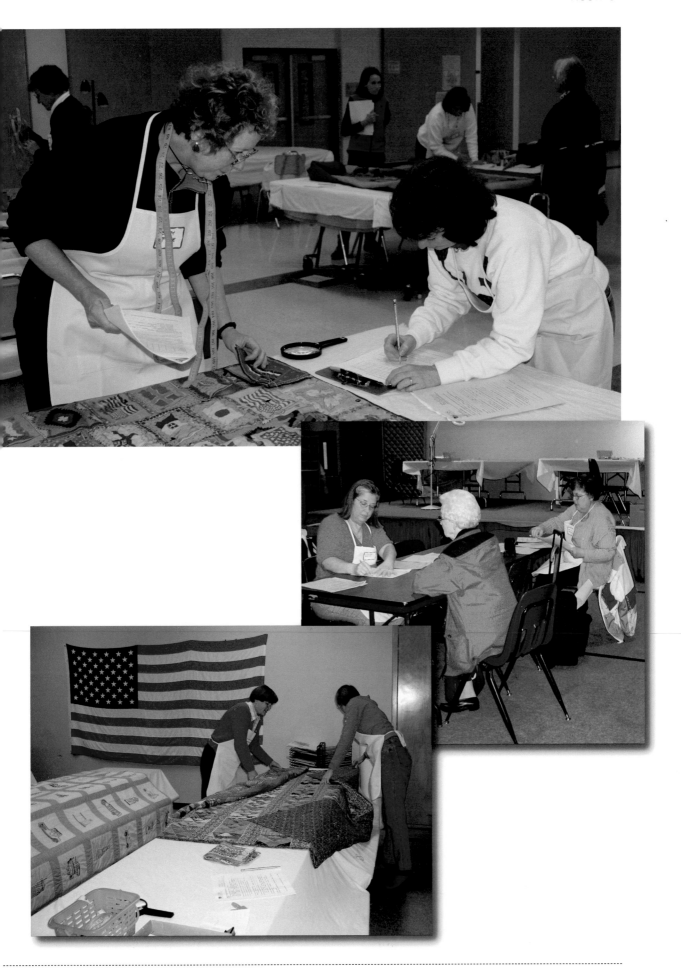

Top) Fig. 1. Unionville High School, Kennett Square, December 2002. Betty Fiske and Sandy Day describing physical characteristics

Center) Fig. 2. Bethany Christian School, Oxford, June 2003. Lynne Hoyt and Jane Davidson collecting provenance from quilt owner.

Below) Fig. 3. Bethany Christian School, Oxford, June 2003. Julie Powell and Mary Kay Hitchner describing physical characteristics

few log cabin quilts." The number of crazy quilts, "a style [Waldvogel] once thought was an 'urban' style" surprised her, and provided an important reminder: "Even in the rural areas, women were tuned in to fashion and trends."[7]

In Chester County, the surprise to me was the large number of turkey-red prints in so many of the mid-nineteenth-century quilts (fig. 4). All around the county, we saw quilts with one, two, three, or even four dozen different turkey-red prints, a sharp contrast to the limited number of red prints used in quilts made beyond southeastern Pennsylvania. This raised numerous questions. How did the makers obtain all these prints? The fabrics would have been imported from England, France, or Scotland, as there is no strong evidence that America's textile industry perfected the complex process of turkey-red printing. Did Chester County quiltmakers have stores dedicated just to fabrics like the quilt shops we have today? What led to this trend of "the more prints the better?" How widespread was this practice? Personally, I have seen

it in an 1841 signature quilt made in Philadelphia for a Methodist church, as well as several quilts from Lancaster County, and a quilt from Carroll County, Maryland. But even quilts made in nearby New Jersey during the same time period were much less likely to have as many different prints.

Although the accomplishments of the quilt project movement are substantial, the puzzle is still incomplete, especially in Pennsylvania. Philadelphia and the remaining counties of southeastern Pennsylvania are largely undocumented. The same goes with most other urban areas. There were documentation efforts in Delaware and Lebanon counties; however, the results remain unpublished, so the data are missing. There is a hope by many quilt enthusiasts that the momentum that flowed through Lancaster, York, and now Chester counties will continue throughout Pennsylvania, establishing a factual foundation for the rich legacy of quiltmaking in Pennsylvania. Jeannette Lasansky, who spearheaded the first documentations in

Fig. 4. Appliquéd turkey-red quilt blocks, mid-1800s
Probably made in the Coatesville area.
Cotton; 13" x 12 ½" each
Courtesy of Barbara Huston

Pennsylvania in 1984, says of the state's quilt riches, "We are really in the heart of it all … deep, broad, and diverse, on both newer and older quilts … incredible design aspects, good colors—even good standard stuff." She recalls going to the first major quilt exhibition, at New York City's Whitney Museum: "I turned to my husband and said 'We've got better stuff in Pennsylvania.'"[8]

The documentation movement continues to evolve, as technology and expertise develop. Several experts believe it is important to prepare for that growth to maximize the accomplishments made in looking back in time. They see an acute need to make information from quilt search projects and museum collections accessible to scholars everywhere. Some records are computerized, but formats have changed over the decades. Patricia T. Herr, who wrote the book based on Lancaster County's Quilt Harvest, says information there was computerized; however, the images of the quilts predate the introduction of digital photography and the trove of data is "on old floppy discs, and, for all intents, unusable. We do have the hard copies, but I'm not sure they are easily accessible."[9]

One solution to that need is the Quilt Index, an online searchable database of information from projects around the country, created by the Alliance for American Quilts and Michigan State University. It already includes data from many documentation projects and several museums, and it is continually updated and expanding. Those shepherding the Quilt Index hope one day it will also include data from historical societies and private quilt collections throughout the United States.

Several quilt historians suggest future search project organizers be open-minded in the scope of their documentations. Jeannette Lasansky and Shelly Zegart say projects need not be defined by state, when a county or regional approach would be more workable, or would better capture the quiltmaking legacy of an area. For *Lest I Shall Be Forgotten*, by Nancy and Donald Roan, documenters of the Goshenhoppen Historical Society focused solely on the Perkiomen Valley region of eastern Pennsylvania, encompassing parts of three counties. The group's efforts in that small region yielded an astounding 1,500 quilts.

Lasansky also cautions against relying too heavily on documentation days, because those only yield what quilt owners think is important enough to share. During projects in New Mexico and with the "white topper" Amish of central Pennsylvania,

Quilt borders.

she went directly into homes, getting a much better perspective on all the quilts made and the role of quiltmaking. Of the white topper Amish, she says, "being in their homes, seeing them make cultural decisions was essential. You must get beyond the approved view of quilting to see what's really done." Lasansky believes that solid fieldwork is the only way to delve into important Pennsylvania communities, such as the African American, the Amish, and the Hmong.[10]

Historian Merikay Waldvogel advises more flexibility in the timelines of future projects. Assessing her experience in the statewide Tennessee effort, she reflects: "We missed many quilts (with a 1930 cut-off date). We also did not value at the time the embroidered, cross-stitch, and kit quilts, which make up a large and important body."[11]

Fortunately, in Chester County, our team set out to capture more of those quilts and their accompanying stories, by focusing on quilters born before 1930, not just on quilts created prior to that date. It gave us the opportunity to piece together Chester County's quilt legacy not just as it was, but also as it is happening, from those practicing their art today. It is crucial that as new documentation projects are conceived, the timeline moves forward to ensure that quilts made in the late twentieth and twenty-first centuries do not languish in boxes, drawers, and closets for a century before they, too, are "discovered."

Layers of cotton backing fabric.

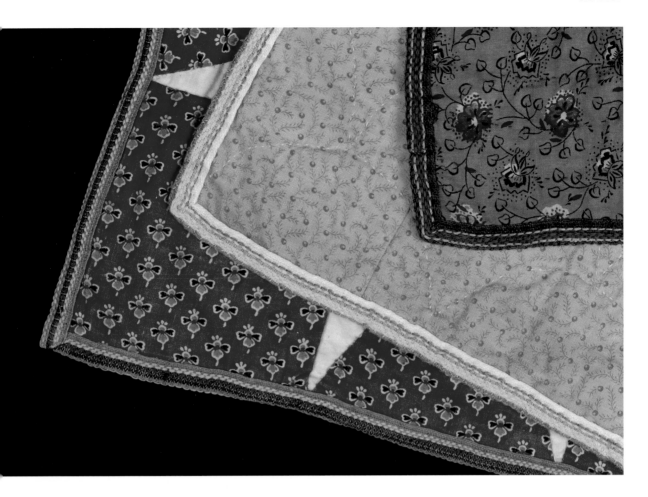

Endnotes

Dawn Heefner is a quilt historian and AQS-certified Quilt Appraiser; she also works as a television news producer and writer specializing in health and medicine.

. John Finley, historical essay, in Jonathan Holstein and John Finley, *Kentucky Quilts, 1800–1900* (Louisville: Kentucky Quilt Project, 1982), 16.

. Shelly Zegart, telephone conversation with author, May 5, 2008.

. Zegart conversation.

. Hazel Carter, e-mail to the author, May 5, 2008.

. Merikay Waldvogel, e-mail to the author, May 5, 2008

. Waldvogel e-mail.

. Waldvogel e-mail.

8. Jeannette Lasansky, telephone conversation with the author, May 15, 2008.

9. Patricia Herr to the author, n.d.

10. Lasansky conversation.

11. Waldvogel e-mail.

Corners with woven tape bindings.

❧ The Lone Star quilt was placed in my keeping in 1984 when my aunt died. She
stipulated that I am to pass it on to my youngest daughter, Kathryn Maereta (Martin)
Phillips. It was made about 1844 by Sarah Pusey (1823–1858), kept by her mother
Eliza (Ogle) Pusey (1792–1870), passed to her granddaughter Annie (Thomas)
Hershey (1850–1929), passed to Annie's granddaughter, C. Maereta Hershey
(1910–1984) and then to me. ❧ When I see and handle this marvelous work of art I
appreciate the patience and character of the woman who made it. I'm humbled to
have been chosen to guard this quilt and perpetuate Sarah's memory. And I'm
encouraged that my daughter recognizes her privilege of being the next link in this
chain between generations of women, past and future.
—*Nancy (Hershey) Plumley, quilt owner*

Lone Star, 1840 – 1850
Made by Sarah Jones Pusey (1823 – 1858) of Parkesburg
Cotton top; cotton back; 97" x 95 ⅝"
Courtesy of Nancy Plumley

Students wrote reactions to several styles of quilts for possible publication in the Chester County Historical Society's book and museum exhibit.

Quilts and Stories
Unfolding the layers

Quilts tell stories about people and people tell stories about quilts. This message has been an important part of the Chester County Quilt Documentation Project and the Chester County Historical Society's educational outreach. Throughout the documentation (2002–2008), owners generously shared stories about their quilts. Some knew the stories of many generations past, others simply found the quilt in a closet and, in some instances, it seemed as though the quilt found the owner. The emphasis of the fieldwork was Chester County quilts but some were made in the region by former Chester County residents. When asked to name their quilts, owners suggested the formal pattern name or, more often, simply offered the name by which the family refers to it. Those names are reflected here.

In 2008 the quilt outreach expanded as a team of volunteers visited public and private schools throughout Chester County. Students of all ages learned about quilts and quilting traditions before looking at photographs of quilts from the documentation. Unlike the quilt owners, the students knew nothing about the history of the objects. Instead, they wrote about the visual impression. They completed creative writing exercises, composed poetry or wrote a few sentences about how the quilts made them think or feel. Some wrote stories from the quilt's point of view.

There are far too many stories to capture within the covers of this book. However, it is hoped that these examples provide a glimpse into the inspiration that the quilts have produced within people of all ages. Perhaps they will inspire a story of your own.

❧ I was working on a crazy quilt in 1999 when my husband passed away. The quilt became a mourning quilt with dark colors and black borders. This quilt, however, made in 2004 has bright colors, photos and quotes and is a celebration of my husband's life.
—*Barbara Perrone, quilt owner and maker*

Charlie's Quilt, 2004
Silk top; rayon back; 39" x 39 ¼"
Courtesy of Barbara Perrone

The sampler was done by Sarah (Webb) Cloud (1817 – 1900) in 1837 when she was 20. Her parents were Thomas Webb (1781 – 1860) and Esther (Paxson) Webb (1781 – 1868).

❧ Quilt blocks were made in 1847 for Jane (Webb) Taylor by her sister Sarah (Webb) Cloud (1817-1900). The quilt was put together in 1896 after death of Dr. Thomas Allen Cloud in 1896. He was the eldest son of Sarah and was never married. His initials "T A C" are stitched in black on the quilt.
—Sara Meadows, quilt owner

(Photograph) The quiltmakers Sarah (Webb) Cloud (1817 – 1899) and her daughter Mary Belle (1862 – 1934) are in this Cloud family photo taken about 1897 or 1898 at Clifton Farm. Sarah is the Quaker lady in front row seated next to her husband James Cloud, Jr.

(Top) Friendship Quilt, 1847 – 1896
Made by Sarah Webb Cloud (1817 – 1899), East Marlborough Township near Unionville. Cotton top; cotton back; 93" x 90"
Courtesy of Sara Meadows

❧ Imagining a Quilt Story. ❧ "Grammy, what's this?" I questioned eagerly. ❧ "It's my family quilt," she told me. "My great-great-grandmother's mother made it, and it has passed down through the daughters of this family ever since. My mother gave it to me, as her mother gave it to her." ❧ Being a mere five years, I could not find words to express how beautiful this quilt was. "It's very pretty," I said finally. ❧ My grandmother smiled. In 12 years I graduated from high school. Joyfully accepting congratulations from friends and family, I turned to see that my grandmother had hobbled into the room. ❧ "Oh, Gram," I exclaimed. "You're wearing your family quilt!" ❧ "No," she said, smiling. "It was my family quilt. Now I am passing it on to you." With that she lifted the quilt from her shoulders and wrapped it around me.
—Natalie, middle school

Nine-Patch Pinwheel, 1880 – 1930
Descended from the Heistand and
Yeager families of East Pikeland Township.
Cotton top; cotton back; 84 ½" x 83 ½"
Courtesy of Anna Wilson

❧ Snowfall. ❧ This quilt is great for when there are snowfalls or starry
nights! Maybe this quilt is 5 or 10 years old. Why [do I call it] Snowfall? It
looks like snow is falling from the sky. Did you know this quilt tells a story?
I think it tells when a woman saw a snowfall. It looks like she really was
amazed by the snow. That is what I think about how this quilt came
together.
—*Lydia, grade 3*

Star Quilt, 1860s
Maker unknown.
Cotton top; cotton back; 94 ¾ x 81 ¼"
Courtesy of Wendy Lofting

❥ Our name dictated the pattern of this quilt made for my son. I researched the Jacobs genealogy. To make this quilt special, the seven Jacobs generations of men have been embroidered around the center J. There are three colors: tan for Grandpaw's big farm barn; red because he loved his red truck; and the rich brown represents the good earth.
— *Ina Jacobs, quiltmaker and owner*

Jacobs' Ladder, 1980 – 1981
Made by Ina Ruth Hippensteel Jacobs (b. 1928).
Cotton, synthetic top;
synthetic blend back; 89 ½" x 72"
Courtesy of Ina Jacobs

❥ This is a beautiful natural collage. It looks like it got good use. The color gives it a warm interesting pretty look. The colors blend in like a warm spring day. The pattern is a magnificent stripe. What I also like about this quilt is that it has different patterns. In the center of each block it has pretty black writing. The quilt of this fabric looks as if the person who owned it put it in a sunny spot. I think that because it looks a little faded. These are the thoughts I have on this most fascinating quilt.
—*Victoria, grade 4*

Friendship Quilt, 1845
Made by the family and friends of Jane Carpenter Webb and Jonathan Gamble of Chester County. Family names include Webb, Darlington, Parker and Haines. The wedding was held in Delaware County, PA.
Cotton top; linen back; 90" x 94 ½"
Courtesy of Lois Bassett

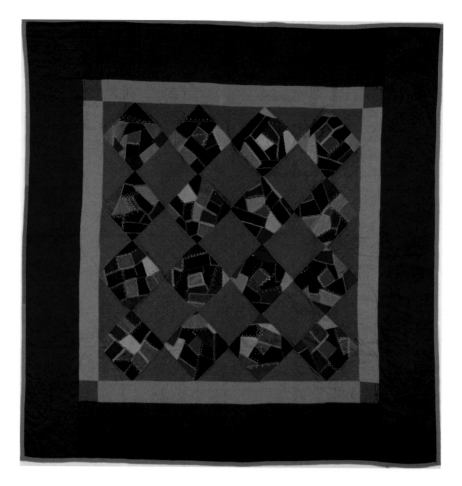

🍃 After piecing the squares and embroidering the patches, the quiltmaker decided on a plain background to further enhance the random patching of the crazy quilt squares. The next design decision was to keep the borders fairly neutral in color, with no piecing. The plain border makes us look longer at the pieced squares.
—*Marion Mackey, quilter*

(Above) Pieced Block Quilt, 1929
Maker unknown; probably Chester County quilt.
Wool top; cotton back; 83 ¼" x 80 ¼"
Courtesy of Wendy Lofting

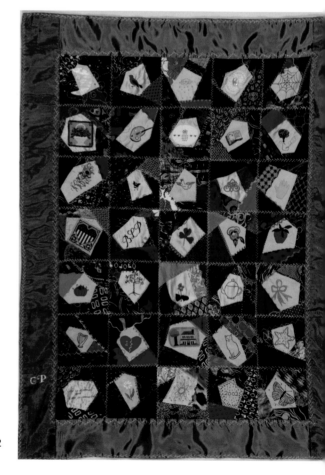

🍃 This quilt has many small boxes in which small pictures are stitched. It makes me wonder about the maker of this quilt. Are there stories that go along with each picture? What does each picture signify? I also like the way that each picture is cut and stitched differently.
—*Paige, grade 7*

(Right) My Favorite Things Crazy Quilt, 2002
Made by Barbara Loftus Perrone (b. 1930)
of West Chester. Silk, synthetic blend top;
synthetic blend back; 45" x 34"
Courtesy of Barbara Loftus Perrone

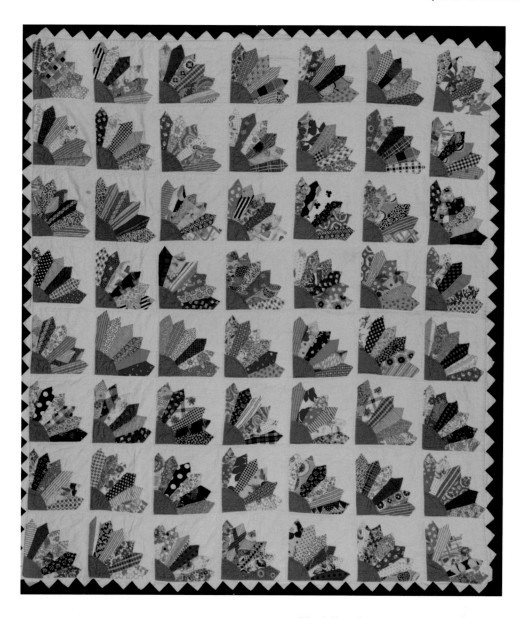

(Top) Fan Quilt, 1900 – 1950
Made by Annie Jane Whitaker
(1869 – 1957) who was married to
William Nelms (1863 – 1953), a
blacksmith in Honey Brook.
Cotton top; cotton back; 72" x 62"
Courtesy of Mary Ann Zeiders

(Above) Fan Quilt Top, 1870 – 1890
Probably from the Heistand or Yeager
families of East Pikeland Township.
Silk; 60" x 60"
Courtesy of Anna Wilson

❯ This quilt was made by my great-grandmother, Sarah (Sally) Lehman Rooke, about 1855. Sally and her husband, Bob, had a farm on Fellowship Road, West Vincent Township. The quilt was a wedding gift for her niece Lydia Lehman and her husband, Sam Rhoads. The Rhoads went, with this quilt, to homestead in Kansas. They returned after the first tornado and settled near Valley Forge.

—Helen Rooke Ferrantello, quilt owner

Log Cabin Quilt, 1855 – 1900
Made by Sarah Lehman Rooke
(1836 – d. early 1900s), North Hill Farm,
Chester Springs.
Silk top; cotton back; 78" x 76"
Courtesy of Helene Rooke Ferrantello

(Above) Sara (Sally) Rooke, quiltmaker

(Left) Lydia Lehman Rhoads, quilt recipient

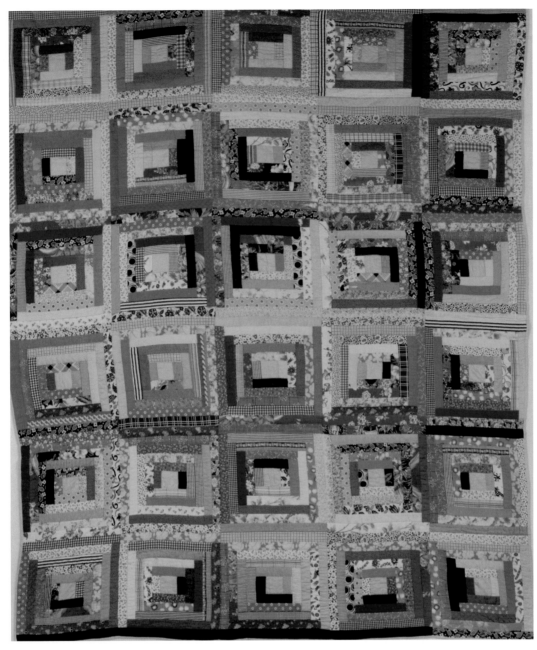

(Above) Log Cabin, 1940s
Made by Eva Viola (Cloud) Delaney (1883 – 1965),
Philadelphia, PA and passed down to Dorothy
Augusta Delaney Close of Honey Brook.
Cotton, linen top; cotton back; 74 ½" x 88"
Courtesy of Susan Cloud Schofield Sleichter

❧ This quilt was passed down through my wife's family,
mainly her Dad's side. The name was Quay. The Quay
family lived in Phoenixville. It was probably made by my
wife's great-grandmother around 1880 or later. My wife,
Pat, is deceased. We have it as an heirloom and for its
sentimental value. We always appreciated the time,
thoughts and skills of our ancestors. It is an important
part of our heritage.
—Rene Cottrell, quilt owner

(Right) Log Cabin, 1870 – 1890
Descended in the Quay family of Phoenixville.
Wool top; wool back; 75 ¹⁄₁₆" x 75 ¾"
Courtesy of Rene Cottrell

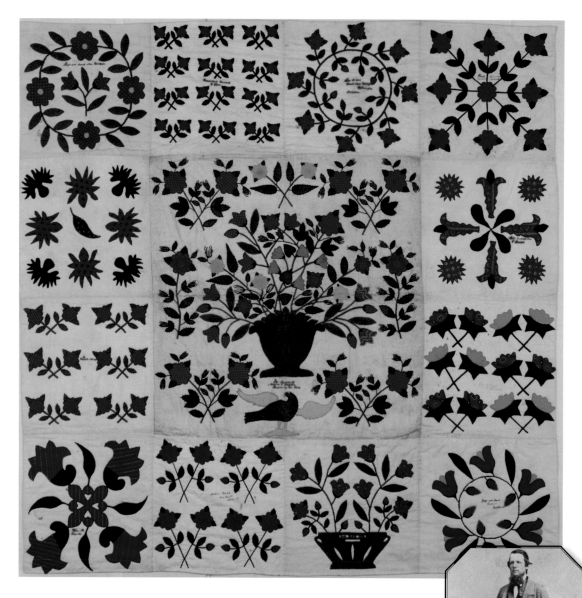

❧ I am overwhelmed by the existence of this quilt, its creation, journey and existence today. One of the signers of the quilt was probably the mastermind of the project. ❧ Its journey began June 2, 1850 as a gift to Matilda Evans Taylor (Cann) by friends who shared that Kemblesville area space and time. It was protected along the way by Matilda's daughters, Pamelia (Foy), Mary (Campbell), then Hannah (Ewing) and Hannah's daughter, granddaughter, and great-granddaughter. Mended and discolored, the quilter's work and materials were strong. ❧ The brilliance of its color and intricacies of pattern testify to the people who set it on its way and those who cared for it.
—*Sharon Fogg, quilt owner*

(Above) Friendship Quilt, 1850
Cotton top; cotton back; 68" x 68"
Courtesy of Sharon Fogg

(Photographs from left to right) Matilda Evans Taylor Cann (1826 – 1901) and Samuel E. Cann (1822 – 1901)

➤ If this quilt could talk [it] would say to me, "I am the very essence of spring and summer. When you look at me, rows and rows of tulips will form as an image in your mind. I am relaxing, calming, peaceful."
—Marli, high school student

(Left) Tulips, 1870 – 1890
Descended through family of Martha Jones of the Chadds Ford area.
Cotton top; cotton back; 82" x 65 ½"
Courtesy of the Chadds Ford Historical Society

➤ Our Tulip Quilt was a kit I ordered from *American Home Magazine* in the late 1960s. My mother-in-law's friend, Esther Graham, living in Phoenixville, PA, put it all together. She and the quilting group from her Kimberton church quilted it. Esther called us to say it was done and we went to her home to pick it up on a very gray, cold day in February. It was like a breath of spring spread out before us. A lovely memory in my heart.
—Carolyn W. Wonderly, quilt owner

(Right) Tulips, 1970
Made by Esther Graham of Phoenixville and a Kimberton church quilt group.
Cotton top; cotton back; 97" x 84"
Courtesy of Carolyn W. Wonderly

❧ We had five children and I made a large bed quilt for each of them. This Baltimore Album quilt was made for our youngest. I took a class about machine appliqué and knew I wanted to make this quilt. It's a large queen size. I used patterns from several authors—Mimi Dietrich and Elly Sienkiewicz—for the 25 blocks. The border and the pillow designs were mine. It took six years (with many interruptions) to do the machine appliqué and hand quilting. I consider all my quilts a labor of love.
—*Gladys Mosteller, quiltmaker*

Baltimore Album Quilt, 2002
Made by Gladys Mosteller of Phoenixville.
Cotton top; cotton back; 103 ½" x 89 ¼"
Courtesy of Gladys Mosteller

(Left) Summer Spread, 1845 – 1875
Possibly made by Elizabeth Oberholser
Robinson Boyer (1860 – 1953/54) of Gap,
located on the border of Chester and
Lancaster Counties. Cotton; 69 ½" x 68 ¾"
Courtesy of Naomi R. Catanese

(Below) Friendship Quilt, 1840 – 1850
Descended through Jane Jones Smedley
of Sugartown. She was the great-aunt
of the present owner.
Cotton top; cotton back; 104 ¾" x 101 ⅝"
Courtesy of Lois Thatcher

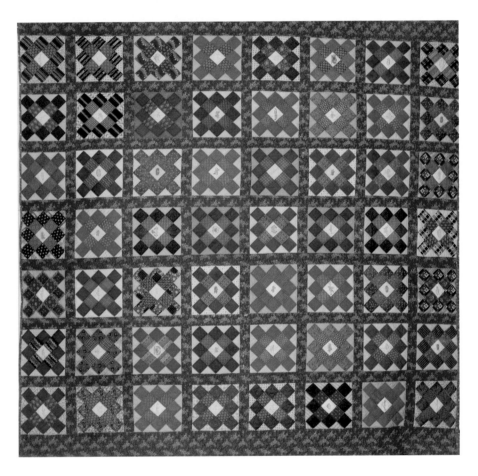

❧ This quilt looks like it was made by an entire town because the
signatures on the quilt all have different last names. It was probably
made for one individual family on an important occasion. Considering its
colors, it might have been a gift for a baby shower, a get well soon gift,
or a present for moving away. It probably wasn't a quilt where you
collect scraps. It looks heavily used, as if it was on someone's bed. The
names are not very faded away, so it was probably made in the early
1900's. Adjacent to the names on the quilt, there are town names, the
most common one being East Goshen.
—Tommy, grade 3

The quilt has white squares with red maple leaf type things in them and red borders. In the middle it has a green wreath with red berries. I think of the Canadian flag and I would name it "O Canada." I would use it to keep me warm. I think this would be easy to make because it has the same pattern. If this quilt could talk it would say, "Yo, what's up?"
—Matt, age 14

(Top) Bear Paw, 1892
Top pieced by Kate M. Liggett Potts, East Nantmeal Township and quilted by the Nantmeal Baptist Church Ladies.
Cotton top; cotton back; 86" x 86"
Courtesy of Edith McElroy

In this quilt I see a gift being given. I see a heart being shared. This quilt reminds me of love and peace, and how special some things are. I favor this quilt because it stands out and shows true meaning. Its bright colors, I believe, stand for unity.
—Emily, grade 5

(Above right) Friendship Quilt, 1840 – 1860
Unknown Chester County maker.
Cotton top; cotton back; 97"x 94"
Courtesy of Connie Webster

❧ The "Civil War" quilt came to me from my parents T.F. Fields, Jr. and Helen Worrell Fields. The maker was Margaret Haycock Kugler (1826-1906) of Media, PA. She was the maternal grandmother of my father's cousin, Margaret Fields. Emma, her only sibling, died in childhood. ❧ In studying my family history, so many times there seem to be just dates. But dates say so much: young widows and widowers; children born at the same time but two lost to illness; men at war; women alone. This quilt connection wraps me in the warmth and strength to carry on, knowing they, too, had joy and pain in life and courage to overcome their failures and adversity.

❧ As a footnote, Margaret Fields lived with her parents, Benjamin Franklin Fields and Elizabeth Kugler Fields, at Idle Moments Farm where Granite Run Mall in Media, PA is today. It was a farm and granite quarry.

—Diane Fields Funk, quilt owner

Trip Around the World, 1875 – 1890
Descended in the Kugler and Fields families.
Cotton top; cotton back; 100" x 96"
Courtesy of Diane Fields Funk

(Photograph) Margaret Haycock Kugler
(1825 – 1906), quiltmaker seated in chair,
Margaret Fields standing

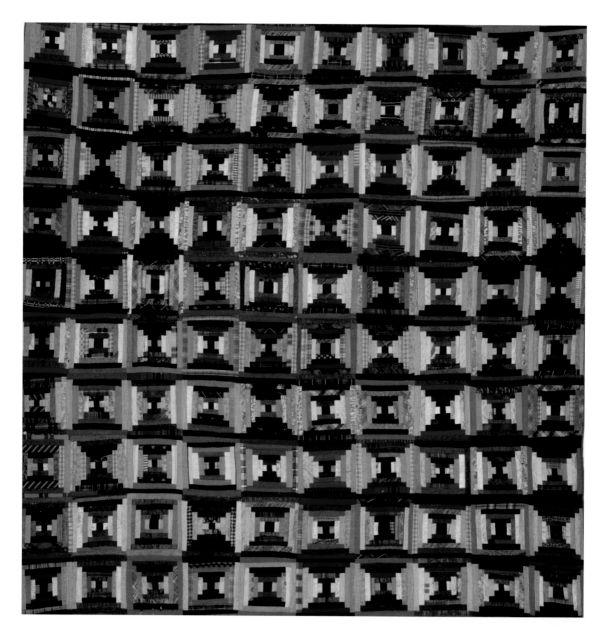

❧ This quilt reminds me of how fast I have to get ready to go to somewhere. If this quilt could talk it would say you better go quicker, time's running out. When I first saw this quilt I thought that the person who did this tried to do it fast.
—Brett, grade 5

(Top) Court House Steps, 1860 – 1880
Made by Eliza Jane Rees Kendig (1831 – 1917),
East Fallowfield Township.
Cotton, wool, silk top; cotton back; 84" x 85"
Courtesy of Eliza Jane Scott Dering

❧ Before moving into our home in 1969, we bought all the furniture left there. There were several quilts in the bureau drawers. We knew the former owners for many years and were very fond of them. Both died here at a very old age. Therefore, we have no idea who made this quilt. We use this quilt for a bed cover because of the color and pattern.
—Nell Jameson, quilt owner

(Above right) Blue Quilt, 1880 – 1890
Possibly made in Downingtown.
Cotton top; cotton back; 67" x 83 ½"
Courtesy of Nell Jameson

❧ This quilt is very plain, but very beautiful. The edges are rigid like triangles, and with a pretty pattern of squares or diamonds.
It stands out to me. The yellowish color has dots of brown, and the green has diamond imprints. It doesn't look like it would go on your bed but it really looks good on the wall!
—*Samantha, grade 4*

(Left) Diamond-in-Square Quilt, 1880 – 1900
Made by Barbara Andes Morris (1849 – 1935), Sadsburyville. Cotton top; cotton back; 83" x 85 ½"
Courtesy of Barbara Morris Zorn

❧ To me this quilt tells a story of a pond when your whole life splashes before your eyes. Your life would land in the middle and it just keeps going on and on. You just try to make it better. As it goes on it gets bigger and soon just stops as if your life is over. After you think of something very happy and colorful it is as if your life is perfect and never ending.
—*Allison, grade 6*

(Above) Log Cabin, 1880 – 1900
Maker unknown probably of London Grove. Silk top; cotton back; 70 ½" x 69"
Courtesy of Chadds Ford Historical Society

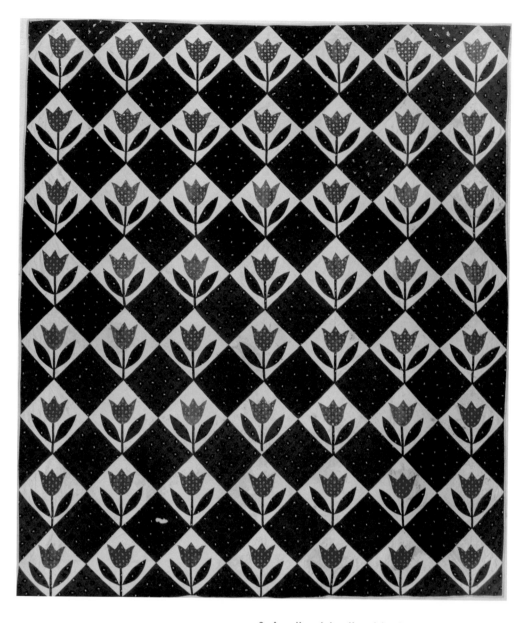

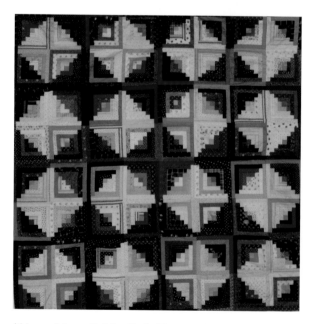

➤ Appliquéd tulips blocks are set on point alternating with plain set blocks. Although slanted at different angles, the maker was careful to cut the set blocks on grain creating a subtle uniformity. That the tulip leaves and stems are cut of that same fabric continues that feeling. Care was also taken to make certain the points would meet. The degree of difficulty in making this quilt is not in the block itself, but rather in the repetition of making 56 identical blocks.
—*Sandy Day, quilter*

(Top) Tulip Quilt, 1830 – 1840
Made by Peniniah Druman Shirk Irwin
(1818 – 1905) of Honey Brook reportedly
in 1835 while in her teens.
Cotton top; cotton back; 96" x 82"
Courtesy of Rev. O.L. Hampton, Jr./Mary Ann Zeide

(Above) Log Cabin Quilt Top, 1894 – 1897
Made by Miriam L. Evans (1872 – 1920) who
lived on a farm near Charlestown. A note
attached reads, "Miriam L. Evans This is the 1st
square. This quilt begun Feb. 3, 1894. Finished
Wednesday evening Feb. 24, 1897 Aldham
Chester County." Cotton; 80" x 79"
Courtesy of Esther Grealey Wise

❧ Red fabric called "Turkey Red" is used in this Whig Rose appliqué quilt made in a 12-block set. The use of double pink fabric and chrome yellow electrify the overall beauty of the quilt. Perfect points of the appliquéd petals are achievable by only the most experienced quilter. Biased fabric strips make the curved stems. Exquisite quilting outlines the appliquéd motifs with fine quilting lines over the background of the quilt.
—*Vickie Brown, quilter*

(Right) Democrat Rose, 1840 – 1850
Unknown maker from Chester County.
Cotton top; cotton back; 102" x 80"
Courtesy of Virginia Musser

(Left) "Rettie" Quilt, 1879
From the Coatesville area.
Cotton top; cotton back;
45" x 34 ½"
Courtesy of Jane Hamilton

❧ A very rare exquisite example of early inked botanical drawings and religious verses captivated my interest from the first time I saw this quilt. A steady hand and a heart, dedicated to God, spent long hours creating this masterpiece for "Rettie" in 1879. ❧ Reading the inscriptions, largely direct quotes from the King James Version of the Bible, the maker implores the recipient to live her life serving God. The complexity of the creator's artistic talents are in stark contrast to the simplistic world of "God and nature" the piece represents. The simple refined beauty, mystery, and intrigue of this piece compelled me to purchase it.
—*Jane Hamilton, quilt owner, lecturer, artist and pattern designer*

❦ To me this quilt makes my head hurt.
That's why I chose it and it reminds me of
the desert in Egypt. It even makes me dizzy.
I think the colors are really cool though it still
makes my head hurt.
—*Josh, grade 3*

(Right) Desert Mirage, 1995
Made by Joanne C. Brown (b. 1925)
of Phoenixville for her daughter-in-law.
Designed by Liz Porter.
Cotton top; cotton back; 84" x 96"
Courtesy of Joanne C. Brown

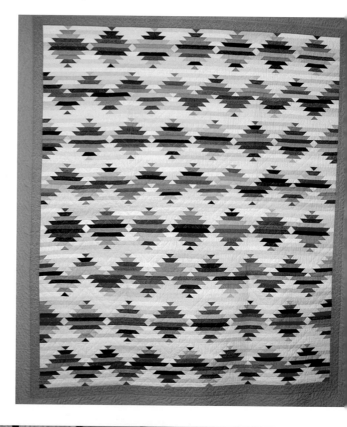

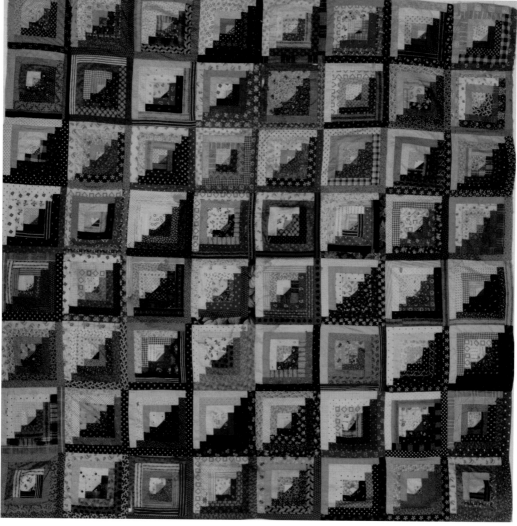

Log Cabin Quilt Top, 1890 – 1920
Made by Miriam L. Evans (1872 – 1920)
who lived on a farm near Charlestown.
Cotton; 79" x 79"
Courtesy of Esther Grealey Wise

❧ This quilt reminds me of many different fireworks going off at one time. It is such a simple design but all of the colors and size of the quilt are so elaborate. The quilt also reminds me of the United States. Every color is a different person or state and it shows how everybody in the world is different represented by the colors used in the quilt. I think the person that made this quilt loved simple shapes and designs so they applied them to their quilt.
—Evan, grade 7

Star, 1840 – 1850
Made by Guenne S. Hall (1806 – 1875) of East Goshen.
Cotton top; cotton back; 106" x 103"
Courtesy of Ron and Nancy Harper/Doug and Amy Harper

(Right) Crazy Quilt, 1880 – 1900
Made by Margaret C. Jones Styer (1825 – 1912)
of Concordville.
Cotton, silk top; cotton back; 65 ½" x 85"
Courtesy of Katharine Burton Way

❧ At first glance this crazy patch quilt seems to have its pieces
sewn on in a random manner. However, by stepping back we can
see that the colors are evenly balanced throughout the quilt. The
quiltmaker may have collected fabrics left over from making
clothing and traded some with friends to accomplish this work. It
was also a good place to practice her new hand stitches.
—Marion Mackey, quilter

(Above) Crazy Quilt, 1880 – 1900
Maker unknown.
Wool, silk top; cotton back; 70" x 59"
Courtesy of Ruth Harrison

❧ This quilt makes me feel like someone was doing their laundry and it was a big mess.
—*Mike, grade 10*

(Top) Crazy Quilt, 1936
Made by Eliza Newhard Evans Walton, Charlestown
Silk, rayon top; cotton back; 69" x 64"
Courtesy of Esther Grealey Wise

❧ Can You?
Can you see me?
All simple
Yet complicated.
Can you tell,
How many shapes I have.
Can you think.
Differently
Like me.
Can you?
—*Anonymous, middle school*

(Right) Crazy Quilt, 1892
Maker unknown.
Silk top; cotton back; 93½" x 83¾"
Courtesy of Hibernia House Museum,
Chester County Parks

❥ Quilters often create quilts where part of the design "pops" out. Nearly 2,000 squares are arranged randomly on point in this quilt. Your eyes tend to focus on the black squares, but the blues also stand out, as do the patterned fabrics.
—*Suzy Brody, quilter*

(Top) Silk Pieced Quilt, 1870s
Made by Mrs. Samuel Haines, Mickletown, NJ, English Quaker ancestor of current owner. Silk top; cotton back; 78" x 77 ¼"
Courtesy of Edith Sumner

❥ This vivid red and white Ohio Star quilt is visually striking. But it is the faded signatures that draw my attention. They make me wonder, "Who are the people who signed this quilt and what are their relationships to the quilter? Are they family, friends, or members of the same church or organization?"
—*Kathleen Wagoner, quilter*

(Above) Friendship Quilt, 1843
Believed to be made by a Society of Friends quilting group with names from Waynesborough, and surrounding area including Rockville, Philadelphia and Pequea. Passed down through Haines or Kent families. Cotton top; cotton back; 104" x 105 ½". Courtesy of Sara H. Kent

❥ A Quilt
I am a quilt
Under a tree with bright lights shining
     on me
On a mantel ouch don't put that on me
Laying on a bed
Over a table
A friendship quilt don't scare me away
Hanging on a wall out best of all
Mommy + me in front of the fire on
     a cold winter's night
—*Christine, grade 5*

(Left) LeMoyne, 1840 – 1870
Possibly Chester County.
Cotton top; cotton back; 96" x 85 ¾"
Private Collection

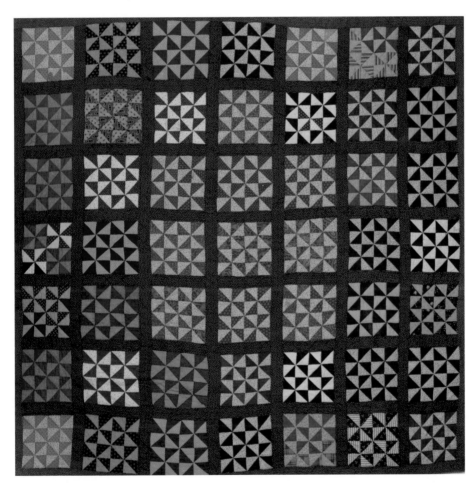

❥ I like this quilt because of the color variety. The person who made this didn't just use several colors but all different colors. The triangle pieces are not all solid either. Some have dots, some have stripes, some are plaid, and some are paisley. I would title this "Pinwheels" because the triangles make a pinwheel shape. The colors remind me of the long socks I get at the Rendezvous [Pioneer and Native American encampment].
—*Maddy, grade 5*

(Above) Pinwheel, 1880 – 1900
Possibly Chester County. Cotton top; cotton back; 88" x 87"
Private Collection

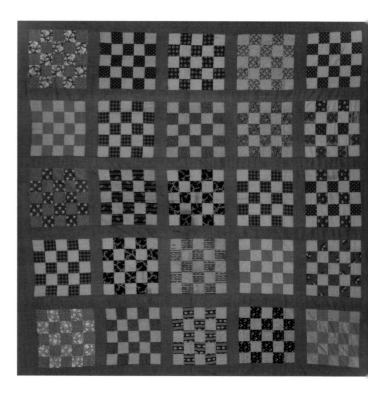

❧ I think that the person who made this quilt liked patterns because this quilt has many different patterns. It is also like a checkerboard because it is an A B pattern.
—*Michael, grade 2*

(Right) Twenty – Five Patch, 1900 – 1910
Made by Eliza Newhard Evans Walton
(1870 – 1943), Charlestown.
Cotton top; cotton back; 80" x 74"
Courtesy of Esther Grealey Wise

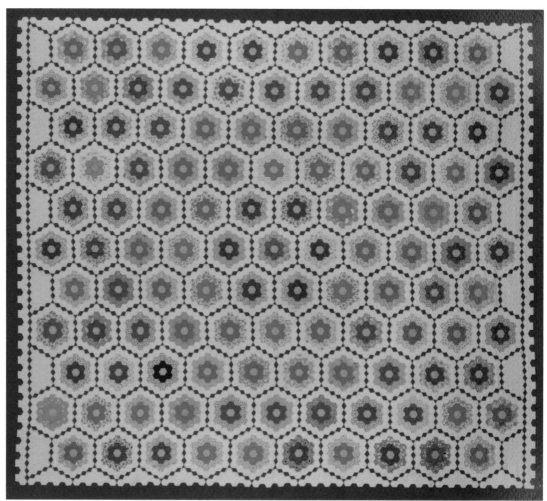

(Above) Grandmother's Flower Garden, 1930s
Made by Blanche Miller Littlewood (1905 – 1999) of Philadelphia and later Malvern. Descended through her daughter Elizabeth Littlewood Beaver of Honey Brook to current owner. Cotton top; cotton back; 104 ½" x 91 ½". Courtesy of Leslie O'Brien

(Top) Sixteen-Patch, 1940 – 1950.
Possibly made by Mrs. Johnson, great-grandmother of owner's
husband, from Lancaster County, PA. May have attended the Society
of Friends Meeting in Oxford. Cotton top; cotton back; 72" x 68"
Courtesy of Barbara P. L. Hill

 It is so peaceful
I am amazed with this quilt
It is so soothing

❧ When I first saw the quilt it reminded me
of plants growing with the sun shining on
them. I wonder if it had any meaning to the
person who sewed it, if it reflected their life
in any way. When I try to imagine the owner
I think of a hard working family, owning a
farm, barely putting food on the table.
—Alia, middle school

(Above) Christmas Cactus, 1850 – 1860
Maker unknown.
Cotton top; cotton back; 100" x 95"
Courtesy of Ruth Harrison

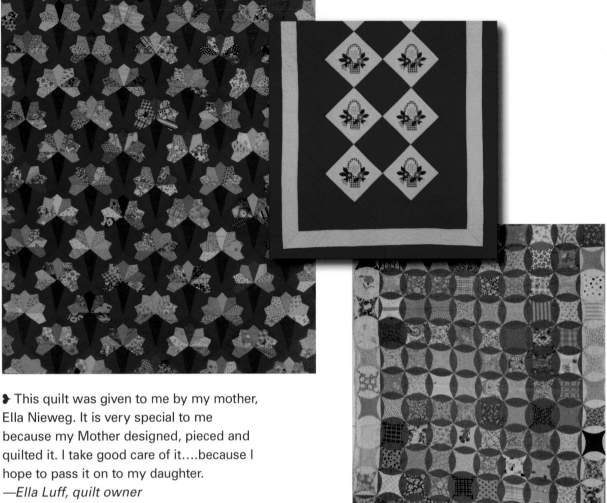

❧ This quilt was given to me by my mother, Ella Nieweg. It is very special to me because my Mother designed, pieced and quilted it. I take good care of it....because I hope to pass it on to my daughter.
—Ella Luff, quilt owner

(Top left) Flower Bouquet, 1956
Made by Ella Weir Crowl Nieweg (1890 – 1965) and given to her daughter Ella Luff. Ella Nieweg passed on the appreciation of quilts and the love of quilting. Members of the extended Nieweg family still quilt today on their own and as a family quilting group.
Cotton top; cotton back; 78" x 58"
Courtesy of Ella Luff

(Top right) Appliqué Flower Basket, 1930 – 1960
Made by Sarah Jane Powell Nieweg (1866 – 1962) of Elkdale, an early generation of Nieweg quilters.
Cotton top; cotton back; 70" x 69 ¼"
Courtesy of Beatrice Thomas and Denise Rash

(Center) Orange Peel, 1960
Made by Ella Nieweg (1889 – 1965) of the Lincoln University area. It was brought to the documentation by daughter Marguerite Nieweg Rector, sister of the present owner. Cotton, feedbag top; cotton back; 79" x 63"
Courtesy of Velma Wilson

❧ "Quilting is a craft our mother [Ella Nieweg] taught us. It is a way to pass on our history to future generations."
—Ella Luff, quiltmaker and owner

(Left) The Broken Star, 1930 – 1960
Made by Beatrice "Bea" Nieweg Thomas (1918 – 2007), daughter of Ella Nieweg, who moved from the Elkdale area to Rising Sun, MD.
Cotton top; cotton back; 72" x 86"
Courtesy of Beatrice Thomas and Denise Rash

❥ "Quilts are made with a lot of love, patience and time. They provide companionship with and an interest in others."
—*Marguerite Rector, quilter*

(Right) Crazy Quilt, 1934
Made by members of the Nieweg family of the Elkdale area: Ella Weir Crowl Nieweg, Beatrice Ellen Nieweg Thomas, Fred Levi Nieweg, Velma Ruth Nieweg Wilson, Marguerite Nieweg Rector and Muriel Jane Nieweg Thomas.
Wool, silk top; cotton back; 80 ½" x 75 ¾"
Courtesy of Beatrice Thomas and Denise Rash

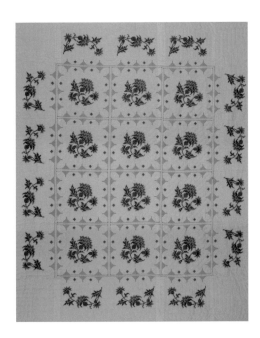

❥ I got the quilt top from my mother-in-law, Muriel Thomas, when she passed away. It was meant for my daughter, Susie Thomas. Upon receiving it, I had to quilt it. It will mean a lot to Susie because her grandmother and I spent time making it. She will have something of her grandmother to remember her for many years to come. It's a part of her history.
—*Terry Thomas, quilt owner and maker*

(Above) Embroidered Flowers, 2001
Cross stitched by Muriel Thomas (1921 – 2001) of Kelton and quilted by daughter-in-law Terry Thomas. Muriel Thomas, daughter of Ella Nieweg, has a daughter, Jennifer Watson, who also continues to quilt.
Cotton top; cotton back; 94" x 55"
Courtesy of Terry Thomas

(Right center) Family Album Quilt, 2008
The blocks were embroidered and quilted by three generations of the Nieweg descendants of Ella Crowl Nieweg and Ernest Powell Nieweg. It was designed and constructed by Carol Luff Biggs (b. 1955).
Courtesy of Carol Biggs

(Bottom) Kitty Cat, Late 1900s
Made by Carol Biggs (b. 1955) of Elkton, MD who carries on the Nieweg quilting tradition.
Cotton top; cotton back; 32" x 32"
Courtesy of Carol Biggs

(Above) Appliquéd Bird, 1840 – 1850
Probably descended in the Reynolds family of Oxford or possibly the
Wilson family of Nottingham.
Cotton top; cotton back; 89" x 90"
Courtesy of Margaret R. Schmoyer

❥ I believe that this quilt should be called
"American Dream." It seems to show visions of
a better tomorrow. It's a vision of peace, a vision
of prosperity, a vision of a better world.
—Sarah, grade 7

American Eagle, 1956
Made by Evora March Stoner Dowlin
(1888 – 1980), Sadsburyville.
Cotton top; cotton back; 97 ½" x 81 ¼"
Courtesy of Marian Stoner and
Susan Stoner Spotts

❧ This quilt reminds me of Christmas. It has a beautiful pattern of red and green shapes. Holly has these colors and patterns too! Christmas is a time of joy and happiness and this person must have been really happy when they designed this quilt! The quilt caught my eye because I look forward to Christmas and seeing my whole family again!
—*Noah, grade 6*

(Left) Currants and Coxcomb Variation, 1840 – 1860
Possibly from Schuylkill County, PA.
Cotton top; cotton back; 85 ½" x 82 ½"
Courtesy of Barbara Breen

❧ This was given to Charles Buster McAfee by his grandmother Mary Elizabeth (Summons) McAfee. She lived in Nantmeal Village for 84 of her 86 years. Mary was the granddaughter of Frank Prizer. His name and the name of his first wife Annie are signed on this "summer spread." Annie died the year she signed it. Frank then married Julia (Potts) Gartley in 1888. Mary McAfee was her granddaughter. The Ortlips, whose names are also on the quilt, were Frank's mother's family. The Ortlips owned land across from Warwick High School. Abram Prizer, Sarah (Ortlip) Prizer's husband, was Nantmeal Village's wheelwright for 67 years at the same address of Mary (Summons) McAfee. My brother is honored to have his quilt included.
—*Ann Bedrick, sister of quilt owner*

(Below) Album Quilt, 1860 – 1886
Probably made in St. Peter's Village or Knauertown area.
Cotton top; cotton back; 68 ½" x 68"
Courtesy of Charles McAfee

❧ The quilt pattern is a deviation from Wild Goose
Chase. Made from coordinating scraps of fabric, each
block is constructed of 6 triangles hand pieced together.
There are over 1,300 triangles in the quilt. Popular
fabrics from the time period, such as bubble gum pinks,
indigo blues and madder browns are pieced in the quilt.
Wool batting is between the quilt top and quilt back.
We consider this a family heirloom. The quilt provides a
connection to our past and provides inspiration to the
next generation of quilters in our family.
—*Vickie Brown, quilter and daughter of owner*

(Top) Flying Geese, 1880 – 1910
Made by Mabel E. Brown (1880 – 1925) of Oxford.
Cotton top; cotton back; 82 ½" x 80 ½"
Courtesy of Jane Brown

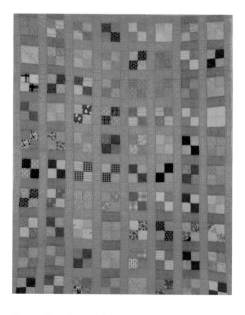

Four-Patch, 1920 – 1940
Made by Mame Rambo who lived in
Birmingham Township near the
Birmingham Meeting House.
Cotton top; cotton back; 76" x 72"
Courtesy of Helen Hickman

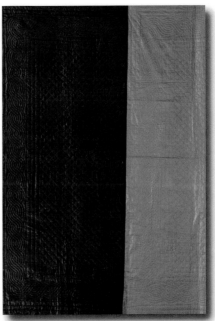

❧ These quilts descended from our Quaker ancestors, the Levis, Miller and Mickle families of Chester and Delaware Counties. Henry Miller and his wife Sarah Deeble Miller settled in Chester County in 1714 (the section later became Delaware County when the two were divided in 1789). The Mickle family arrived in what was then called West Jersey in 1682 and slowly moved westward to Chester and Delaware Counties. ❧ Though it's difficult to say who made these quilts, there are writings from Sarah Levis Miller (1803-1890) where she recollects, "I remember sitting on a stool at my Grandmother Levis' feet and sewing patchwork when I could not have been more than 4 or 5 years." ❧ I first saw these quilts when my mother inherited them from her mother. They were packed away in trunks with other textile treasures. My sister, Sidney Matthews, and I have taken care of the family quilts since they were passed on to our generation. We have always treated them as works of art—family treasures that our ancestors, several generations ahead of us, painstakingly created. They are links to our past that we can touch, see and admire.
—Linda Hawley, quilt owner

(Top) Strip Quilt with Puss in Corner Blocks, 1846
Note on quilt: "Quilt made by Grandmother Mary Miller, 1846."
Cotton top; cotton back; 99" x 96"
Courtesy of Linda Hawley

Whole Cloth Quilt, folded to show reverse, 1810 – 1830
Made by a Miller or Mickle family member, Quakers in the Chester and Delaware County area.
Cotton top; cotton back; 105" x 115"
Courtesy of Linda Hawley

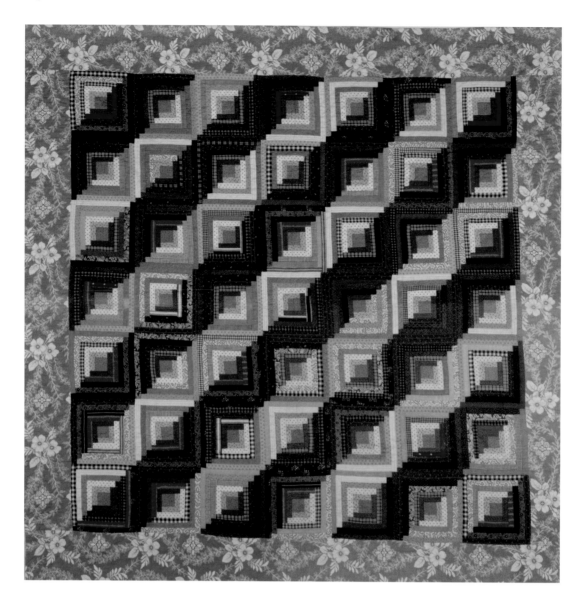

❧ As I look at this quilt, I wonder what inspired the maker to make the quilt this way. I imagine the quiltmaker cooped up inside her house waiting for winter to finally be over and for spring to come. The quiltmaker is going crazy because she can't wait to be outside again, plant beautiful flowers, feel the heat of the sun on her back, and experience the feeling of bare feet in the grass again. So, she starts making this quilt the way she wishes the weather was outside.

Colors all throughout
Flowers over here and there
Spring is coming soon

—*Marley, age 13*

Log Cabin Quilt, 1870 – 1900
Made by Catherine Good Horning (1845 – 1900s)
who lived near Bowmansville, Lancaster County, PA.
Cotton top; cotton back; 76" x 76"
Courtesy of Roberta L. Pettit

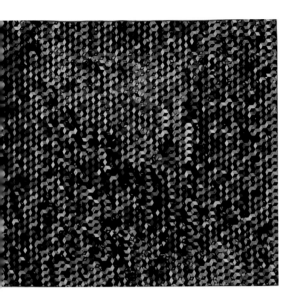

> This stunning silk quilt shows off the quiltmaker's skill, with its many, many small diamond-shaped pieces. The pattern, usually called Tumbling Blocks or Baby's Block, gives a very 3-dimensional appearance. The arrangement of color in each block determines which side looks like it is "on top." It was constructed using a method called English paper piecing. The edges of the fabric diamonds are first folded over paper templates and then sewn together using a tiny overcast stitch. This type of fancy silk quilt is frequently not actually quilted.
> —Barb Schneider, quilter

(Left) Tumbling Blocks, late 1800s
Unknown Chester County maker.
Silk top; cotton back; 85 ½" x 78"
Courtesy of Hibernia House Museum, Chester County Parks

> Many stars,
Many colors,
Many shapes,
Many others.

Shades of green,
Shades of blue,
All of which,
Are laid out for you.

Every stitch,
Every square,
Shows more and more,
Things to share.

Time after time,
You take another glance,
You find new things,
Your're in a trance.

It tells many stories,
Deep down within,
It tells some good
    things,
And shows some sin.

But this piece is the most
special of all,
Because when you look
at it you hear its call.

—Stephanie,
middle school

Star Quilt, 1840 – 1860
Unknown Chester County maker.
Cotton top; cotton back; 93" x 92"
Courtesy of Hibernia House Museum, Chester County Parks

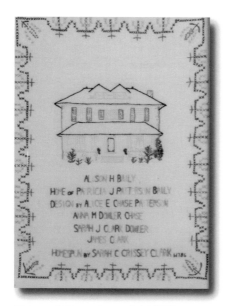

(Above) Sampler, mid-1900s
Designed and stitched by
Alice Chase Patterson
depicting the Oxford home of
her daughter Patricia Baily.
Linen fabric believed to by
homespun by ancestor Sarah
C. Crissey Clark (b. 1786).
Linen, cotton
Courtesy of Patricia Baily

Album Quilt, 1991
Made by family members of Alice Chase Patterson of the
Oxford area for her 89th birthday.
Cotton, synthetic blend top; cotton back; approx. 60" x 48"
Courtesy of Patricia Baily/Ruth Patterson

❥ My mother, Louise Burrows Taylor (1909 – 1998), was always doing some type of
needlework. She belonged to the "lady's sewing social" and enjoyed sewing. In the
1960s when Louise started having health problems and had to stay off her feet she found
comfort in quilting. Her first quilt was a counted cross stitch "wedding quilt." From
there her quilting just took off. In her lifetime she quilted fourteen plus quilts. I think part
of her driving force was to be sure each family member had their own quilt, such as my
husband Joe and I, her grandchildren, Stacy and Scott, plus her nieces and nephews.
She succeeded in passing on her love of sewing to those she loved.
—Sarah T. Finnaren, quilt owner

Redwork Quilt and Matching Pillows, 1997
Made by Louise Burrows Taylor (1909 – 1998) of West Chester.
Cotton top; cotton back; 84" x 72"
Courtesy of Sarah T. Finnaren

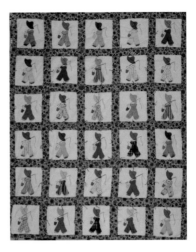

❧ This quilt interests me a lot. Different fabrics are used to create children with fishing rods. The children are arranged in rows all heading in the same direction. It makes me wonder if the children are fishing for food or if they are just going to spend a nice day in the sun fishing for fun and throwing back everything they catch.
—*Paige, grade 7*

Overall Sam, 1960s
Made by Mary Hickman Milliron (b. 1916)
who grew up in the West
Chester/Birmingham area.
Cotton top; cotton back; 91" x 76"
Courtesy of Barbara Hickman Carozzo

❧ My mother, Sarah Lynn Fulton, born in 1911 on a farm, was the youngest of 8 children. She had a career in banking. She married my father, Sharp Fulton in 1935 in Unionville, where they lived. I'm not sure when she started quilting but her mother, Mary Lynn, also quilted. One of my mother's favorite patterns was the Dresden pattern. She also liked to embroider quilts. Her quilting frame was made of clothes props and was set up in the bedroom. My Mother worked full time so her quilting had to be done in the evenings. It was relaxing for her and gave her quiet time after a long day. The embroidered quilt of the birds of Chester County radiates in the vibrant colors and each bird seems to be joyfully singing. I cherish each quilt my mother made because they were made lovingly. She graciously shared her talent, interests, patience and love with her family.
—*Marlene Baker, quilt owner*

Birds, 1970
Made by Sarah Lynn Fulton (1911 – 1995)
of West Chester.
Cotton and synthetic blend top; cotton back
36" x 58 ½"
Courtesy of Marlene Baker

❧ My first response to this quilt is it is beautiful and has very vibrant colors. I wonder—did someone make the quilt to represent a garden, flowers or nature? I imagine the owner as being someone who likes flowers, plants, nature and art. I would name this quilt "The Ruby Red Flower Garden." If it were a song I would call it "Nature in Red." This explains how beautiful nature is explained in art.

Red so beautiful
So vibrant in the light
Nature at its best.

—*Katherine, grade 7*

Album Friendship Quilt, 1848 – 1849
Made by relatives and friends of Rachel Spencer and James Michener from New London, London Grove and London Britain. Descended in the Michener and Pusey families.
Cotton top; cotton back; 88" x 85"
Courtesy of Barbara Hood Pusey

(Right) Log Cabin, 1922
Made by Susann Faucett
Henderson Cloud
(1855 – 1934) of Waterview
Farm, West Chester.
Cotton top; cotton back;
80" x 69"
Courtesy of Susan Cloud
Schofield Sleichter

Susanna Faucett
Henderson Cloud
(1855 – 1934)

Eva Viola Cloud Delaney
(1883 – 1965)
*See her quilt on page 38,
fig. 12.*

➤ This quilt is a wish waiting to come true. If my quilt could talk it
would say you have eleven wishes for every pattern on me. If my quilt
could fly it would fly in space really fast like a shooting star so
someone could wish on it. All of the patches are colorful in many
ways. There's orange, blue, yellow, purples, and pinks and lots of
greens. I think the person that made this quilt was thinking of a wish.
—*Taijah, grade 5*

(Above) Quilt Top, 1930s
Made by Ethel Pauline (Hilton) Gray (1911 – 2005) of Oxford,
daughter of Emma (McMichael) and Elmer S. Hilton.
Cotton; 69" x 69"
Courtesy of Iris Gray Dowling

❧ I would give this quilt the title of "Spinning Stars" because in my imagination it looks like the stars are spinning. If the quilt could talk it would say, "Be comfy and cozy. Stay awhile."
—*Danielle, middle school*

(Right) String Star, 1910 – 1930
Possibly made in Schuylkill County
by Bertha Geise or her family.
Cotton top; cotton back; 79 ¾" x 78 ¼"
Courtesy of Susan Bravo

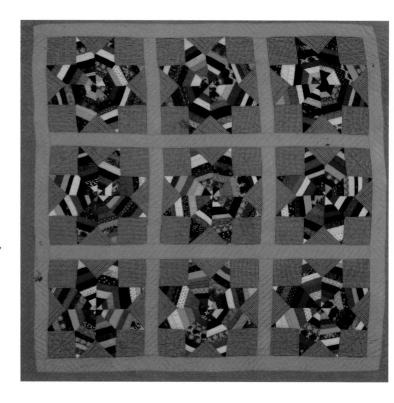

❧ I enjoy this quilt because it reminds me of happy times like when my brother or sister was born and they could be wrapped up in it or one day it might be used for donating to people who live on the streets. The colors are the real part that strikes me mostly because it looks like somebody took some scraps she bought from a craft store and made it into a quilt. To me the quilt looks like it was taken very good care of and might have been made a long time ago. Or it might just be a today quilt with all mixes of colors. That's what I think of this quilt.
—*Olivia, grade 3*

(Left) Many Roads to the White House, 1930
Made by Harriet Andora Deitrick Hawk of Elverson. Cotton, linen, polyester, synthetic blend top; cotton, polyester back; 82" x 72"
Courtesy of Viola M. Patton

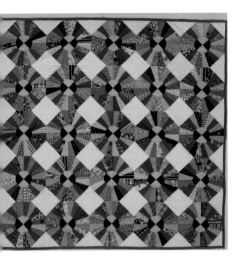

(Top) Dresden Plate Variation,
1940 – 1960
Made by Alice Stilwell Cameron
(1901 – 1976) of Oxford.
Cotton top; cotton back; 78 ½" x 80"
Courtesy of Martha M. Cameron

❧ This quilt was made by Alice Stilwell Cameron circa 1960. Alice was the wife of William H. Cameron. Having lived through the depression, Alice believed in using everything to its fullest until it could no longer be used. That is why feed bags were used for this quilt. She left a note stating that this quilt was to go to her only grandson, Kenneth C. Cameron, and his wife Martha (Mason) for a wedding gift. Little did she know that Ken would marry someone who had been sewing since the age of eight and in her twenties would become a quilter. Knowing all the time, skill, work and love that was put into this quilt makes it a very treasured gift.
—Martha M. Cameron, quilt owner

❧ I Am a Quilt ❧ I am finally done, no more late nights on her lap becoming alive. I have been growing every afternoon at twelve o'clock. Mary, my creator, made me into a beautiful quilt, for her young grandson. I can't believe it though, getting into the brown paper boxes, and getting shipped off like I was a birthday invitation. I would rather stay here and warm Mary up. She did work extremely hard on me, and made me what I am today. A hand stitched quilt, with different designs throughout my body. Other quilts like me are shaped as a measly square, but not me, I have rhombuses all over me: my edges are filled with triangles, and little balls hanging off the sides. I have to admit that I am a unique looking quilt. I'm not that big but not that small, my edges are red like a rose petal falling from your hand. I know I am only a quilt getting shipped off to a little boy's house, but inside, and all over, I am a crafty, creative masterpiece.
—Tessa, middle school

(Above) Crazy Quilt, 1884
Made by Louisa Hanna Menough (b. circa 1840s) of Oxford
and given to her daughter Emma Louise Menough Wales (b. 1860).
Silk top; cotton back; 54" x 56"
Courtesy of Margaret R. Ireson

❥ I think this quilt could represent a night sky. I think this because the stars and the blue trim make it look peaceful and calm. Whoever made this quilt might have hung it by his window. It looks like the evening sky.
—*Sophie, grade 3*

(Photograph) Anne Thomas, mid-1800s

(Top) Block Pattern, 1840 – 1860
Made by Anne Thomas sister of Charles Thomas
through whose family it descended.
Cotton top; cotton back; 123" x 105"
Courtesy of Anne Hollingsworth Thomas Moore

❧ This quilt was purchased by John R. and Linda V. Hicks at the estate sale of Casper P. Hicks (1892-1974). Casper was one of eleven children, born to William H. Hicks (1865-1927) and Anna Marshall Pratt (1862-1927). Most of the family became Chester County farmers, but Casper was West Chester's funeral director. If people could not afford to pay for their loved one's funeral, he would bury them for free or for bartered goods. We believe this quilt was given to Casper to pay for a funeral. ❧ Casper helped all of his family. He came to the farms on hot summer hay-baling days, with cold drinks and watermelons. He gave them all turkeys at Thanksgiving and often helped with farm repairs. Each of the brothers would help Casper with funerals. As a child, my husband John remembers his dad leaving, dressed in a black suit, and returning just in time to milk the cows. We cherish this quilt as a tie to his happy childhood.
—Linda Hicks, quilt owner

Sixteen-Patch Quilt, 1871
Made by the grandmother of Morris H. Eldridge, probably from the West Chester area.
Silk top; cotton back; 91" x 90". Courtesy of Linda Hicks

Postage Stamp, 1950
Made by Folcroft Women's Group to raise money for needy families and other good works. Won in a raffle by Eleanor L. Bair of Folcroft, Delaware County.
Cotton top; cotton back;
82 ½" x 74"
Courtesy of Jacqueline Robinson

➤ This quilt was pieced together by Helen McCuskey in Mount Carmel, Northumberland County, PA. It was quilted by Helen, her mother Frances McCuskey, her sister Constance von Wening, and probably by an occasional neighbor or relative who stopped to visit. Most likely it was quilted during the winter of 1944. Helen married Julius Pryzblinski in April, 1944. Until they moved to Phoenixville in 1957, I remember it being placed on their bed on Sundays.

—Dorothy Lammer, quilt owner and daughter of Helen and Julius Pryzblinksi

(Top) Twenty-five Patch, 1930s
Made by Helen Prysblinski (b. 1907) who moved to Phoenixville as an adult and lives in Berwyn.
Rayon top; rayon back; 85" x 89"
Courtesy of Dorothy Lammer

(Photographs from top to bottom)
Constance Von Wening, mid-1900s

Helen McCuskey, mid-1900s

Frances McCuskey, mid-1900s

(Above) Gather Ye Rosebuds and detail, 1998
Made by Elizabeth S. Voorhees (b. 1929) of
West Chester.
Cotton top; cotton back; 11 ½" x 12"
Courtesy of Elizabeth S. Voorhees

(Left) Broken Dishes, 1990s
Made by Jean Carol MacKinnon
Billet (b. 1934) of Devon.
Cotton top; cotton back; 102" x 78"
Courtesy of Jean Billet

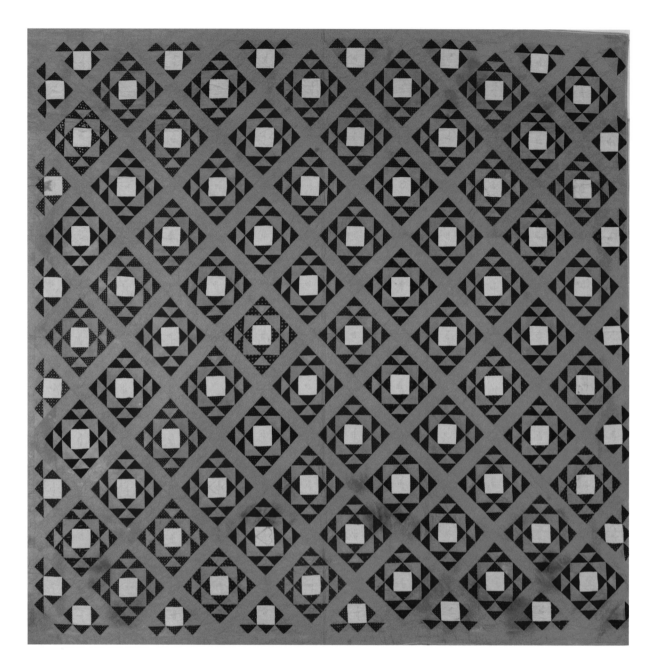

❥ This quilt is very pretty. It reminds me of a farm. It reminds me of all the cheerful animals in the barn. The reason why I picked this quilt is because I love the color combination. The colors look great together. I would name this "Back at the Barnyard." I imagine the maker being very creative but very quiet. I imagine the maker loves animals because of the "barnyard." I just have to say I love this quilt. It is absolutely dazzling and beautiful.
—*Meg, grade 4*

Friendship Quilt, 1845
This quilt was probably made by members of the Society of Friends in Willistown and surrounding Chester and Delaware Counties. It is descended from the family of Samuel Kirk (1860 – 1944) and his wife, Katie Cornog Bond, both of Willistown Township. Samuel was the son of Thomas Kirk (1826 – 1906) and Isabella Black Hannum (1825 – 1914) of Newtown Square, Delaware County. Samuel and Katie were members of and are buried at Willistown Monthly Meeting. Family names include Thomas, Williamson, Lewis, Taylor, Garrett, Sharpless and Seal among others. Place names include Willistown, East Bradford, Birmingham, Newtown, and East Goshen among others.
Cotton top; cotton back; 116" X 115"
Courtesy of Cynthia Pyle Dixon and Mark Dixon